MODERNIST WORK

MODERNIST WORK

Labor, Aesthetics, and the Work of Art

Edited by John Attridge and Helen Rydstrand

BLOOMSBURY ACADEMIC
NEW YORK • LONDON • OXFORD • NEW DELHI • SYDNEY

BLOOMSBURY ACADEMIC
Bloomsbury Publishing Inc
1385 Broadway, New York, NY 10018, USA
50 Bedford Square, London, WC1B 3DP, UK
29 Earlsfort Terrace, Dublin 2, Ireland

BLOOMSBURY, BLOOMSBURY ACADEMIC and the Diana logo
are trademarks of Bloomsbury Publishing Plc

First published in the United States of America

Copyright © John Attridge, Helen Rydstrand, and Contributors, 2019

For legal purposes the Acknowledgments on p. xi constitute
an extension of this copyright page.

Cover design by Eleanor Rose
Cover image: Sybil Andrews, Winch, 1930, linocut on paper © Estate of Sybil Andrews,
Glenbow, Calgary, Alberta, 2019

All rights reserved. No part of this publication may be reproduced or
transmitted in any form or by any means, electronic or mechanical,
including photocopying, recording, or any information storage or retrieval
system, without prior permission in writing from the publishers.

Bloomsbury Publishing Inc does not have any control over, or responsibility for,
any third-party websites referred to or in this book. All internet addresses given
in this book were correct at the time of going to press. The author and publisher
regret any inconvenience caused if addresses have changed or sites have
ceased to exist, but can accept no responsibility for any such changes.

Names: Attridge, John, 1976–editor. | Rydstrand, Helen, editor.
Title: Modernist work: labor, aesthetics, and the work of art / edited by
John Attridge and Helen Rydstrand.
Other titles: Labor, aesthetics, and the work of art
Description: London; New York, NY: Bloomsbury Academic / Bloomsbury
Publishing Inc., 2019. | Includes bibliographical references and index.
Identifiers: LCCN 2019003738 (print) | LCCN 2019012917 (ebook) |
ISBN 9781501344039 (ePDF) | ISBN 9781501344022 (eBook) |
ISBN 9781501344015 (hardback: alk.paper)
Subjects: LCSH: Modernism (Literature)—History and criticism. | Modernism
(Music) | Film criticism. | Work—Social aspects. | Modernism (Aesthetics)
Classification: LCC PN56.M54 (ebook) | LCC PN56.M54 M618 2019 (print) |
DDC 700/.4112—dc23
LC record available at https://lccn.loc.gov/2019003738

ISBN: HB: 978-1-5013-4401-5
PB: 978-1-5013-7830-0
ePDF: 978-1-5013-4403-9
eBook: 978-1-5013-4402-2

Typeset by RefineCatch Limited, Bungay, Suffolk

To find out more about our authors and books visit
www.bloomsbury.com and sign up for our newsletters.

CONTENTS

List of Figures — vii
Notes on Contributors — viii
Acknowledgments — xi

AN INTRODUCTION TO MODERNIST WORK
    John Attridge — 1

Part I
THE WORK OF ART

Chapter 1
THE ABSOLUTE AND THE IMPOSSIBLE WORK: FRANZ KAFKA'S "THE BURROW"
    Robert Buch — 21

Chapter 2
AUTONOMY, DIFFICULTY, AND THE WORK OF LITERATURE IN WYNDHAM LEWIS'S *TARR* AND ANDRÉ GIDE'S *THE COUNTERFEITERS*
    Emmett Stinson — 35

Chapter 3
MIMESIS AND THE TASK OF THE WRITER FOR LAWRENCE AND WOOLF
    Helen Rydstrand — 49

Part II
ARTISTIC LABOR

Chapter 4
RICHARD STRAUSS AT WORK IN HIS WORKS
    David Larkin — 65

Chapter 5
STEIN'S IMMATERIAL LABORS
    Kristin Grogan — 83

Chapter 6
TRACE AND FACTURE: LEGACIES OF THE "READY-MADE" IN
CONTEMPORARY SOUTH AFRICAN ART
    Alison Kearney   95

Part III
REPRESENTING WORK AND WORKERS

Chapter 7
JOSEPH CONRAD'S *NOSTROMO*: WORK, INHERITANCE, AND
DESERT IN THE MODERNIST NOVEL
    Evelyn T. Y. Chan   113

Chapter 8
MAGIC, MODERNITY, AND WOMEN AT WORK
    Caroline Webb   131

Chapter 9
THE DISCLOSURE OF WORK IN THE POETRY OF RON SILLIMAN
    Christopher Oakey   145

Part IV
CLASS IDENTITY AND CLASS CONFLICT

Chapter 10
SWEDISH SOCIAL MODERNISM: THE INWARD AND OUTWARD
TURN IN EYVIND JOHNSON'S *STAD I LJUS*
    Niklas Salmose   163

Chapter 11
PERCUSSION AND REPERCUSSION: THE HAITIAN REVOLUTION
AS WORKER UPRISING IN GUY ENDORE'S *BABOUK* (1934) AND
C. L. R. JAMES'S *BLACK JACOBINS* (1938)
    Sascha Morrell   179

Chapter 12
DOMESTIC HOLOCAUST: MICHAEL HANEKE'S INTRACTABLE
CLASS WAR
    Paul Sheehan   197

AFTERWORD: WORK, MODERNISM, AND THINKING THROUGH
THE AESTHETIC
    Morag Shiach   211

Index   217

FIGURES

4.1	Strauss, *Symphonia Domestica*, transcribed for piano by Otto Singer (Berlin: Bote & Bock, 1907), bars 1–22	75
4.2	Strauss, *Symphonia Domestica* (Berlin: Bote & Bock, 1904), bars 410–422 (reduced score)	75
4.3	Strauss, *Symphonia Domestica* (Berlin: Bote & Bock, 1904), bars 559–570	76
6.1	Alan Alborough, *Beautiful Objects: Ellipses and Asterisk*, 1997. Installation view, University of the Witwatersrand Art Galleries, University of the Witwatersrand. Image courtesy of the artist	99
6.2	Alan Alborough, *Beautiful Objects: Hyphen*, 1997. Plastic pegs, cable ties, coins, electric cable. Dimensions variable. Image courtesy of the artist	100
6.3	Alan Alborough, *Beautiful Objects: Ellipses*, 1997. Detail. Plastic pegs, mixing bowls, cable ties, coins, electric cable. Image courtesy of the artist	100
6.4	Penny Siopis, *Patience on a Monument: A History Painting*, 1988. (Detail). 180 × 200 cm, oil and collage on board. Collection: William Humphreys Art Gallery, Kimberley. Image courtesy of the artist	102
6.5	Penny Siopis, *Reconnaissance 1900–1997*, 1997. Detail of installation at Goodman Gallery, Johannesburg. Image courtesy of the artist	103
6.6	Penny Siopis, *Reconnaissance 1900–1997*, 1997. Detail of installation at Goodman Gallery, Johannesburg. Image courtesy of the artist	104
6.7	Usha Seejarim, *50 Stories*, 1997. (Detail) Dimensions variable. Found objects, pigment, Perspex, steel. Image courtesy of the artist	106
6.8	View from the "Top of Africa": the 50th floor of the Carlton Centre, looking west onto Johannesburg. Photo: Alison Kearney	107

CONTRIBUTORS

John Attridge is a Senior Lecturer in English at the University of New South Wales. His main research field is modernist literature, with a particular focus on modernist conceptions of authorship and the relationship between literature and specialization. He is co-editor, with Rod Rosenquist, of *Incredible Modernism: Literature, Trust and Deception* (2013) and his essays have appeared in journals such as *ELH*, *Modernism/modernity*, *Modern Fiction Studies*, and *The Henry James Review*.

Robert Buch is a Senior Lecturer in German and European Studies at the University of New South Wales. His research and publications focus on modern European literature and intellectual history, with a particular interest in the afterlife of theological figures and topoi in modern poetics. His main publications are *The Pathos of the Real: On the Aesthetics of Violence in the Twentieth Century* (2010) as well as the essay collection *Blumenberg lesen* (2014), co-edited with Daniel Weidner.

Evelyn T. Y. Chan is Associate Professor of English at the Chinese University of Hong Kong. Her publications include *Virginia Woolf and the Professions* (2014) and essays on Joseph Conrad.

Kristin Grogan recently completed a DPhil in English at Hertford College, Oxford, where she wrote a thesis on American modernist poetry and labor. From October 2018, she will be a Junior Research Fellow at St. Catharine's College, Cambridge.

Alison Kearney is a scholar of contemporary African art. She obtained her PhD in 2016 from the University of the Witwatersrand in Johannesburg where she is currently full-time Lecturer. Through focusing her research on the use of found objects by contemporary African artists, Kearney explores the trajectory of the modernist avant-garde in contemporary African art. She has written numerous articles and writes education materials for Wits Art Museum. Her recent publication *Art History is Dead! Long Live Art History!* (2017) considers ways of overcoming the seeming impossibility of writing about contemporary African art from a decolonial perspective.

David Larkin is Senior Lecturer in Musicology at the Sydney Conservatorium of Music, University of Sydney. His research focuses mainly on the music of

Liszt, Wagner, and Richard Strauss, exploring issues such as intertextuality, ideologies of progress, and relationships with literary and visual cultures. His work has appeared in *19th-Century Music, Music and the Moving Image, The Cambridge Companion to Richard Strauss*, and *The Musical Quarterly*. He gives regular pre-concert talks at the Sydney Opera House and is active as a reviewer of classical music concerts and opera.

Sascha Morrell is Lecturer in Literary Studies at Monash University. She completed her PhD at the University of Cambridge and was a Visiting Research Scholar at New York University in Fall 2015. She is the co-editor of *Flann O'Brien and Modernism* (2014) and has published widely on American and modernist literatures while completing a book project on race, labor, historiography, and visual culture in the fiction of Herman Melville and William Faulkner. She has a special interest in the appropriation of Haitian history and cultural motifs (including the zombie) in US fiction, theater, and film.

Christopher Oakey completed his PhD in 2017 on the philosophical influences of Martin Heidegger and Ludwig Wittgenstein on late-modernist American poetry, specifically focusing on George Oppen and Ron Silliman. He has published previously on Oppen's Heideggerian poetry and on the epistemological poetry of William Carlos Williams. His current research focuses on changing conceptions of the interpretive capacities of poetry in modernist and post-modernist America.

Helen Rydstrand received her PhD in 2016 from the University of New South Wales. Her first book, *Rhythmic Modernism: Mimesis and the Short Story* was published by Bloomsbury in 2019. She is currently working on a new major project, focusing on the concept of mimesis as a point of contact between early twentieth-century anthropology and modernist culture.

Niklas Salmose is Senior Lecturer in English Literature at Linnaeus University, Sweden, where he is an active member of the Linnaeus University Center for Intermedial and Multimodal Studies (IMS). He is part of the international research project "Nostalgia in Contemporary Culture" and is currently guest editor for a special issue on contemporary nostalgia for the journal *Humanities*. His recent publications include work on F. Scott Fitzgerald, animal horror, translation, nostalgia and modernism, Nordic Noir, Alfred Hitchcock, and the Anthropocene. He is currently editing a volume titled *Transmediations. Communication across Media Borders*.

Paul Sheehan is Associate Professor at Macquarie University, Sydney. He is the author of *Modernism and the Aesthetics of Violence* (2013), and the editor of "Post-Archival Beckett: Genre, Process, Value" (2017), a special issue of the

Journal of Beckett Studies. As well as recently publishing essays on Marcel Proust, Albert Einstein, and cryptographic modernism, he has been working on a book-length study of late, postwar modernism that examines cinematic and musical works as well as literary works.

Morag Shiach is Professor of Cultural History in the School of English and Drama at Queen Mary University of London, where she also directs Network: QMUL's Centre for the Creative and Cultural Economy. Her books include: (co-edited with Tarek E Virani) *Cultural Policy, Innovation and the Creative Economy*, *Modernism, Labour and Selfhood in British Literature and Culture, 1890–1930*, (ed.) *The Cambridge Companion to the Modernist Novel*, and *Discourse on Popular Culture: Class, Gender and History in Cultural Analysis 1730 to the Present*. Her current research is on immaterial labor, language reform in the early twentieth century, knowledge exchange with the creative economy, and marginal modernisms.

Emmett Stinson is the author of *Satirizing Modernism* (2017) and has also edited two collections of essays on Australian publishing. He is a Chief Investigator on the ARC Discovery Project, "New Tastemakers and Australia's Post-Digital Literary Culture." He is currently researching the late novels of Gerald Murnane.

Caroline Webb is Associate Professor in English Literature at the University of Newcastle, Australia, where she specializes in English fantasy literature (including children's literature) and modern literature. She has published articles on a range of authors, including Virginia Woolf, James Joyce, Lewis Carroll, Jeanette Winterson, and Angela Carter. Her book *Fantasy and the Real World in British Children's Literature: The Power of Story*, examining the children's fiction of J. K. Rowling, Terry Pratchett, and Diana Wynne Jones, was published October 2014. In 2010–14 she served as Secretary of the Australasian Children's Literature Association for Research.

ACKNOWLEDGMENTS

This collection grew out of a conference held at UNSW Sydney. The many wonderful presentations and discussions that took place at that event provided the project with its initial momentum. We would like, in particular, to thank our co-organizers, Jasmin Kelaita, James Dutton, and Trish May, as well as Susan Best, Christopher Nealon, and Morag Shiach, who all traveled from afar and contributed generously. We are grateful for the material support of the Australasian Modernist Studies Network, the Centre for Modernism Studies in Australia, the Faculty of Arts and Social Sciences, and the School of the Arts and Media, which collectively made the conference possible. A timely grant from the School of the Arts and Media was also instrumental in this book's final stages.

AN INTRODUCTION TO MODERNIST WORK

John Attridge

"Work" is a modernist keyword. In the phrase "work of art," it designates one of modernism's most actively debated aesthetic and ontological questions, calling to mind such topics as the artwork's status in an age of mechanical reproduction, its famous (supposed) autonomy, and, in the case of a Dada ready-made, a Surrealist *poème automatique,* and many other novel pretenders to the category of art, the extent to which a modernist art object can be considered a "work" at all. As these two examples imply, the concept of the work of art as a product is closely tied to the idea of work as an artistic practice: the labor performed by an artist.[1] Always a vexed topic in modern aesthetics, the question of how to understand the relationship between artistic or literary "work" and other forms of productive activity was one that modernist artists and writers posed and answered in new ways. If some strands of modernism refused the model of artisanal making altogether, others fashioned an image of the artist or writer as a conscientious laborer or a highly skilled technician. "Work," finally, is a modernist keyword because the *Arbeitswelt* itself underwent a series of fundamental transformations in the late nineteenth and early twentieth centuries—the era traditionally thought to coincide with the modernist movement in art and literature. While in some ways a chapter in the long history of industrialization, the half-century from 1880 to 1930 was also a period of innovation and upheaval for both manual and intellectual labor—one which presided over the birth of the modern "scientific" production line as well as the modern office. Not incidentally, the same period was a crucial one in the emergence of the labor movement, socialist politics, and class consciousness. The meanings of these new social and technical developments were by no means given. To consider how twentieth-century work was mediated in the period's art and literature is to examine one of the arenas in which these meanings were formed.

In bringing together chapters that address labor or class with essays on the concept of the modernist work of art or the idea of the working artist, the aim of this book is not to argue that the nature of artistic work is reducible to changes in the means of production or the history of labor. Our intention, rather, is to position the concept of "work" at the nexus of multiple discourses—as a keyword, in fact—that inform one another without being mutually determining. A keyword is a crossroads: some senses of work might pass through this junction unimpeded, but the word itself serves to mark a point of intersection, making it possible to identify deviations, meetings, and collisions. The task of this introduction is less to proffer a unifying definition of "modernist work" than to give a sense of lay of the land—to sketch the common background against which the book's case studies stand out as figures. One part of this background is more theoretical, involving an introduction to the concept of the work of art in modernist aesthetics and some of the ways in which this concept has been theorized. The other part is more historical, consisting of a (necessarily selective) survey of developments in the social history of work around the turn of the twentieth century, and a review of these themes in recent modernist studies.

"Around the turn of the twentieth century": it would once have been possible to write, "during the modernist period." As a large body of recent work on "late modernism" attests, however, modernism's clear temporal boundaries are not what they once were. While the majority of the essays collected here deal with the "paleo-modernist" era, to use Frank Kermode's term, the reader will also find chapters on the Language poet Ron Silliman, the contemporary artists Alan Alborough, Penny Siopis, and Usha Seejarim, and the film-maker Michael Haneke.[2] It is evident that the conditions of global capitalism encountered by, say, Silliman in the post-war United States are very different from those that obtained in 1910, 1913, 1922, or any of the other dates that have been proposed as modernist watersheds. But if, as Jasper Bernes cogently argues, the art and literature of the 1960s and after can be read as a response to a new, "*post industrial*" phase of capitalist development, this large-scale paradigm shift inevitably conceals partial continuities and fractal similarities.[3] In some respects, for instance, the "new forms of technocratic management and control" that characterize middle-class work in the postindustrial era continue an "office revolution" that began in the early twentieth century.[4] Modernism's typists, telegraphists, clerks, bureaucrats, and insurance workers bear witness to the birth of a modern "informatic" society, which anticipates in many ways the full-blown information economy of the late twentieth century.[5] In focusing the brief historical section of this introduction on the decades either side of 1900, I don't mean to assign a unique explanatory value to these developments, as though 1880 to 1930 could give us the key to modernism in all of its various adjectival or prefixal iterations—late, inter-, neo-, etc.[6] Nonetheless, the attitudes that formed in response to these conditions had long afterlives, while the effects of changes that originated or matured during this period would continue to be felt during the era of deindustrialization.

"[T]he inevitable collapse of all technique"

Let me begin with a micro-episode in the reception history of the European avant-gardes, which will serve as well as any other to remind us why the received category of the work was one of modernism's most productive irritants. In April 1920, the popular French monthly *Les Hommes du jour* published a reproduction of Francis Picabia's ink splash *La Sainte Vierge* (*The Holy Virgin*) (1920) alongside Ingres's identically titled 1841 religious painting, under the dead-pan heading "Deux écoles" ("Two schools"). Picabia's splatter belongs to the heroic age of Dada agitation, and is often cited as a touchstone of that movement's anti-art project. But although *La Sainte Vierge* counts as an extreme case within the spectrum of early-twentieth-century artistic disruption, and the sardonic response of the magazine's editors adhered to an already well-worn script, the incident provides a useful introduction to one of this collection's *idées mères*. For while, of course, the comparison was intended to chastise Picabia's irreverence, the force of the contrast also depends upon Ingres's status as a great technical master, *chef d'école* of the French Neoclassicists and a paragon of technical discipline. It foregrounds, in other words, the extent to which a consecrated work of art was precisely that: the product not only of spontaneous genius but also of arduous, highly skilled facture. In a short piece published in *Les Ecrits nouveaux* the following year, Picabia's Dada associate, Louis Aragon, derided the *Hommes du jour* centerfold, offering, in the process, an explanation of the beliefs that informed it. Aragon dismisses the comparison of the two works as a typically flat-footed example of "the criticism of our era" ("la critique de notre époque"), which judges only by "analogy" ("analogie") and "pun" ("calembour").[7] What such judgments failed to comprehend was that the avant-garde break with tradition had brought with it the "inevitable collapse of all technique" ("faillite inévitable de toute technique").[8] Failing to understand this aspect of the contemporary situation, the bourgeois public responds to a work of art like Picabia's *Sainte Vierge* by complaining that it is not one: "everyone would make as much of it" ("tout le monde en ferait autant"), grumbles the indignant spectator.[9]

This stereotypical Dada anecdote serves to illustrate a more general problematic in the history and theory of modern art: modernism, many critics and theorists have observed, demanded new ways of thinking about the category of the work. Peter Bürger, for instance, in a chapter of *Theory of the Avant-Garde* (1974) devoted to this topic, argues that "[w]e must distinguish" between "a general meaning of the concept 'work' and differing historical instantiations," like those formulated by the avant-gardes.[10] Such Surrealist techniques as *le hasard objectif*, *l'objet trouvé* and constructive montage rebelled, not against the artistic category of the work itself, but against a received "organic" version of this concept, in which "the unity of the universal and the particular is posited without mediation."[11] In *Aesthetic Theory* (1970), likewise, Theodor Adorno returns repeatedly to the problem of conceptualizing the artwork during the era of modernism. The avant-garde axioms of "experimentation" and "construction," for instance, introduce a distance between the "subjective imagination" and the product of artistic labor, necessitating "solutions that the imagining ear or eye does not immediately encompass or know in detail."[12] Emulating the scientist's "conscious control over materials," artistic experimentation is "primarily concerned with means," rather than with the telos of the finished work.[13] Hence,

> [i]n sharp contrast to traditional art, new art accents the once hidden element of being something made, something produced. The portion of it that is θεσει (posited, put) grew to such an extent that all efforts to secrete away the process of production in the work could not but fail.[14]

The modernist work of art both flaunts its own madeness and replaces the ideal of a seamless organic whole with the image of a constructive process. Contemporary art, Adorno observes, embraces "the pleasure of substituting for artworks the process of their own production," so that "[t]oday every work is virtually what Joyce declared *Finnegans Wake* to be before he published the whole: *work in progress.*"[15]

For Adorno and Bürger, like their Frankfurt School comrade Walter Benjamin, the status of the work of art was one of the research questions that an emergent aesthetics of modernism needed to address: how, they asked, should this category be understood in the age of ready-mades and experimentalism, photography and cinema, industrial reification and technological hubris? The themes of these canonical interventions may no longer set the agenda of aesthetic debate, but, as Emmett Stinson's essay in this volume demonstrates, the concept of the work continues to attract theoretical attention in contemporary modernist studies. Lisa Siraganian's *Modernism's Other Work: The Art Object's Political Life* (2012), for instance, posits that "modernism's core aesthetic problem" is still "the artwork's status as an object and a subject's relation to it"—a problem which poses "fundamental questions of agency, freedom, and politics."[16] *Pace* Bürger, Siraganian argues that the critical commonplace of the work's aesthetic "autonomy" should be construed, not as "the art object's removal from life praxis," but rather in terms of meaning and interpretation: for writers like Gertrude Stein and Wyndham Lewis, autonomy implies "the beholder's irrelevance to an object's meaning."[17] Another recent reconsideration of the status of the modernist work of art, Todd Cronan's *Against Affective Formalism: Matisse, Bergson, Modernism* (2013), focuses on the history of claims about the work's intentionality. Cronan argues that theories of the artwork as an affect machine, generally associated with postmodern art criticism, are in fact continuous with "a set of failed beliefs of modernist theory and practice," which likewise substituted the direct affective agency of color and line for an idea of the work's intentional expressiveness.[18] Contra this discourse of "affective formalism," Cronan concludes that art's intentional character is precisely what distinguishes the work of art from other objects in the world. Although their angles of intervention differ—the postmodern aesthetic that Siraganian terms "incorporation" belongs, indeed, to the school of thought that Cronan argues against—these recent studies suggest that the work of art remains a contested concept in contemporary modernist aesthetics.

Arts and crafts

Changing attitudes towards the category of the work of art are closely related to changing conceptions of the process of artistic production. Thus, for Adorno, the modernist emphasis on experimentation tends to produce artworks that are self-evidently constructed, "[i]n emphatic opposition to the illusion of the organic nature of art."[19] This contrast between the modern artist's "conscious control over materials" and the traditional "image of the artist's unconscious organic labor" evokes the specter of a familiar problem in the definition of artistic work, to do with the vexed distinction between art and craft.[20] As is often pointed out, the Ancient Greek word *"technê"* made no distinction between these different kinds of production, denoting the practical knowledge used for "bringing something into being," as Aristotle put it in *The Nicomachean Ethics*, whether that something is a house or a poem.[21] The concept of *technê* thus marks an obvious point of intersection between art and certain kinds of work: like other expert makers, practitioners of the modern fine arts use a knowledge-based skill to fashion their works. But if the affinity between art and craft served in the nineteenth century to bolster the idea of art as a special kind of unalienated labor—a "saving clause in a bad treaty," as Raymond Williams has it—the modern discourse of aesthetics also enshrines a distinction between mere technique (Adorno's "conscious control over materials") and the capacity to produce a work of art.[22] In *Aesthetics* (1835), for example, Hegel observes that while "all the arts require lengthy study, constant industry, a skill developed in many ways," the "genuine artist" combines technical "execution" with a "natural gift"; "a purely learnt proficiency," on the other hand, "never produces a living work of art."[23]

The art/craft distinction is one way of approaching the question of artistic work; historically, indeed, the question and the distinction might be said to arise simultaneously, at a moment when the "genuine artist" and the skilled artisan split apart into different social identities. For Adorno in *Aesthetic Theory*, this familiar aesthetic distinction has little relevance for the art of modernism, which is enmeshed in different conditions of production than those that pertain to artisanal making. In this respect, Adorno's modernist aesthetics contrasts sharply with another influential twentieth-century meditation on the nature of the work of art—one that engages explicitly with the idea of *technê* and the art/craft divide. In "The Origin of the Work of Art" (1935–6), Martin Heidegger rejects the proposition that the concept of art can be derived from that of craft, at least as it is conventionally understood. Whereas such a connection might be inferred from the Greek use of *technê* to designate both spheres of activity, Heidegger famously reinterprets *technê* to mean "mode of knowing," in the sense of *alêtheia*, or unveiling: both works of art and products of handicraft cause "beings in the first place to come forward."[24] This is a construction of *technê* to which Heidegger returns in another well-known paper, "The Question Concerning Technology" (1953). Here, again, he sublimates the conventional opposition between art and craft by defining *technê* as "revealing, and not as manufacturing": contra the modern art/craft dichotomy, all *technê* implies *poiêsis* (making or, as Heidegger has it, "bringing-forth").[25]

"The Question Concerning Technology" is doubly pertinent in the context of modernist work because it addresses the effect of modern technology—"the first technology based on physics as an exact science"—on the concept of artistic production as *technê*. For Heidegger, modern technological objects like an airplane, a hydroelectric dam, or an atomic bomb signify a fundamentally different mode of unveiling than that involved in the work of a peasant or an artisan. Modern technology is not a "bringing-forth in the sense of *poiesis*," but rather a "setting-upon that challenges the energies of nature."[26] In a concluding section, Heidegger suggests that the dangerous "objectlessness" of this technological world, which alienates man from his "essence," may be counteracted by art: a return to a certain conception of artistic work—art as *technê*, as a mode of knowing and unveiling that is common to both art and craft—holds the remedy for technological alienation and the reduction of nature to a "standing-reserve."[27] In this respect, Heidegger's understanding of the relationship between artistic work and industrial technology is diametrically opposed to Adorno's demanding conception of modernism. For Adorno, art cannot be a sanctuary from the technological forces of production. Rather,

> [t]he substantive element of artistic modernism draws its power from the fact that the most advanced procedures of material production and organization are not limited to the sphere in which they originate.... [Rather], they radiate out into areas of life far removed from them, deep into the zones of subjective experience, which does not notice this and guards the sanctity of its reserves. Art is modern when, by its mode of experience and as the expression of the crisis of experience, it absorbs what industrialization has developed under the given relations of production.[28]

From Adorno's perspective, the Heidegger of "Question" would resemble those "traditionalists" who revile the "technologization of art" as a "loss of soul": it is only a conservative, expressivist conception of artistic work that regards such "technologization" as anti-aesthetic.[29] By radicalizing "reification," "absorb[ing] what industrialization has developed," accepting the alienation of the creative subject, modern art wins access to "the expression of what no significant language can achieve."[30]

For both Heidegger and Adorno, modern technology exacerbates the tension between art and craft, creating the need for new formulations of the nature of artistic work. For Heidegger, technology has become alienated from *technê*, so that the responsibility of preserving a traditional ontology of productive labor falls to the artist. For Adorno, conversely, a modernism worthy of the name will not flinch from "the most advanced procedures of material production." What Adorno calls the "technologization of art" is thus a natural continuation of avant-garde experimentation and construction, which is "primarily concerned with means" and generates formal "solutions that the imagining ear or eye does not immediately encompass or know in detail."[31] The modernist emphasis on technique, as a program or plan executed by the artist, breaks with the idea of an organic shaping of materials; rather, like the pilot of an airplane or a worker in a hydroelectric power station, the modern artist submits to the mediation of an opaque technical process. Although they seem to move in opposite directions, the "technologization of art" and Aragon's "collapse of all technique" perform an identical destabilization of artistic work. Picabia's ink splash might thus be said to reflect the "most advanced procedures of material production" just as well as a hyper-technical artistic practice like, say, serial composition: in neither case is a nostalgic idea of work as craft allowed to structure the concept of artistic production.

"[T]he most advanced procedures of material production"

In insisting that changes in industrial practices necessitate corresponding changes in artistic practices, Adorno draws a characteristically radical inference from what is a relatively unexceptionable proposition about modernism: modernist art and literature were shaped in important ways by the developing "procedures of material production"—by changes, that is, in the conditions and meaning of human work. By any measure, the period traditionally associated with the emergence of modernism was also a time of rapid and tumultuous change in work's social, political, and economic history. In the sphere of manual labor, the half-century from 1880 to 1930 witnessed a host of transformative developments: the rise of large industrial concentrations in a growing number of industries, the spread of mechanization and continuous-process manufacturing, and the uneven but inexorable adoption of what the engineer F. W. Taylor called "scientific management," to name a few.[32] Partly as a result of these changes in the material conditions of manufacturing and industry, and partly in response to the various strains of socialism that flourished in the wake of the Second Paris International, the decades that straddle the turn of the twentieth century were also critical ones for the formation of a sense of collective working-class identity, or class consciousness, in many industrial societies. Hence, in the British context, argues Eric Hobsbawm, "the so-called 'traditional' working class with its specific patterns of life and views of life did not emerge much before the 1880s and took shape over the next couple of decades."[33] A notable manifestation of this mass class identity was the rise of modern trade-unionism and an upsurge of *industrial action*— itself a novel term, which made its first recorded appearance in 1914 (*OED*). As Richard J. Evans observes, "[l]abour unrest reached unprecedented heights in the last decade and a half before the outbreak of the First World War, fuelled by a renewal of economic growth that reflected not least the increasing demand from governments for arms and ammunition."[34] If the outbreak of war brought the worsening industrial strife of the Edwardian period to an artificial conclusion, this was a temporary cessation of hostilities, rather than a lasting settlement. In Britain, in particular, the 1926 General Strike seared the ideas of class conflict and worker solidarity ineffaceably into the imaginations of the period's cultural elites.[35]

A number of studies over the past two decades have addressed the relationship between modernism and the changing nature of manual labor in industrial societies. Largely, although not exclusively, focused on physical work is Morag Shiach's important *Modernism, Labour and Selfhood in British Literature and Culture, 1890–1930* (2004), which examines the ways in which work came to define notions of selfhood in the modern era. Modernist texts are read as sites for the "cultural contestation of the meanings of labor," especially those meanings concerned with the impact of mechanization and the changing position of women in the workforce.[36] Similarly engaged with the question of what is distinctively modern about work during the moment of high modernism is Evelyn Cobley's *Modernism and the Culture of Efficiency* (2009). Building on previous studies like James Knapp's *Literary Modernism and the Transformation of Work* (1988) and Martha Banta's *Taylored Lives: Narrative Productions in the Age of Taylor, Veblen, and Ford* (1993), Cobley charts an extensive network of connections between Fordist and Taylorist theories of management and modernist writing. As Shiach points out, however, it is important not to overstate the degree to which such processes of modernization were universal: if new technologies introduced labor-saving machines into the home and created new forms of waged work for women, it was equally true that 40 percent of British working women in 1901 were still engaged in domestic service.[37] This social fact provides the starting point for another recent study of modernist representations of manual labor, Mary Wilson's *The Labors of Modernism: Domesticity, Servants, and Authorship in Modernist Fiction* (2013), which explores the complex relationship between "a domesticity supported by servants" and the critique of that domesticity in modernist women's writing.[38] Work as manual labor is also the primary focus of Valerie Mainz and Griselda Pollock's valuable edited collection *Work in Modern Times: Visual Mediations and Social Processes* (2000), which tracks representations of work in the visual arts and film, from the painting and sculpture of the classical avant-garde to feminist documentary in the 1970s. Also relevant in this connection, finally, are studies that challenge the methodological barrier between the received modernist canon and what Nick Hubble calls, after William Empson, "proletarian literature." Hubble revives this label to define a "heterogeneous category" of 1930s writing that includes not just texts by working-class authors but also other works that engage with the "intersubjective connections between the worker and people of other classes."[39]

The transformation of work during the late nineteenth and early twentieth centuries was not, of course, confined to the sphere of manual labor. Indeed, one of the period's most notable social changes was the growth of white-collar occupations as a proportion of waged employment. To take the British context once again as an example, the number of white-collar employees increased more than threefold in the United Kingdom between 1871 and 1911, from 262,084 to 918,186.[40] As both businesses and state bureaucracies became larger, more complex, and more interconnected, this demographic shift was accompanied by a rationalization of office work practices, driven in part by the adoption of new efficiency technologies: devices such as "loose-leaf ledgers, card indexes, vertical filing systems, typewriters, telephones, Dictaphones, adding machines [and] duplicators" all became standard office equipment in the years between 1880 and 1920.[41] The transformation of office culture during this period has been the subject of a growing body of scholarship in recent years, driven in part by the research concerns of modernist media studies.[42] In Friedrich Kittler's influential account, the arrival of the typewriter, along with the gramophone and the cinematograph, signaled the demise of a certain Romantic conception of literary presence, premised on, inter alia, the immediacy of hand-writing: "Typewriters do not store individuals; their letters do not communicate a beyond that perfectly alphabetized readers can subsequently hallucinate as meaning."[43] Critics such as Shiach and Mullin have shown how early-twentieth-century literary culture responded with ambivalence to both the typewriter and the typist, which were seen by some authors as an incursion of inauthenticity and commercialism into the domain of artistic creation.[44]

The world of white-collar work was also transformed in the twentieth century by the consolidation of what the historian Harold Perkin has called "professional society": a social formation in which accredited knowledge-workers both represent an expanding proportion of the workforce and command a disproportionate share of cultural authority.[45] Professionalism has often been invoked as an explanatory context for modernism, seeming to provide an analog for its deployment of esoteric knowledge as symbolic capital and its squeamishness about unadulterated market relations. Thomas Strychacz, for instance, argues that professionals and modernist writers both used "special, esoteric discourse[s]" to "demarcate a space that exists culturally, economically, and linguistically apart from mass culture and the imperatives of the mass market."[46] As Evelyn Chan points out, however, applying this "hermeneutics of suspicion" too crudely to modernist culture as a whole risks overlooking the specificity of particular responses, such as, for instance, Virginia Woolf's self-conscious ambivalence about professional ideology.[47]

The advent of new communication technologies, the modernization of office work, and the rise of professionalism were all implicated in another important historical shift: the changing nature of women's work and the gradual erosion of barriers between the feminine domestic sphere and the masculine sphere of the workplace. Two of the technologies that transformed the way that modern offices stored and transmitted information, for instance—the telegraph and the typewriter—also created new, emblematically modern employment opportunities for women. The late nineteenth and twentieth centuries saw a massive influx of women into the clerical labor force, with female clerks accounting for 29 percent of all clerical workers in the United States by 1900.[48] This process of "feminization" occurred somewhat later in Britain, where the proportion of clerks who were women grew from 13 to 60 percent during the first half of the twentieth century.[49] Although not all women clerks operated typewriters, the figure of the "typewriter girl" or "typist" emerged towards the end of the nineteenth century as a recognizable social type, considered one of the few occupations that did not entail a loss of "class standing" for middle-class women.[50] As Mullin persuasively shows, the typist was the "younger sister" of the telegraphist, another new occupation for women, which likewise assumed the status of a gendered social identity.[51] Together, these forms of work became the kernels of new, potentially transgressive "sexual personae," ambiguously located within the masculine sphere of the office.[52] Like the other social identities Mullin considers, "shopgirls" and "barmaids," typists and telegraphists became the object of a prolific representational discourse, spanning both popular and canonical literature.

By contrast with these modern forms of information work, professional identity at the turn of the twentieth century was still overwhelmingly identified with masculinity, although legislation like the 1919 Sex Disqualification Removal Act in Britain was a sign of incipient change. As Francesca Sawaya has argued, a variety of American women writers in the late nineteenth and twentieth centuries deployed the interlocking discourses of domesticity and professionalism to "authorize and shape" their own forms of professional work, laying claim, for instance, to a "feminized transcendent expertise" for women as social workers.[53] When Virginia Woolf contemplated the entry of women into the professions around the time of the 1919 Act, Chan notes, she displayed a comparable form of ambivalence, recognizing the material advantage to women of the new professional opportunities, but also mistrusting the nature of existing professional institutions, which were insufficiently attuned to the individual and the "private sphere."[54]

"[M]aking and seeing"

We have seen that Adorno's *Aesthetic Theory* and Heidegger's "The Question Concerning Technology" represent conflicting responses to the predicament of art in an advanced technological society, delineating, in the process, divergent theories of the modern work of art. By way of conclusion, I want to consider a more recent aesthetic theory of the relationship between art and work—one which also takes its bearings from the Greek concept of *technê*, but which unpacks the implications of this etymon in a different way. The final chapter of Jacques Rancière's *The Politics of Aesthetics* (2004; French edition 2000), entitled "On art and work," begins with an unusual reading of Book III of Plato's *Republic*. For Rancière, the poet is a danger to the Platonic republic, not because he fashions simulacra, but because he violates the proper distribution of *technês*. Whereas Plato's civic order restricts each individual to the practice of a single function, excluding artisans, for instance, from political decision-making, the poet is a double being: by imitating the *technês* of others, he brings the hidden domain of labor into the political realm of speech and representation. Transposing this classical schema to the industrial era, Rancière makes a distinction between fabrication and production, playing on the meaning of "to produce" (*produire*) as showing or making something public. If "manufacturing" (*fabriquer*) means "inhabiting the private and lowly [*obscur*] space-time of labour for sustenance" [*travail nourricier*], "producing," by contrast, "unites the act of manufacturing with the act of bringing to light, of defining a new relation between making and seeing."[55] Modernism, too, instantiates this paradigm. At the moment of the 1917 Russian Revolution, for instance, "art and production would be identified because they came under one and the same principle concerning the redistribution of the sensible."[56] The Soviet avant-garde provides a convenient shorthand for the modernist making-public of work, but Rancière might also have adduced the interpretation of modernist experimentalism we find in Adorno's *Aesthetic Theory*. As a movement that is concerned with means and processes, that embraces "the pleasure of substituting for artworks the process of their own production," Adorno's modernism internalizes the principle of visible work as a formal procedure. In this way, modernism's concern with technique would continue a narrative that begins, for Rancière, with Plato, and the idea of poetry as the imitation of a *technê* in the public sphere.

No single theory or methodology informs the chapters that comprise this book. Nonetheless, Rancière's construction of the art/work binary articulates a question that concerns them all. Seeing art as fabrication-plus-publicness is a way of understanding aesthetics as intrinsically political—concerned with the differential distribution of the sensible—but it also engages with the more general problem of the representability of work. The idea of a primordial separation between manual labor and the public sphere, which Rancière ascribes to Plato's republic, is also an allegory of work's resistance to representation: work, by definition, whether because of technical opacity or cumulative hardship, is what only the worker knows, what the layperson or the sociologist can grasp only theoretically. With respect to manual labor, we sometimes call the dangers associated with this problem "romanticization" or "primitivism": however free they are from pastoral idealism, representations like *L'Angelus* or *Des Glaneuses*, for example, can still be accused of a certain sentimentality, even if it is only the aestheticizing beam of the painter's gaze. For a book like ours, one of the virtues of Rancière's schema is that it approaches the distinction between art and work, not in terms of utility, for example, or genius, but as a problem of representation. Like Millet's paintings of peasants, modernist representations of labor come up against the problem of work's "private and obscure space-time": they engage, to a greater or lesser extent, with the Platonic trope of drawing hidden *technês* into the light. But modernism's own characteristic aesthetic concerns—its preoccupation with the technical conditions of its own possibility, its predilection for means and processes, its uneasiness with the category of the work of art—also imply an engagement with the question of work's visibility.

The same question is posed negatively in an artwork like Picabia's *La Sainte Vierge*. By invoking the visibility of art without the sanction of technique, Dada attacks the distinction between labor that circulates in a public economy of images, like Ingres's masterful painting, and labor that is deemed unworthy of representation—the labor congealed in a ceramic urinal, for example. We might indeed say that making the artist's work visible—teaching a public how to read, or how not to read, the traces of avant-garde artistic work—is one of modernism's abiding concerns. If what we moderns call art has always been defined by its separateness from the adjacent territory of work, modernism was a period of exceptional volatility in the terms of this settlement. Modernism was instrumental in producing the texts and images that mediated the meanings of twentieth-century labor. But these same changes in the meaning of work are also internal to the narrative of the modern movement itself, which might well be told as a series of attempts by artists and writers to understand their own ambiguous status as producers, their own strange privilege of visibility.

Overview

The first group of essays below is concerned in different ways with the modernist aesthetics of the work. Robert Buch's chapter, "The Absolute and the Impossible Work: Franz Kafka's 'The Burrow'" introduces this topic by examining Kafka's ambivalent engagement with the trope of the absolute or perfect work of art. "The Burrow," in which a badger-like creature works tirelessly to perfect its labyrinthine dwelling, seems to represent a "fantasy of symbiosis between maker and work." This ideal is shown to be maddeningly unachievable, however, the burrow's "autonomy" inevitably yielding to "the pressure from without." Autonomy is the central question considered in Emmett Stinson's chapter, "Autonomy, Difficulty, and the Work of Literature in Wyndham Lewis's *Tarr* and André Gide's *The Counterfeiters*." The autonomy of the work is traditionally supposed to be a modernist axiom, but novels like *Tarr* (1916–17) and *The Counterfeiters* (1925), Stinson argues, mobilize "autonomy claims" as "confrontational rhetorical assertions," rather than sincere statements of intent. Helen Rydstrand's chapter, "Mimesis and the Task of the Writer for Lawrence and Woolf," also questions a received idea about modernist aesthetics. The modernist work of art is conventionally supposed to eschew mimesis in favor of significant form, but the rhythmic conception of the universe elaborated by these two canonical modernists complicates the binary opposition between work and world.

The second cluster of essays focuses on the idea of artistic labor. In "Richard Strauss at Work in his Works," David Larkin explores the tension between methodical bourgeois industry and heroic self-aggrandizement in Strauss's musical self-representations. Strauss's *A Hero's Life* (1899), sometimes read as a hymn to creative genius, in fact takes up an ambivalent attitude towards this romantic trope. His *Symphonia Domestica* (1904), meanwhile, goes even further in the direction of demystification, suggesting that Strauss's "hyper-romantic sound-worlds originated … in mundane domesticity." In "Stein's Immaterial Labors," Kristin Grogan argues that Gertrude Stein fashioned an alternative conception of poetic labor, defined in opposition to the Poundian aesthetic of craft-based object-making. Challenging "masculinist orthodoxies around what aesthetic work means," Stein's poetry also asks questions about the definition of work itself, and the habitual separation between productive labor and our affective lives. In "Trace and Facture: Legacies of the 'Ready-Made' in Contemporary South African Art," Alison Kearney examines how the anti-art aesthetic of the found object has been adapted and reimagined by three twentieth-century artists: Alan Alborough, Penny Siopis, and Usha Seejarim. Like the classical avant-garde, these artists use found objects to interrogate traditional assumptions about artistic facture, but their work also shows how this avant-garde practice can be made to take on new connotations.

The section entitled "Representing Work and Workers" shifts the focus from the labor of the artist to artistic representations of work. In "Joseph Conrad's *Nostromo*: Work, Inheritance, and Desert in the Modernist Novel," Evelyn Chan argues that the novel's titular character imagines work, not as the exchange of labor for wages, but as the guarantee of an inheritance. Nostromo's paradoxical belief that he can earn his inheritance allows the novel to "critique assumptions of meritocratic desert," which formed an important part of the Victorian ideology of work. Caroline Webb's chapter, "Magic, Modernity, and Women at Work," examines the representation of women's work in two post-war fantasy narratives, Stella Benson's *Living Alone* (1919) and Ronald Fraser's *Flower Phantoms* (1926). In different ways, both novels engage with the changed attitudes towards work for women that came about as a result of the war, as well as exploring the relationship, central to this volume's concerns, between ordinary labor and the idea or practice of art. Christopher Oakey's chapter, "The Disclosure of Work in the Poetry of Ron Silliman," examines the connection in Silliman's poetry between working-class labor and quotidian forms of violence. Drawing on Heidegger's notion of poetic "disclosure," Oakey reads Silliman's paratactic "new sentence" as a means of disclosing "the material and social Enframing of individuals within certain contemporary forms of work."

The final set of essays focuses on "Class Identity and Class Conflict." Niklas Salmose's chapter, "Swedish Social Modernism: The Inward and Outward Turn in Eyvind Johnson's *Stad i ljus*" (*City in Light*), engages with the question of working-class writing in Swedish literary history. Questioning the conventional antithesis between so-called proletarian literature and aesthetic modernism, Salmose reads Johnson's 1926 circadian novel as an example of "social modernism," which combines modernist stylistic features with the depiction of "social consciousness." In "Percussion and Repercussion: The Haitian Revolution as Worker Uprising in Guy Endore's *Babouk* (1934) and C. L. R. James's *Black Jacobins* (1938)," Sascha Morrell shows how two socialist intellectuals reimagined the events of the Haitian Revolution as a prototype of "worker solidarity and revolutionary organization." Both Endore and James sought to reclaim the image of "voodoo" from its primitivist associations, "presenting it instead as a positive medium for worker solidarity and revolutionary organization." Paul Sheehan's chapter, "Domestic Holocaust: Michael Haneke's Intractable Class War," traces the Austrian director's abiding preoccupation with the habitus of the European bourgeoisie. Haneke's "anti-bourgeois cinema," Sheehan argues, is based around his corrosive representation of two sacrosanct bourgeois "milieux": work and home.

Morag Shiach's Afterword begins by revisiting the modernist office worker considered in Chapter 1: Franz Kafka. Its fantastic premise notwithstanding, Kafka's 1915 story *Metamorphosis* is much concerned with the banal realities of Gregor Samsa's job as a traveling salesman, so that Gregor's transformation opens an imaginative space for "autonomy and agency." This mini-reading of *Metamorphosis* is followed by a survey of new developments in critical work studies, including the theory of immaterial labor, the prospects for a postwork future, and movements that aim to reimagine work itself outside of a capitalist model. At once tools of critique and forms of world-building, art and literature will have an important role to play in these projects.

Notes

1 In Hannah Arendt's influential interpretation, it is the fact that "work" can denote both a process and a product that distinguishes it from its synonym, "labor." Hannah Arendt, *The Human Condition* (Chicago: University of Chicago Press, 1998), 80. For a discussion of the different values that have been assigned to these terms, see Kathi Weeks, *The Problem with Work: Feminism, Marxism, Antiwork Politics, and Postwork Imaginaries* (Durham, NC: Duke University Press, 2011), 14–15. Like Weeks, we assert no systematic distinction between the two in this book.

2 Frank Kermode, "The Modern," in *Modern Essays* (London: Fontana Books, 1971), 60.
3 Jasper Bernes, *The Work of Art in the Age of Deindustrialization* (Stanford: Stanford University Press, 2017), 3.
4 Bernes, *Work of Art*, 7. Joanne Yates, *Control Through Communication: The Rise of System in American Management* (Baltimore: Johns Hopkins University Press, 1993), 63.
5 The "informatic revolution," writes James Purdon, "was as much a legacy of early twentieth-century bureaucracies as a post-industrial achievement." James Purdon, *Modernist Informatics: Literature, Information, and the State* (Oxford: Oxford University Press, 2015), 6–7.
6 Kristin Bluemel, ed. *Intermodernism: Literary Culture in Mid-Twentieth-Century Britain* (Edinburgh: Edinburgh University Press, 2011). "Neo" is Kermode's counterpart to "paleo."
7 Louis Aragon, "A quoi pensez-vous?," *Les Ecrits nouveaux* 8, no. 8–9 (1921), 151.
8 Aragon, "A quoi pensez-vous?," 150.
9 Aragon, "A quoi pensez-vous?," 150.
10 Peter Bürger, *Theory of the Avant-Garde* (Minneapolis: University of Minnesota Press, 1984), 56.
11 Bürger, *Theory of the Avant-Garde*, 56.
12 Theodor Adorno, *Aesthetic Theory* (London: Continuum, 2004), 31.
13 Adorno, *Aesthetic Theory*, 47.
14 Adorno, *Aesthetic Theory*, 33.
15 Adorno, *Aesthetic Theory*, 33–4.
16 Lisa Siraganian, *Modernism's Other Work: The Art Object's Political Life* (Oxford: Oxford University Press, 2012), 3.
17 Siraganian, *Modernism's Other Work*, 14–15.
18 Todd Cronan, *Against Affective Formalism: Matisse, Bergson, Modernism* (Minneapolis: University of Minnesota Press, 2013), 27.
19 Adorno, *Aesthetic Theory*, 44.
20 Adorno, *Aesthetic Theory*, 47.
21 Aristotle, *The Nicomachean Ethics*, trans. J. A. K. Thompson and Hugh Tredennick (London: Penguin, 2004), 149. R. G. Collingwood: "The Greeks and Romans had no conception of what we call art as something different from craft; what we call art they regarded merely as a group of crafts, such as the craft of poetry." R. G. Collingwood, *The Principles of Art* (Oxford: Clarendon Press, 1938), 5.
22 Raymond Williams, *Culture and Society 1780–1950* (Harmondsworth: Penguin, 1961), 81.
23 G. W. F. Hegel, *Aesthetics: Lectures on Fine Art*, trans. T. M. Knox (Oxford: Clarendon Press, 1975), 286.
24 Martin Heidegger, "The Origin of the Work of Art," in *Basic Writings*, ed. David Farrell Krell (London: Routledge, 1978), 184.
25 Martin Heidegger, "The Question Concerning Technology," in *Basic Writings*, ed. David Farrell Krell (London: Routledge, 1978), 315, 318.
26 Heidegger, "The Question Concerning Technology," 320–1.
27 Heidegger, "The Question Concerning Technology," 332.
28 Adorno, *Aesthetic Theory*, 43.
29 Adorno, *Aesthetic Theory*, 78.

30 Adorno, *Aesthetic Theory*, 78.
31 Adorno, *Aesthetic Theory*, 47, 31.
32 For an account of some of these changes in American industry from a business-historical perspective, see Alfred Chandler, *The Visible Hand: The Managerial Revolution in American Business* (Cambridge, MA: Harvard University Press, 1977). On deskilling, see Harry Braverman, *Labor and Monopoly Capital: The Degradation of Work in the Twentieth Century* (New York: Monthly Review Press, 1975).
33 E. J. Hobsbawm, *Worlds of Labour: Further Studies in the History of Labour* (London: Weidenfeld & Nicolson, 1984), 200. As Andrew Miles and Mike Savage point out, however, it is important not to underestimate the "slowness and unevenness" of these changes. *The Remaking of the British Working Class, 1840–1940* (London: Routledge, 1994), 22.
34 Richard J. Evans, *The Pursuit of Power: Europe, 1815–1914* (London: Penguin, 2016), 548.
35 The Strike "was that rare phenomenon, a truly public or universally experienced event." Charles Ferrall and Dougal McNeill, *Writing the 1926 General Strike: Literature, Culture, Politics* (New York: Cambridge University Press, 2015), 2.
36 Morag Shiach, *Modernism, Labour and Selfhood in British Literature and Culture, 1890–1930* (Cambridge: Cambridge University Press, 2004), 2.
37 Shiach, *Modernism, Labour and Selfhood*, 8.
38 Mary Wilson, *The Labors of Modernism: Domesticity, Servants, and Authorship in Modernist Fiction* (Burnham, VT: Ashgate, 2013), 3.
39 Nick Hubble, *The Proletarian Answer to the Modernist Question* (Edinburgh: Edinburgh University Press, 2017), 30, 7. A comparable study of proletarian literature in the United States is Barbara Foley's *Radical Representations: Politics and Form in U.S. Proletarian Fiction, 1929–1941* (1993), which sets out to rescue interwar proletarian fiction from the modernist-friendly proscriptions of New Criticism.
40 Jonathan Wild, *The Rise of the Office Clerk in Literary Culture, 1880–1939* (Basingstoke: Palgrave Macmillan, 2006), 3.
41 Lawrence Rainey, "More Office Affairs," *Modernism/modernity* 16, no. 1 (2009), 161.
42 See, for example, Christopher Keep, "The Cultural Work of the Type-Writer Girl," *Victorian Studies* 40, no. 3 (1997); Pamela Thurschwell, "Supple Minds and Automatic Hands: Secretarial Agency in Early Twentieth-Century Literature," *Forum for Modern Language Studies* 37, no. 2 (2001); Leah Price and Pamela Thurschwell, eds., *Literary Secretaries/Secretarial Culture* (Aldershot: Ashgate, 2005); Wild, *Rise of the Office Clerk*; Katherine Mullin, *Working Girls: Fiction, Sexuality, and Modernity* (Oxford: Oxford University Press, 2016), 17–94; Matthew Schilleman, "The Bureaucrat Inside: Kafka, Office Media, and the End of Authorship," *Symploke* 24, no. 1–2 (2016).
43 Friedrich Kittler, *Gramophone, Film, Typewriter*, trans. Geoffrey Winthrop-Young and Michael Wutz (Stanford: Stanford University Press, 1999), 14.
44 Shiach, *Modernism, Labour and Selfhood*, 59–78; Mullin, *Working Girls*, 54–94.
45 Harold Perkin, *The Rise of Professional Society: England Since 1880* (London: Routledge, 1989).
46 Thomas Strychacz, *Modernism, Mass Culture and Professionalism* (Cambridge: Cambridge University Press, 1993), 26.

47 Evelyn Chan, *Virginia Woolf and the Professions* (Cambridge: Cambridge University Press, 2014), 19.
48 Keep, "The Cultural Work of the Type-Writer Girl," 154.
49 Shiach, *Modernism, Labour and Selfhood*, 63.
50 Keep, "The Cultural Work of the Type-Writer Girl," 155.
51 Mullin, *Working Girls*, 24.
52 Mullin, *Working Girls*, 19.
53 Francesca Sawaya, *Modern Women, Modern Work: Domesticity, Professionalism, and American Writing, 1890–1950* (Philadelphia: University of Pennsylvania Press, 2003), 16.
54 Chan, *Virginia Woolf and the Professions*, 5.
55 Jacques Rancière, *The Politics of Aesthetics: The Distribution of the Sensible*, trans. Gabriel Rockhill (London: Bloomsbury Academic, 2013 [2004]), 41.
56 Rancière, *Politics of Aesthetics*, 42.

Part I

THE WORK OF ART

Chapter 1

THE ABSOLUTE AND THE IMPOSSIBLE WORK: FRANZ KAFKA'S "THE BURROW"

Robert Buch

One of the preferred targets of the avant-garde's cheerful and occasionally triumphalist iconoclasm was undoubtedly the category of "work," both in the sense of the artwork and in that of the activity aimed at producing it. What came under attack as the category of work was dismantled were, on the one hand, the putative ideals underlying it, notions of coherence, closure, unity, and self-sufficiency, in short, the artwork's lofty detachment and self-contained character. On the other hand, the iconoclastic critique, according to the well-known thesis of Peter Bürger's classic *Theory of the Avant-Garde*, aimed at the special status accorded to the work of art, the bourgeois sacralization of art, its removal and isolation from the spheres of everyday life and everyday practice.[1] Against the institutional seal, both in the sense of consecration—the stamp of approval conferred by cultural authorities and the institutions of art—and in the sense of sealing art off by placing it in a circumscribed domain, the protagonists of the avant-garde advocated more permeable boundaries between work and beholder, art and audience, unsettling the latter's expectations and presumed complacency. In Bürger's account this effort amounted to nothing less than revoking the autonomy of the artwork and collapsing the boundary between art and life. The ideal of disinterested contemplation was to be replaced with a sense of exposure and disquiet on the part of the spectators; passive receptivity would yield to more unsettling and possibly transformative experiences.

Equally under attack was the work of the artist, her creative labor and the related notions craftsmanship, discipline, practice, and virtuosity. These characteristics had to give way to less elevated, less controlled, and more spontaneous modes of creation: opening the door to chance, contingency, and violence as important elements in the creative process. Ironically, the modernist clearing operation also swept up the opposite of the traditional values of craftsmanship and skill, namely the ideas of genius and inspiration, replacing them at times with a more sober and cerebral approach, at times with more exalted and visceral conceptions.

The avant-garde's iconoclastic impulse was not pervasive, however. As a matter of fact, some paradigmatic modernist artists and writers stuck to the notion of work in a rather emphatic manner. Once more, I think, in the double sense of the term, work as in the single and singular artwork (less in the sense of an entire *oeuvre*) and "work" in the sense of the creative activity, the effort required to bring the artwork into being, to make it appear. It is an activity that is typically experienced as difficult, the hard work that is necessitated by the fact of resistance, whether it be the resilience of the material or the elusiveness of form.

There are many examples of the search for *the* work and the effort and despair spent on it. Often it is a search for nothing less than the perfect, the ultimate work, the absolute painting, for instance, "the one picture that will annihilate all the other ones," as Francis Bacon put it in conversation with David Sylvester, but also "the one that sums up all the others."[2] It is a search, though, that is haunted by failure, dogged by a sobering sense of shortcoming, and perpetual self-repudiation. Among the most dramatic accounts of this process are Francis Bacon's own depictions of his effort to wrest new configurations from the canvas in a peculiar mix of marshaling models from the great tradition of easel painting and of a late-modernist investment in chance and the material properties of oil paint, spurted randomly on the canvas. It is as though Bacon sought to continually thwart his own virtuosity in oil painting by hurling paint on the figures and faces he had just finished and then smudging the paint so as to see what possibilities this technique produces. It comes as no surprise that abandoning and even destroying works would come to be an inevitable part of this procedure. So is an unmistakable repetitiveness and seriality in Bacon's production, returning to the same motifs over and over, as though to something constitutively unfinishable.

A similar dialectics of achieving the perfect and indisputable work through a process of creation and destruction can be found in James Lord's fascinating account of sitting for a portrait by the Swiss sculptor and painter Alberto Giacometti or in W. G. Sebald's story in *The Emigrants* about the British painter Frank Auerbach.[3] Both Giacometti and Auerbach proceeded by painting or drawing over the previous day's work, adding and erasing at the same time, in an unending effort to capture the appearance that condenses all appearances in one. Whether in Bacon, Giacometti, or Auerbach, it seems as though the ostensibly old-fashioned search for perfection, if still in place, tends to unfold via its opposite: negation, reduction, elimination. The gesture of erasure which appears to be such a typical feature of this effort is at once a deletion that makes room for starting from scratch, as though the perfect work had to be achieved *ex nihilo*, in a few decisive strokes, and a verdict on the efforts thus far, forcing a new departure. Perfection has its counterpart in repeated failure, the dream of completion and closure never comes to an end but prompts ever-renewed beginnings. And yet, this failure and the seemingly compulsive self-denial accompanying it constitute an approximation of the absolute work flickering through in its ephemeral appearances. It is something like an infinite, an unending approximation because the absolute by definition does not manifest itself in the world of relations and particulars, or if it does, it does so only by repudiation, through denial and withdrawal.

The dynamic sketched here is not limited to the visual arts. In literature too, it is not difficult to think of a number of modernist authors who clung to an emphatic notion of work and an emphatic notion, if not of perfection, then at least of supreme achievement. The two such perfectionists that come to mind immediately are Flaubert and Proust, whose novels, while not necessarily seeking to "annihilate" all precursors and contenders, were nevertheless thought to constitute a kind of summa, a summation of the possibilities of their art: from the former's *livre sur rien* to the latter's *œuvre cathédrale*. In the first case, it is a work whose accomplishment is supposed to be entirely independent of its apparent subject matter and one that refuses to conform to any worldview or impart any kind of message. Flaubert's ideal is one of an absolute work in that it has absolved itself from the tutelage of ideas or, in his words, conclusions. In the case of Proust, rather than a book built on, and ostensibly about, nothing, patently oblivious to meaning and content, the ideal work at once encompasses and transcends the world. It is, in short, a book about everything. The novel outlined in the last volume of the *Recherche* is claimed to subsume, absorb, and sublimate the narrator's life of trials and tribulations into a vast structure. Like a cathedral, it would synthesize and integrate not only different arts but also organize and connect the different themes and motifs into a coherent unified whole, joining different discourses, genres, and media into a new form of *Gesamtkunstwerk*.[4] But the summative and totalizing gesture at the conclusion of Proust's novel is misleading. As many critics have pointed out, the closing prospectus of alignment and convergence is strangely at odds with the actual work the reader is about to end and which, they argue, ought not to be mistaken for the one so emphatically invoked on the last pages.[5] As is well known, Proust was working on the proofs of the penultimate volume, *Albertine disparue*, until his last breath. Rather than the relief and redemption adumbrated in the surprising revelation of the work's climactic finale, written at about the same time as he wrote the first part, *Du côté de chez Swann*, the penultimate volume seemed to expand uncontrollably, hypertrophically, a searching but also sprawling exploration of the circumstances and ramifications of a separation, the narrator's lover's abrupt departure, indeed escape, a loss that clearly defied any closure and integration, eclipsing the triumphant vision of denouement and fulfillment. Here too then we find a curious dialectic between the notion of a definitive and indeed summative achievement and a creative process that turns out to be interminable and all-consuming, undercutting the very idea of the absolute work.

The notion of the absolute, with its unmistakable theological overtones, has a long lineage.[6] It encompasses the aspiration of a work, as in Proust's *Recherche*, of ultimate breadth and comprehensiveness, an echo of the encyclopedic dream to create works that would be as wide in scope and as abundant in content as the world itself. We have also seen the quasi-Platonic dream of matching the elusive ideal, of painting, in Giacometti, Bacon, and Auerbach, the perfect head, the perfect scream, the perfect portrait, indeed the perfect, that is, the absolute and final painting itself. Then there is the notion of the work that is absolute in terms of its detachment, its radical independence and self-sufficiency, as in Flaubert's *livre sur rien*. And there is also, finally, the notion of the artist's unconditional commitment, the single-minded pursuit of a calling irreconcilable with any other vocation.

In the following, I want to pursue the categories of work *and* work, of work as consummate achievement and of work as painstaking labor, as an arduous process that requires discipline, dedication, and skill, with regard to the case of another high modernist, Franz Kafka, who seems to fit seamlessly in the paradoxical logic of creation and destruction, the definitive confirmation of creative power and its perpetual revocation. A pattern that gives the distinct impression that self-realization, self-effacement, success and failure are not antithetical but coincide, effecting one another in a peculiar form of reciprocity. The aim is to develop a better understanding of the curious crossing, or concurrence, between the notion of an ultimate accomplishment and its opposite, an almost inescapable sense of defeat. Perhaps this is merely an understandable psychological dynamic of the overly ambitious, part of the myth and self-stylization of the artist, setting the bar unrealistically high so as to indulge themselves in the pleasures of self-denigration. But while this is certainly a pattern very much in evidence in Kafka's writerly obsessions, the ideal he was aiming for was not a figment of the imagination. He had himself written some things that matched his expectations and that would serve as the measure of his other works. The question of "work" and its multiple meanings of creative process, its result (*the* work), but also the apparent drudgery of his daily work at the office form an interesting complex whose parts are by no means simply at variance with one another.

Kafka's perfectionism is notorious, part and parcel of the image we have of the writer. Its notoriety is to no small extent due to the fact that Kafka rarely thought that he had reached it. As you will recall, all three novels Kafka wrote remained unfinished and weren't published during his lifetime. The same is true for a large part of his prose fiction. The famous last will communicated to Max Brod was to destroy all manuscripts, the author's final and definitive verdict on his production. As a matter of fact, this too, the final act as a vanishing act, though left, not without reason, to someone else to perform, has become part of the myth revolving around Kafka: the specter of a literary self-annihilation. The author certainly knew that his long-time confidant and executor Brod, whose admiration was so unconditional it would at times discomfort the subject of its praise, was definitely never going to carry out his dying friend's last instruction.

Kafka's *modus operandi* seems to have been a largely intuitive kind of writing, one starting not from a preconceived plan but rather from a scene, or sketch or phrase that would then hopefully unfold into something longer, more sustained. This sometimes worked. Often it didn't. Hence the many beginnings or narrative fragments breaking off, in Kafka's notebooks. Unlike his hero Flaubert, Kafka did not obsess over style or word choice, *le mot juste*. There are, as a look at the facsimile edition of Kafka's manuscripts confirms, many traces of later revisions and reworkings in the manuscripts.[7] But Kafka did not "chisel" his prose nor did he, as far as I can see, rewrite larger sections in their entirety. Writing was to give oneself over to the flow of language and imagination. To achieve this surrender successfully was the incalculable part, always at risk of not unfolding properly or getting stuck.

While the ideal of the perfect work mostly eluded Kafka, there are a few notable exceptions which afford us the unfamiliar sight of a contented Kafka, a Kafka brimming with confidence and pride over his writerly abilities. One is the writer's account of writing "The Judgement," his breakthrough story, which would remain the touchstone of all further achievement. The other is a remark in the diaries apropos of the stories in *A Country Doctor* (1920). Both remarks, each of them cited so frequently in the scholarly literature that quoting them once more seems almost unnecessary, are in fact not particularly revealing when it comes to understanding what Kafka found so compelling about these particular stories. Instead, the insights they provide concern the outright ecstatic, if not oceanic, experience successful writing meant for the writer: "Nur so kann geschrieben werden, nur in einem solchen Zusammenhang, mit solcher vollständigen Öffnung des Leibes und der Seele"; "This is the only way to write, in such a continuum, and with such complete opening of body and soul."[8] They also give an idea of how writing that reached this level transformed the world: lifting or transfiguring it, in Kafka's words, into something "pure, true, and immutable" ("die Welt ins Reine, Wahre, Unveränderliche heben").[9] Kafka's jubilant account of his breakthrough provides a number of suggestive characterizations, however brief, of the creative process highlighting the extraordinary gratification writing of this quality could produce. Apart from the insistence on the experience of bodily and mental abandon in view of the story's continuous progression, the writing of "The Judgement" is described as a great fire in which the most capricious conceits were consumed and resurrected. The result of this process of destruction and resurrection was, as Kafka's diary declared two days later, after reading the story to a group of friends and his sister, "indisputable." The reading, he writes, confirmed the "Zweifellosigkeit der Geschichte" (September 25, 1912): it was beyond doubt, unassailable, incontrovertible, and with all this, it confirmed Kafka's sense of his sweeping abilities as a writer.[10] Writing "The Judgement" came as something like a positive shock to his system, jolting him out of his habitual stance of self-doubt and self-denigration, into a sense of mastery at one stroke, exhilarating and exhausting at the same time. The impossibility of doubt, error, failure, positively attested by this work, was indeed the very opposite of the countless shortcomings so readily confessed and eagerly "owned" by Kafka whenever the opportunity arose.

As I noted, the brief entries in Kafka's diary do not say much about what it is that makes "The Judgement" into the indisputable and unsurpassable exemplar of writing of the highest order of which he was capable. What do predicates such as these even mean? "Zweifellosigkeit," undoubtedly (!), implies that the story was done, finished, not in need of alterations. This accords with a minimal definition of perfection as that which cannot be improved, neither through expansion, subtraction, or further elaboration. The work is complete and its parts cohere. But such a quasi-logical definition hardly captures what Kafka's unmistakable commotion and positive sense of fulfillment were about. To understand them one needs to see "The Judgement" in relation to his early texts; to the concurrent work on his first novel, *Der Verschollene* (*The Man Who Disappeared*, formerly known as *Amerika*); as well as to his subsequent output. Unlike, the rather minimalist and understated prose of his first book publication, *Betrachtung* (1912; *Contemplation* in English), the story staged an outright confrontation and it culminated in a most dramatic denouement: Georg Bendemann's suicide, a radical and shockingly harsh ending whose violence is quite foreign to the early prose, yet quite familiar if one thinks ahead to the later works. The work on *The Man Who Disappeared* had stalled and Kafka's excitement over the creative momentum with which this story seemed to propel itself forward is clearly a response to the feeling of being stuck with the novel. "The Judgement" also, and perhaps this is the most important, features many of the key motifs and themes, opening up the world of his future fictions: the trial situation, the mixture of ridicule and revolt (a revolt against a revolting and ridiculous authority figure), the juxtaposition of intimacy and estrangement, indeed of love and hatred, the main protagonist's eager self-indictment and self-sacrifice, but also a certain poise in the delivery of all of this, treating the profane and the dreadful on the same plane.

With the possible exception of "The Judgement" and perhaps "The Stoker," Kafka did not particularly fetishize any of his works nor did he seem particularly invested in the idea of work in the "Spirit of Protestantism," made famous by his contemporary Max Weber. While a diligent and by all accounts brilliant legal expert, Kafka disliked his work because it was antithetical to his writing. In this sense, writing is the opposite of work, that is, his office work. This is a sentiment one finds echoed in many of his letters.[11] In spite of the ostensible compartmentalization between his own writing and the work done at the office, it would be a mistake to regard the partition that sought to keep them apart as constituting an impermeable barrier. As a matter of fact, Kafka's office work itself consisted to a large extent of writing and his professional successes in turn were owed to his writerly aptitude, his ability to put things into words, to argue complex cases. Even a cursory reading of the office writings, many of which were not published under his name, can't fail to pick up a certain resemblance with Kafka's other writings, resemblances in terms of tone, register, and perspective.[12] From writing, or rather dictating, in the office to writing hundreds of private letters to friends, and especially the women in his life, Felice Bauer and Milena Jesenská, to writing literature, there was in fact a continuum, Kafka's mind continually exerting and casting itself in the written word. For all his resistance to and dislike of the office, it also seeped into his literary writing in numerous ways: in terms of characters, scenes, and situations, but also, of course, in its lawyerly dimensions, preoccupation with the law and legal matters as well as, in certain instances, a diction and argumentation that were, unmistakably, those of a lawyer.

For Kafka, however, work was patently in the way of writing as were the expectations of his family and the practical exigencies of the world of the everyday. All of this was a distraction from writing, though "distraction" might be too weak a word; from Kafka's point of view, the many obstacles in the way of his writing were indeed taking a toll, aggravating his habitual sense of distress and anxiety. It might be worth recalling the extent to which the worry and frustration over being unable to devote enough time to writing unsettled and alienated Kafka. He had, in fact, devised a schedule he describes in one of his first letters to Felice.[13] He would work in the office from eight in the morning until two in the afternoon; after lunch, he would go to bed around three to sleep; rising again around seven-thirty to do some exercises or go for a long walk, followed by dinner with his parents and sisters to then finally get to his writing which he wouldn't stop until late at night. Unable to achieve the proper concentration in the afternoons because of the noise and commotion in his parents' apartment (Kafka's room was a walk-through), with this schedule, he effectively inverted the order of night and day, limiting and, in a sense, cordoning off the claims of work and family to create something of an extraterritorial space for the solitary and demanding business of writing.

As opposed to his day job, the work at the offices of the Worker's Accident Insurance, Kafka described his writing as a nocturnal, devilish service, undoubtedly with irony, but the term service suggests an activity on behalf of a higher calling, a different kind of office and a different form of officiating, one that ideally, if it could be pulled off, culminated in transfiguration, absorption, self-dissolution: the transformation of the self into writing.[14] Kafka's writerly ideal was, in a word, a form of *excarnation*, the bodily self being absorbed and transformed into *Schrift*.[15] For writing, *Schrift*, always means both the act of writing and that which is written: text, scripture. Many of Kafka's stories, including some of the best-known ones, are about this kind of transformation. One of the most gruesome examples of this is, without a doubt, *In the Penal Colony* (1919). The convicted man's body is tied onto an apparatus that is nothing but a monstrous writing machine. It is supposed to inscribe the law that was transgressed into the body of the criminal and culminate in a sort of epiphany, not only of the man whose body is disfigured but also in the onlookers who are said to partake, as if by osmosis, in the spectacle of transfiguration.[16]

In spite of such remarkable ambition, Kafka's relation to his writing was ambivalent. As I mentioned before, it was an activity that set him apart from his family (though not from his friends), and he tended to regard the virtually exclusive preoccupation with it as yet another symptom of his unmistakable shortcomings vis-à-vis the demands of the world, the conventions of everyday life, the obligations of sociality. But he also considered it as an alternative to the readily conceded failures on his part, the ultimate achievement that compensated for and was bound to redeem the countless deficiencies of Kafka the son, the fiancé, the Jew, the office worker.[17] We thus have writing as an absolute ideal and as an impossible endeavor, the escape from and overcoming, but also extension and culmination of constitutive failure.

The oscillation and tension between supreme achievement and the impossibility of perfection is one of the major motifs in Kafka's penultimate narrative, the unfinished fragment known as "The Burrow" ("Der Bau" in German, a title chosen by Max Brod).[18] In the story, a badger-like animal thinks about the elaborate underground construction it has devised. Two countervailing tendencies characterize the animal's taking stock of its burrow: a sense of utmost gratification in light of the sophistication of the structure, surveyed with the homeowner's philistine pride in "a work well done." The burrow features various tunnels, a hidden entrance, ample space for storing the animal's bloody provisions of prey, and something called the castle court, a dome-like center space. But the sense of gratification and pride is routinely unsettled by nagging doubts as to the structure's vulnerability to potential intruders from the outside. The first half of the story swings back and forth between, on the one hand, the self-congratulatory satisfaction with a life's work affording its creator the peace and tranquil enjoyment of old age and, on the other, sudden bouts of panic that trigger frantic building or rather renovation activity. The burrow and its inhabitant are portrayed as living in a symbiosis, creation and creator forming a whole, with the animal rolling and somersaulting through the tunnels in sheer enjoyment of its existence, feasting on the plentiful provisions of cadavers amassed in the castle court, or drifting away in deep and dreamless slumber, as though cradled by the burrow. But, as I said, such spells of pure bliss are disturbed and superseded by the compulsive search for flaws and oversights in the construction. For instance, the castle court, first touted as the structure's crowning achievement (whose walls the animal had fortified by banging its forehead against them until it was bloody), suddenly appears utterly deficient. It would be far more sensible, the animal now reasons, to have a set of chambers like it, rather than just one. But it is too late.[19]

The animal's relentless vigilance and self-scrutiny make for the narrative's frantic pace and neurotic energy, at times generating a sensation of veritable vertigo in the reader. The narrative continuously pivots from a sense of optimism and self-assurance into its opposite. It is a pendulum swing that seems inescapable. But at the same time, in many instances the transitions and reversals from one state of mind to the next take place imperceptibly. Every stance, including the most positively self-assured, is shaded, and before long eroded, by doubt, anxiety, and self-recriminations. The perfectly camouflaged entrance turns out to be misconceived: it is in fact the most vulnerable spot of the entire structure, a token of the burrow-dweller's mortality, "there, at that one place on the dark moss, I am mortal";[20] the maze close to the burrow's entrance, designed to trap intruders, once a cause for pride, appears dangerously inadequate, "the work of a beginner,"[21] not worthy of the burrow; the allocation of provisions for defense purposes, whether strategically distributed throughout the burrow or stockpiled centrally in the castle court, turns out to be intractable and triggers mindless activity.[22] The animal's worries over potential attackers are particularly acute and eventually culminate in the realization that the safest spot for the burrow-dweller is actually outside the burrow, so the animal posts itself near the entrance to determine how the entry and exit point might attract enemy passers-by in spite of its inconspicuous moss cover.

> I look for a good hiding place and stealthily watch the entrance to my house—in this instance from the outside—for days and nights at a time. You may call it foolish, but it gives me ineffable pleasure; even more, it consoles me. It feels to me, then, not as if I were standing outside my house but outside myself while I am asleep and knew the joy of sleeping deeply and at the same time of being able to keep close watch.[23]

Even though, ironically, a spot on the outside is deemed the best vantage point to assess the burrow's problems, soon enough here too unforeseen and incalculable complications proliferate and make a retreat into the burrow seem the most sensible way out of the predicament, a plan in turn delayed, though, by painstaking considerations of the inevitable risks involved in such a return. As it turns out, observing the burrow from without only provides an incomplete scenario for the animal watches the burrow without its inhabitant, and can thus develop no sense of how its presence inside might manifest itself to the outside. The peculiar and blissful doubling of watching (and watching over) one's own sleep receives a characteristic twist, converting the sense of reassurance and self-control into an unwieldy and indeed uncontrollable threat. "No, I'm not the one, though I thought I was, who watches me sleeping; rather, I am the one who sleeps while the one who wants to deprave me watches."[24]

The pride of owner- and craftsmanship alternates compulsively with all-consuming suspicion and unappeasable paranoia, the convergence of madness and the need for total control poignantly epitomized by the animal's battered and bloodied forehead used to strengthen its fortification. The burrow features at once as the cause of self-aggrandizement, indeed a barely mastered triumphalism, and of self-chastisement over the countless errors and weaknesses that taint the presumed perfection. It is a work that elicits conflicting feelings: calm and soothing contemplation of that which is in need of no further modifications and the opposite sense of an obligation to an infinite task, inevitable oversights necessitating the creator's continual and renewed attention and recommitment.

As I mentioned, "The Burrow" is Kafka's penultimate story, written in the face of death. It is sometimes read allegorically as a story about Kafka's work, a recapitulation of his achievements and failings.[25] Like the later artist stories, "First Sorrow," "A Hunger Artist," and Kafka's last text "Josefine the Mouse Singer," the story, read in this vein, appears to ridicule the mysticism and metaphysics of writing as a transfigurative and redemptive endeavor. "The Burrow" features not only the fantasy of symbiosis between maker and work, creator and creation, but also the dream of their self-sufficiency, well-nigh complete autonomy from the rest of the world. However, the self-sufficient artwork which the author has entered as though a womb, a blissful abode, a safe haven and/or a retirement home turns out to be far from homely or durable. If we read "The Burrow" as a reflection on the work of art that incorporates or absorbs its maker, the final reward for his retreat from the world, we must also acknowledge the numerous other models, shining through the elusive structure that is the burrow, like a palimpsest. For this underground construction does not only invoke a castle but also a dungeon, a high security complex or bunker turned into a trap, a labyrinth as bewildering as the animal's restless ruminations themselves, and, last but not least, a tomb.

The artwork as tomb or crypt is an old topos, one Kafka has actually drawn on himself in a short text titled "Ein Traum" (A Dream).[26] In the dream of "Ein Traum" the dreamer, Josef K., inadvertently finds himself in a cemetery where he sees a freshly dug grave and a tombstone on which an artist who appeared from nowhere inscribes a name in gold letters. When after a moment it dawns on Josef K. that it is his name that is being written he lies down in the grave which receives him gently: it is a death into writing, *excarnation*; it is writing as epitaph, outliving the writer's exit. The twist on the topos of the artwork as tomb, crypt, monument to its creator, given in "The Burrow" is that there is no serenity in the grave either. The afterlife too is disturbed, haunted by turbulence and disquiet. For it turns out that even the thickest of walls are penetrated by an enigmatic interpellation that undoes all the circumspection and caution the materialization of which is the burrow. The second part of the story is about a hissing sound that reaches the animal and, above all, about the latter's strained attempts to locate its source and determine its properties and meaning.[27] The hissing is presumably the sound emitted by an advancing enemy or enemies, indeed an entire enemy army. It confirms the animal's worst nightmares and belies its sense of accomplishment and security. The hissing is the sound of the final reckoning for which the animal had a lifetime to prepare and for which, as it must now admit, it is not prepared.[28] Although the unfinished second part, which breaks off in mid-sentence, on some level, continues in the same vein as the first, featuring the twists and turns of the burrow-dweller's attempts to come to grips with the approaching danger, to somehow rationalize the phenomenon he confronts, it introduces an element familiar from Kafka's other fictions: the hissing is an instantiation of a mysterious, intangible, yet insistent menace so often confronting Kafka's hapless characters. As in other stories too—think, for instance, of *In the Penal Colony* or *The Metamorphosis*—the narrative manages to intertwine pedantry and a sense of panic and utter exposure. The effect is at once hilarious and dire. The animal goes through a dizzying sequence of possibilities as to the adversary it is confronting, but it does not come to any conclusions and is left, as the story breaks off, with a sense of doom and finality in the face of the imminent showdown with its unknown nemesis.

The hissing shatters the dream of the artwork as resting place, as retreat and relief from the demands of the world. If Kafka had pitted the imperative to write against the imperatives of life and if we regard the animal's obsession with work, both the structure and the unending additions, extensions, and corrections it requires, as an instantiation of such unconditional commitment, the hissing shatters the ludic self-absorption in the form of an inescapable yet unintelligible summons. As in many other instances of mystifying disruption in Kafka's fiction, in which a different, more exacting reality, often associated with authority and the law, seems to assert itself—most famously perhaps, the arrest of Joseph K., the metamorphosis of Gregor Samsa, or the condemnation to death of Georg Bendemann by his own father—the protagonist is faced with a power that is at once forbidding and, at the same time, intimately familiar. In spite of the indeterminacy of the hissing, the animal begins to imagine what it is facing as another animal, drilling its pathway through the underground, quite similar to itself, indeed a kind of doppelgänger, except bigger and stronger and operating on a plan that remains utterly unfathomable to the inhabitant of the burrow.[29] Through much of the second half of the story, though, the hissing is not personified but figures as a disembodied force, everywhere and nowhere, seemingly oblivious to the animal and yet closing in on it. It is thus at once a figure of the same, a double of the protagonist, and a figure of radical alterity, the manifestation of something belonging to an altogether different order.

One of the most striking parallels to the "advent" of the hissing in Kafka's prose is the glimpse of the law in the famous parable "Before the Law" in which the law appears as a radiance shining through the closed gate before which the man from the countryside is waiting to be admitted. Like the hissing, the effect is captivating and transfixing as though before an ultimate and definitive revelation, punishment and redemption in one. In both instances, visual and aural, it is a confrontation with something absolute, irrefutable, and maddeningly cryptic, fundamentally inscrutable for the very subject addressed by this ominous other and who is to meet its destiny, its moment of truth, in this encounter. Both episodes feature characters about to die in scenes that have the allure of grand finales but end anticlimactically, undoing the promise of final relief and resolution.

Starting with "The Judgement," it is not difficult to see Kafka's writing revolve around the primal conflict of entering or inscribing the subject in the symbolic order, a process achieved through marriage, procreation, and commitment to work and family.[30] Many of Kafka's texts, from the longer narratives, "The Judgement" and *The Metamorphosis* for instance, to the unfinished novels, feature protagonists failing at this spectacularly, though it is often a failure that could be considered a victory in disguise, releasing the protagonists for a different kind of subjectivation, for entering a different order, and for assuming, as I said earlier, a different kind of office, that of writing. However, the potential liberation into and through writing frequently stays tethered to that from which it was intended to extricate the subject, in that the stories themselves rehearse the very conflict and its violent solutions over and over. "The Burrow" too is a story of withdrawal, of carving out a space of autonomy; the underground maze, half tomb, half retreat, affording its creature freedom from the worries of the life outside. But it is also the story of the spectacular collapse of this elaborate structure. The hissing dispels and disrupts the fantasy of writerly transfiguration, of an ecstatic merger with the work. To a significant extent the fantasies of such continual absorption into writing are sustained, precisely, by their impossibility and Kafka's work clearly draws its energy from the countervailing forces it stages with unmistakable relish. "The clamor of the world" which the construction of the burrow was meant to keep at bay is back with a vengeance.[31] The hissing oscillates between a minor but nagging disturbance, reminiscent of the countless distractions diverting the artist from his work, and an all-consuming menace, inescapable and irrefutable ("zweifellos"): a message all the more pressing for its apparent lack of any specific content. It is reminiscent of the many judgment scenes in Kafka's works in which a punishing fury is unleashed against characters receiving their sentences in an odd mixture of disbelief and resigned acceptance.

It is of course impossible to tell where the unfinished story would have figured in Kafka's canon of his own works. It features many of the characteristics of the kind of deeply satisfying creative experience given in the excited account of the writing of "The Judgement." On the level of form, there is an unmistakable sense of flow, a meandering and turbulent progression. Yet, many readers have wondered if and how the story was supposed to end.[32] The animal's reasoning seems interminable, without definitive conclusions, constantly overturning its own rationalizations and resolutions, while the hissing's effectiveness seems to be predicated precisely on the fact that it does not materialize, on its amorphous ubiquity. As we have seen, on the level of plot and drama the story rehearses the confrontation with an overbearing and mystifying power so typical of many of Kafka's stories and novels written after "The Judgement," even if it doesn't occur. There is also, and above all, the perfectionist exaltation over the elaborate and self-contained structure that is the burrow, the absolute work par excellence, and the terrifying and crushing realization of its constitutional vulnerability, of the inevitability of yielding to the pressure from without, of its impossibility.

Notes

1 Peter Bürger, *Theory of the Avant-Garde*, trans. Michael Shaw (Minneapolis: University of Minnesota Press, 1984), especially 55–9.

2 David Sylvester, *Interviews with Francis Bacon* (London: Thames & Hudson, 1985), 22.
3 James Lord, *A Giacometti Portrait* (New York: The Museum of Modern Art, New York/Doubleday, 1965); W. G. Sebald, *The Emigrants*, trans. Michael Hulse (New York: New Directions, 2010), 147–237.
4 See Luc Fraisse, *L'œuvre cathédrale. Proust et l'architecture médiévale* (Paris: José Corti, 1990); David Roberts, *The Total Work of Art in European Modernism* (Ithaca, NY: Cornell University Press, 2011).
5 See Rainer Warning and Jean Milly, eds., *Marcel Proust. Écrire sans fin* (Paris: CNRS, 1996).
6 See Jean-Luc Nancy and Philippe Lacoue-Labarthe, *The Literary Absolute. The Theory of Literature in Literary Romanticism*, trans. Philip Barnard and Cheryl Leser (New York: SUNY Press, 1988).
7 See the ongoing facsimile edition of Kafka's manuscripts: *Historisch-Kritische Franz Kafka-Ausgabe*, ed. Roland Reuß and Peter Staengle (Frankfurt am Main: Stroemfeld Verlag, 1997ff.).
8 Franz Kafka, *Tagebücher*, ed. Hans-Gerd Koch, Michael Müller, and Malcolm Pasley (Frankfurt am Main: S. Fischer, 1990), 461, September 23, 1912; Kafka, *Diaries*, trans. Martin Greenberg in collaboration with Hannah Arendt (Harmondsworth: Penguin, 1975), 212–13 (translation modified).
9 Kafka, *Diaries*, 187, September 25, 1917 (translation modified); *Tagebücher*, 838.
10 Kafka, *Tagebücher*, 463, September 25, 1912; Kafka, *Diaries*, 214.
11 See, for instance, Franz Kafka, *Briefe 1902–1912*, ed. Hans-Gerd Koch (Frankfurt am Main: S. Fischer, 1999), 296, December 3, 1912 (to Felice Bauer); Kafka, *Briefe 1913–1914*, ed. Hans-Gerd Koch (Frankfurt am Main: S. Fischer, 1999), 158–9, April 7, 1913 (to Felice Bauer); Kafka, *Briefe 1913–1914*, 222, June 26, 1913 (to Felice Bauer); Kafka, *Letters to Felice*, trans. James Stern and Elisabeth Duckworth (London: Secker and Warburg, 1974), 84–5, 238, 278–9.
12 Franz Kafka, *Amtliche Schriften*, ed. Klaus Hermsdorf and Benno Wagner (Frankfurt am Main: S. Fischer, 2004); Kafka, *The Office Writings*, ed. Stanley Corngold, Jack Greenberg and Benno Wagner (Princeton, Oxford: Princeton University Press, 2009).
13 Kafka, *Briefe 1902–1912*, 202–5, November 1, 1912 (to Felice Bauer); Kafka, *Letters to Felice*, 20–3.
14 For writing as "Teufelsdienst," as "serving the devil," see Kafka's letter to Max Brod, July 5, 1922, Franz Kafka, *Briefe 1902–1924*, ed. Max Brod (Frankfurt am Main; S. Fischer, 1958), 384; Kafka, *Letters to Friends, Family, and Editors*, trans. Richard and Clara Winston (New York: Schocken, 1977), 333.
15 See Detlef Kramer, *Kafka: Die Erotik des Schreibens* (Bodenheim: Philo, 1998); Gerhard Kurz, *Traum-Schrecken: Kafkas literarische Existenzanalyse* (Stuttgart: Metzler, 1979).
16 For a more detailed reading of this text see Robert Buch, *The Pathos of the Real. The Aesthetics of Violence in the Twentieth Century* (Baltimore, London: Johns Hopkins University Press, 2010), 39–52.
17 For a "confession" of these countless shortcomings see Kafka's letter to Max Brod, November 14, 1917, Franz Kafka, *Briefe April 1914–1917*, ed. Hans-Gerd Koch (Frankfurt am Main: S. Fischer, 2005), 362; Kafka, *Letters to Friends, Family, and Editors*, 166. For the ambiguity of writing, its supreme significance and its dubious value, see the letter to Brod, from July 5, 1922, cited earlier, as well as the letter to

Robert Klopstock, late March 1923, *Briefe 1902–1924*, 382–7 (to Brod), 430–2 (to Klopstock); Kafka, *Letters to Friends, Family, and Editors*, 332–5 (to Brod); 322–4 (the letter to Klopstock has a different date in the English edition: beginning of April 1922).

18 Franz Kafka, "The Burrow," in *Selected Stories*, ed. and trans. Stanley Corngold (New York: Norton, 2007), 162–89; "Der Bau," in Franz Kafka, *Nachgelassene Schriften und Fragmente*, Vol. II, ed. Jost Schillemeit (Frankfurt am Main: S. Fischer, 1992), 576–632. For the history of this text, commentary, and an overview of the critical literature see Hartmut Binder, *Kafka: Kommentar zu sämtlichen Erzählungen* (Munich: Winkler, 1975), 301–22; Vivian Liska, "Der Bau," in Manfred Engel and Bernd Auerochs, eds., *Kafka-Handbuch* (Stuttgart: Metzler, 2010), 337–43; for a recent collection of critical essays on the story see Dorit Müller and Julia Weber, eds., *Die Räume der Literatur: Exemplarische Zugänge zu Kafkas Erzählung "Der Bau"* (Boston, Berlin: De Gruyter, 2013).
19 See Kafka, "The Burrow," 166; "Der Bau," 584.
20 Kafka, "The Burrow," 162–3; "dort an jener Stelle im dunklen Moos bin ich sterblich" (Kafka, "Der Bau," 577).
21 Kafka, "The Burrow," 168; "dieses Erstlingswerk" (Kafka, "Der Bau," 587).
22 Kafka, "The Burrow," 165–6; Kafka, "Der Bau," 582–3.
23 Kafka, "The Burrow," 169–70; "Ich suche mir ein gutes Versteck und belauere den Eingang meines Hauses—diesmal von außen—tage- und nächtelang. Man mag es töricht nennen, es bereitet mir aber eine unsagbare Freude, mehr noch es beruhigt mich. Mir ist dann, als stehe ich nicht vor meinem Haus, sondern vor mir selbst, während ich schlafe, und hätte das Glück gleichzeitig tief zu schlafen und dabei mich scharf bewachen zu können." Kafka, "Der Bau," 590–1.
24 Kafka, "The Burrow," 171; "Nein, ich beobachte doch nicht wie ich glaubte meinen Schlaf, vielmehr bin ich es der schläft, während der Verderber wacht." Kafka, "Der Bau," 593.
25 See Binder, *Kafka Kommentar*, 308–11; Liska, "Der Bau," 339–42.
26 Kafka, *Selected Stories*, 75; Franz Kafka, "Ein Traum," in *Drucke zu Lebzeiten*, ed. Wolf Kittler, Hans-Gerd Koch and Gerhard Neumann (Frankfurt am Main: Fischer Taschenbuch Verlag, 2001), 295–8. For a reading of this text as an instance of *Schriftwerdung*, the transformation into writing, see Gerhard Neumann, "Franz Kafka: Der Name, die Sprache und die Ordnung der Dinge," in G. Neumann and Wolf Kittler, eds., *Franz Kafka. Schriftverkehr* (Freiburg im Breisgau: Rombach, 1990), 11–29 (12–13).
27 See Mladen Dolar, "The Burrow of Sound," *Differences: A Journal of Feminist Cultural Studies*, 22, no. 2–3 (2011), 112–39.
28 Kafka, "Der Bau," 619–20, and again 624–5; Kafka, "The Burrow," 184–5, see also 186–7.
29 Kafka, "Der Bau," 630–2; Kafka, "The Burrow," 188–9.
30 See Neumann, "Franz Kafka."
31 Kafka, "The Burrow," 184; Kafka, "Der Bau," 621.
32 For speculations regarding the ending see Binder, *Kafka Kommentar*, 322; see also Liska, "Der Bau," 341–2.

Chapter 2

AUTONOMY, DIFFICULTY, AND THE WORK OF LITERATURE IN WYNDHAM LEWIS'S *TARR* AND ANDRÉ GIDE'S *THE COUNTERFEITERS*

Emmett Stinson

This chapter examines the relationship between modernist autonomy claims and the valorization of difficulty that typically accompanies these claims. Autonomy and difficulty have both typically been seen as key aspects of modernism, and I will argue that they remain essential for any understanding of the modernist work of art. Instead of taking modernist autonomy claims at face value, I will argue that difficulty enabled modernists to "frame" their autonomy, thereby enacting what appeared to be a radical break from nineteenth-century aesthetic regimes. Notwithstanding the frequent characterization of modernist literature as impenetrable and insensitive to readerly pleasure, there is often a significant gap between the forms of difficulty modernists explicitly advocated for and the way that difficulty actually manifests within their literary works. Instead, claims of autonomous difficulty are inconsistently applied, ironic, and amplified for rhetorical effect. Difficulty was therefore essential to modernist writers insofar as it exaggerated modernism's own distance from prior traditions. Understanding the modernists' ambiguous and ironic relationship to difficult autonomy complicates the frequent depiction of modernism as a set of austere, esoteric, or wholly elitist aesthetic practices. Acknowledging the hedged and contradictory nature of modernism's difficult autonomy also clarifies the ways in which modernism sought to self-reflexively critique itself—a tendency that was often ignored by subsequent theorists of postmodernism. This presents a more complex and dialogic model for the modernist work of autonomous art, which sought out autonomy not to deny any connection to the social, but as a provocative and provisional means for engaging in specific debates, aesthetic practices, and modes of discourse.

Theorists of the postmodern from the 1970s through the 1990s frequently sought to position modernism as attached to outmoded notions of autonomy, difficulty, and elitism. In his seminal 1984 essay, Fredric Jameson argued aesthetic autonomy was impossible under later modernity's system of commodity production.¹ This implicit assertion of postmodern heteronomy was broadly representative of positions taken by a variety of eminent postmodern theorists. But recent scholarship has returned to the question of autonomy in a different manner, seeking to *historicize* autonomy claims by understanding them within the modernists' own terms. A new group of critics—Jennifer Ashton, Charles Altieri, Nicholas Brown, Lisa Siraganian, Andrew Goldstone—have investigated autonomy in precisely these historicized terms. Their analyses of autonomy are linked by the claim that most twentieth-century accounts have conflated modernist autonomy claims with nineteenth-century articulations of art-for-art's-sake by *Le Parnasse* or decadent writers, such as Oscar Wilde. But modernism did not simply reproduce such claims, and, in fact, modernist notions of autonomy typically sought to differentiate themselves from aestheticism. Difficulty became a key marker of modernism, which distinguished its notion of autonomy from earlier ones—and this has a significant effect on how the modernist work of art is understood.

It is worth briefly surveying the key aspects of these more recent accounts of modernist autonomy. Jennifer Ashton, in *From Modernism to Postmodernism*, argues that modernist autonomy is characterized by an inviolable *intention*, which creates a firm horizon of possible interpretations of modernist works.² Nicholas Brown presents competing accounts of the commodity cycle in Hegel and Marx, and argues that modernist autonomy essentially valorized the Hegelian account, in which the directed intentionality of the artist's work distinguishes it from commodity exchange.³ Charles Altieri argues that modernist accounts of autonomy comprise an aesthetic sublimation of modernism's broader political commitments, including a deep skepticism of purely rhetorical claims of equality and inclusiveness presented by contemporary European nation-states.⁴ Lisa Siraganian argues that modernist autonomy claims are exemplary political statements, which intentionally open onto broader social and political questions by a seeming refusal of such material.⁵ Andrew Goldstone offers the most detailed typology of modernist autonomy, identifying four modes of modernist autonomy that (respectively) seek to differentiate themselves from realist techniques, authorial presence, political affiliation, and mimetic reference; he argues that modernist autonomy was therefore not monolithic but emphatically plural.⁶ As I will argue, however, this plurality can still be unified under a broader modernist aesthetic that is linked by the articulation of difficulty and the tendency to ironize and undermine stringent autonomy claims within specific works. These arguments present a new approach to modernist autonomy insofar as all of them seek to emphasize what is specifically unique about *modernist* presentations of the same and implicitly acknowledge that some modernist claims to separate art from politics should not be taken at face value.

If modernist autonomy, by its nature, is the contextual disavowal of specific connections between the work of art and the world, then it needs to be acknowledged that such autonomy claims are not really consistent philosophical propositions of any kind, but highly contingent provocations. My view is that modernist autonomy claims are almost always aporetic, and often intentionally so. Rather than presenting logical claims of autonomy, modernist writers—as artists interested in rhetoric and affect rather than logic—presented provocative claims of autonomy that they had no intention of supporting, and their works often highlight the *inconsistencies within* claims of autonomy. These aporetic autonomy claims can take a variety of forms.

Elsewhere,[7] for example, I have considered instances in which authors such as André Gide and Wyndham Lewis have intentionally used dialogism to ironize and complicate what seem to be straightforward claims of autonomy. In Gide's *The Counterfeiters* (1925), Edouard calls for an aesthetic of the "pure novel" that is radically different from the nineteenth-century realist novel:

> I should like to strip the novel of every element that does not specifically belong to the novel. Just as photography in the past freed painting from its concern for a certain sort of accuracy, the phonograph will eventually no doubt rid the novel of the kind of dialogue which is drawn from life and which realists take so much pride in. Outward events, accidents, traumatisms, belong to the cinema. The novel should leave them to it. Even the description of characters does not seem to me to properly belong to the *genre*. No; this does not seem to be the business of the *pure* novel (and in art, as in everything else, purity is the only thing I care about) ... The novelist does not as a rule rely sufficiently on the reader's imagination.[8]

While Edouard espouses a notion of the pure novel that Gide—in his various other writings—appears to share, the novel relentlessly undercuts Edouard's pretensions, since his work—also called *The Counterfeiters*—is never completed. The result of this ironic positioning is that the value of Gide's autonomy claim is never settled: it is *both* a sincere yearning for a certain kind of style and a hyperbolically inflated rhetorical position that Gide's own novel never seriously tries to enact.

Another example occurs in Wyndham Lewis's *Tarr*, where the character Tarr articulates a notion of aesthetic "deadness" that has frequently been equated with Lewis's own "external method" of representation:

> deadness is the first condition of art. The armoured hide of the hippopotamus, the shell of the tortoise, feathers and machinery, you may put in one camp; naked and pulsing and moving of the soft inside of life—along with elasticity of movement and consciousness—that all goes in the opposite camp. Deadness is the first condition for art: the second is absence of soul, in the human and sentimental sense. With the statue its lines and masses are its soul, no restless inflammable ego is imagined for its interior: it has no inside: good art must have no inside: that is capital.[9]

Here, what appears to be an explicit claim of autonomy is rendered uncertain by being placed in the mouth of an obviously flawed character. As Nathan Waddell has noted, the notion of "deadness" articulated by Tarr cannot be identified with Lewis, since Tarr, himself, is variously satirized and undermined throughout the novel.[10] At the same time, Lewis—throughout his career—would return to this notion of deadness and claim it as a central element of his own aesthetic process. Tarr's autonomy claim—like Edouard's—is both sincere *and* ironic, comprising a rhetorically charged set of claims that are related to aspects of their authors' aesthetics without being a straightforward statement of artistic intent. This aporetic structure is characteristic of autonomy claims in modernist works of art, which are always both genuine aesthetic positions and rhetorical provocations.

What I want to examine now, however, is the way that both Lewis's and Gide's claims deploy implicit notions of difficulty that interact with this aporetic autonomy in significant ways. But to do this, it's necessary to consider the broader relationship between literary difficulty and the modernist work of art. George Steiner has produced a typology of difficulty, which—although not directed specifically at modernism—is useful for locating the specific modes of difficulty that modernist autonomy claims articulate. Steiner identifies four kinds of difficulty, which he labels contingent, modal, tactical, and ontological. Contingent difficulties relate to minor points of readerly confusion that can be resolved quickly through recourse to external sources, and usually consist of "a word, a phrase or a reference which [readers] will have to look up."[11] These kinds of difficulties require "homework" on the part of the reader, and therefore present a barrier to comprehension because of this extra work, but contingent difficulties are always soluble in practice, and are arguably even easier to resolve in a post-digital era with ready access to information. Modal difficulties require much greater work on the part of the reader; these difficulties result from a lack of knowledge about the broader social, cultural, and historical contexts that inform a piece of writing, and would require intense study to overcome.[12] I suspect—given his references to Borges in this piece of writing—that Steiner might be thinking of the short story "Averroes' Search" in which the Islamic philosopher Averroes fails to understand Aristotle's *Poetics* for the reason that he has no concept of what a play is. Overcoming modal difficulties requires both intense scholarship and access to key historical information; unlike contingent difficulties, modal difficulties may not always be soluble since this information may not always be available. Tactical difficulties constitute situations in which authors intentionally deploy obscure, confusing, or innovative language and literary techniques in order to avoid clichéd forms of expression and produce new modes of literary affect. This is the form of difficulty that relates most directly to modernist autonomy claims, and Steiner appropriately offers Wallace Stevens' "Anecdote of the Jar" as an exemplar of a poem which contains no contingent difficulties but many tactical ones.[13] Steiner also notes a fourth mode of ontological difficulty, which refers to moments in a text that evade any singular interpretation either through obscure personal reference (a gesture that, for Steiner, undermines the communicative function of literature) or because there is no explicit intention or meaning behind these difficulties that can be definitively interpreted.[14] Unlike contingent difficulties, ontological difficulties are inherently insoluble and call into question the very act and purpose of interpretation, which inevitably presumes the existence of the object of its inquiry (i.e., meaning or intent).

The modernists applied various forms of difficulty, but probably their two favorite modes of difficulty within Steiner's typology were the contingent and the tactical. Modernism's infamous preference for obscure references, recondite information, sesquipedalian vocabularies, and polyglot quotations all present contingent difficulties for readers who must "do their homework" to understand the explicit content of modernist works. These contingent difficulties are reinforced by a variety of tactical difficulties that are encountered variously as technique or style, whether it may be stream of consciousness, rotating narrators and perspectival characters, dialogism, the creation of ambiguity around essential contexts, a studied refusal of the traditional narrative structures associated with realism, or a deployment of extreme forms of parataxis that force readers to make causal connections on their own, along with many others. The cumulative function of these techniques could result in forms of ontological difficulty (a mode that certainly appears in the work of such modernists as Samuel Beckett and Gertrude Stein), but it is primarily within the domain of the tactical and the contingent that modernist modes of difficulty pertain.

While Steiner's typology of difficulty helps clarify the specific ways in which modernist works employed difficulty, the most extensive and significant engagement with modernism's difficulty remains Leonard Diepeveen's *The Difficulties of Modernism* (2003). Diepeveen argues that modernists made difficulty "central to art's *direction*" and that claims for difficulty constituted an attempt to emphasize modernism's "refined sensibility" as inherently superior to the sentimental aesthetics of Victorianism.[15] This championing of difficulty constituted modernism's uniqueness but also created new criteria for artistic excellence that enabled modernists to claim pre-eminence over the works of tradition. As Diepeveen notes, this process also worked backwards historically to reshape the canon and revive the reputation of marginal writers who seemed to anticipate modernism's difficult aesthetics, as in the case of T. S. Eliot's championing of John Donne.[16]

But despite the importance of difficulty, Diepeveen notes that modernists rarely produced nuanced accounts of it. Indeed, the tactical and contingent difficulties that are explicated by Steiner, for example, are rarely distinguished or discussed. As Diepeveen explains, modernism's explication of difficulty usually relied on "shorthand" arguments carried out not by "careful thought" but rather by "rhetorical tropes" that he terms "conceptual metaphors":[17]

> Conceptual metaphors encouraged assertions of difficulty's vigor and morality ... with words such as "courage," "terror," "repel," "terrifying,"

"strong," "bold," and "cost." These words recall the anxiety of the difficult experience ... but modernism's apologists, instead of morally condemning the instigator of this experience, lauded the moral courage of those who were able to endure it ... The proponents of difficulty modulated the anxiety surrounding difficulty into a sense of macho pleasure.[18]

For Diepeveen, the modernists presented a gendered aesthetics based on notions of work, courage, and endurance, which were identified against a soft (and implicitly feminine) Victorian sentimental realism that relied on repeated and readily intelligible tropes, diction, and narrative expectations. Here, Diepeveen's claims resonate with David Trotter's identification of a masculine (and frequently misogynist) modernist will-to-technique.[19] As Diepeveen notes, while the arguments *against* difficulty often relied on "common-sense" notions about art, the modernists' own purely rhetorical claims for difficulty relied on similarly ungrounded assumptions, and are therefore problematic in many respects. While I am not disputing Diepeveen's assessment of the rhetorical nature of modernist articulations of difficulty, I do want to extend and complicate this analysis in two ways. Firstly, literature is, by its nature, a rhetorical performance, so the rhetorical nature of modernist arguments for difficulty is neither surprising nor a limitation in the way Diepeveen implies. Indeed, modernists' rhetorical arguments for difficulty only become problematic insofar as they are taken at face value. Secondly, I want to establish that the modernists were often aware of the hyperbolic and rhetorical nature of their claims of autonomous difficulty. They often ironized and complicated such arguments in ways that self-reflexively acknowledged their limitations. This can be seen in the difference between modernist articulations of difficulty and the way that such notions of difficulty were actually applied in modernist *works*. To examine this, I will return to considering the two exemplary articulations of modernist autonomous difficulty in Lewis's *Tarr* and Gide's *Counterfeiters* that I quoted earlier.

The concept of "deadness" in *Tarr* constitutes an aesthetics of difficulty. The new work of art advocated by Tarr presents surfaces that are defensive and impenetrable, associated with machines or animals (the tortoise's shell, the skin of the hippopotamus, birds' feathers) that—although not necessarily threatening—cannot readily be anthropomorphized. These aesthetic forms do not conform to traditional modes of human perception but intentionally draw on strange and alien forms. Moreover, the dead work of art is not "soft" but hard: the rigid and spiky new aesthetics are thus implicitly positioned against what Lewis viewed as soft Victorian modes of sentimentality. Here, it needs to be emphasized that a variety of modernist scholars have argued for a more expansive conception of modernism beyond such masculine aesthetics; Suzanne Clarke offers one such account of the way that modernist aesthetics were intertwined with sentimental modes of affect.[20] Moreover, Martin Hipsky has argued that much of the popular fiction contemporary with modernism actually presents "complex symmetries" with formally experimental works rather than hard oppositions, which complicates such binary distinctions between sentimental literature and difficult forms of modernism.[21]

Nonetheless, Lewis makes an explicit association between Victorianism and a soft sentimentality: Tarr contrasts the hardened forms of this new art with the "soft inside of life," which is to say human emotions and psychology, encompassing consciousness, sentimentality, the ego, the soul, and even pleasing forms of bodily movement. The only further complication is that modern forms of psychology and perspectivalism (including modernist stream of consciousness techniques) are also in opposition to the aesthetics of deadness. This refusal of any anthropomorphism—whether physical or emotional—constitutes the specific difficulty of this conception of art: art, in refusing to conform to human expectations, is necessarily difficult and requires an adjustment on the part of the viewer. In this sense, the deadness advocated by Tarr is absolutely a *tactical difficulty* in Steiner's sense, which results from an artist's choice of specific techniques to achieve new aesthetic ends.

The adjustment needed to understand this new work of art is more difficult still, because the depth model of hermeneutic interpretation no longer applies—and suggests that viewers will have to perform a new and different kind of interpretative work. This is so because the new art is all surface: "it has no inside" and therefore there is no hidden content that requires explication or analysis along traditional lines of criticism. The art described by Tarr is therefore necessarily *difficult* in two different ways: its hard surfaces refuse both "sentimental" responses to art and the intellectual work that has traditionally been associated with interpretation. Traditional modes of interpretation, which look for authorial intent or meaning buried within the work, are to be rejected as an incorrect attentiveness to the surface. Here, Lewis's championing of aesthetic surfaces prefigures aspects of both Greenbergian modernism[22] and Sontag's argument against interpretation,[23] albeit to very different ends. The work of art's self-sufficiency requires readers and viewers to rethink their relationship to the aesthetic object and the kind of "work" that they must perform on it to have an aesthetic experience. In other words, the notion of deadness alters both the work of art, and the work that must be performed by audiences.

In so doing, the notion of deadness equates all forms of nineteenth-century literature, suggesting that all required the same kinds of work. But as Hipsky argues, nineteenth-century realism cannot be equated with the kinds of sentimentality Lewis discusses, since the goal of such realism is to "awaken, disturb, educate, and even galvanize readers into action."[24] This model of writing and reading—which attempts to address social ills through imaginative fiction and encourage action within the real world—implies a variety of forms of readerly work. It necessitates affective labor on the part of the reader, who must identify and empathize with the plight of characters in a fictional narrative. It also requires such a reader to translate this affective, empathetic labor back into action in the real world and employ other forms of labor outside of regimes of reading: the ideal reader of a social realist text translates their affective labor into material advocacy for social change. There is thus an irony here: the modernist notion of "difficult" readerly work, which responds to the autonomous work of art, constitutes a relief both from certain modes of affective, empathetic labor, and from non-readerly forms of political or social action. These kinds of work, which are implied in the form of social realism, are essentially dispatched in favor of a disinterested aesthetic contemplation that examines forms and traditions in an intellectual rather than emotional fashion.

Although *Tarr* does accurately depict the kinds of work done by Victorian readers, the novel's articulation of deadness constitutes an exemplary aesthetics of modernist inhumanism. But, as Andrzej Gasiorek has noted, while the description of deadness "presents the view that has most commonly been attributed to Lewis," it ultimately "is misleading even about his character's aesthetics, to say nothing of" Lewis's.[25] Indeed, the novel itself clearly and repeatedly violates the aesthetics of deadness. *Tarr* is driven by plot and character in ways that are largely traditional; the intellectualized, English artist Tarr is given a foil in the German, Romantic artist Otto Kreisler, whose increasingly self-destructive behavior seems largely comic when he disrupts a dance at the Bonnington club, but eventually becomes violent and criminal: he sexually assaults Bertha, engages in a duel that results in the accidental death of his opponent, and ultimately dies by his own hand in police custody. For all of his intellectual critiques of traditional art, bourgeois-bohemians, and the aesthetics of deadness, Tarr—as Michael Levenson, Toby Avard-Foshay, and others have noted—is nonetheless motivated by emotional and affective factors that the novel categorizes under the concept of "sex."[26] Rather than comprising an explication of the novel's aesthetics, the concept of deadness serves a *dialogic* function. It presents one aesthetic mode that is associated with the intellectual Tarr and opposed to both the romanticism of Kreisler and the messy, affective world of sex. But the novel is driven by the entanglement and conflict between these categories. Here, the difficult autonomy articulated within the work only partially describes its broader aesthetic regimes, which absolutely—despite the book's unusual punctuation, diction, and sentence structure—rely on the traditions of European sentimental realism established in the nineteenth century.[27] The notion of deadness, in this sense, "frames" the novel, by making it seem both more modern and more distant from the tradition of realism than it really is.

A similar disconnection between articulations of autonomous difficulty and their literary execution can be seen in Edouard's description of the "pure novel" in *The Counterfeiters*. The pure novel also implies an inherent difficulty—although one that is of a different kind than in *Tarr*. Deadness in *Tarr* opposes sentimentality, soft forms of affect, and artistic anthropomorphism, but the pure novel constitutes an escape from specific tropes associated with the novel in the late nineteenth century. Interestingly, the pure novel also defines itself *against* popular (and often newer) forms of culture, including photography, phonography, the cinema, and the theater. If *Tarr*'s notion of deadness relies on a sculptural metaphor drawn from the visual arts (although its appearance in a novel suggests that the aesthetic is trans-media), the pure novel is an inherently literary aesthetic that cannot be transposed to other media. The appearance of other more popular forms of media, which might appear to threaten the dominance of the novel, instead frees the novel from the requirement to adhere to the norms of realism. This position therefore can be seen as either elitist or anti-populist (depending upon one's perspective), since it seeks to divide the work of popular culture from a purified and refined literature. Here Gide seems to reflect, at least in part, Fredric Jameson's claim that aesthetic autonomy is an artifact of the division between popular and high culture.[28]

Both Tarr's notion of deadness and Edouard's concept of the pure novel are aesthetic modes at least partially conditioned by the negative. While Tarr argues for "absence of soul" alongside a list of positive qualities, Edouard's definition of the pure novel relies almost entirely on the apophatic logic of negative theology: the pure novel's content is not a presence but an absence of the traditional markers of the novel, including plot, character, dramatic action, and so forth. On one level, the difficulty presented by the pure novel is tactical insofar as it refuses these techniques in favor of a pure *style* that would supplant them. But the tactical difficulty here hedges into the category of ontological difficulty, since a truly pure novel, in abandoning all the markers of the novel, would also seem to *cease to be a novel*, and the impossibility of describing or envisioning it in any concrete way is reinforced by Edouard's recourse to an apophatic logic. The pure novel is beyond positive description, and, so it follows, will also move beyond the traditional field of interpretation requiring a new kind of reader, and, so it would seem, a new form of literary discourse beyond the traditional regimes of hermeneutics.

In a sense, then, Edouard's notion of the pure novel seems to require more radical adjustments even than Tarr's notion of deadness, which is odd because the concept of the pure novel explicitly draws on Flaubert's conceptions of pure style, which he developed in the 1840s. In this sense, the pure novel seems simultaneously modern and already antiquated by the time of the publication of *The Counterfeiters* in 1925. Despite the fact that Flaubert's aesthetics seem to belong to a pre- or proto-modernism, the notion of difficulty attached to the pure novel remains inherently modernist insofar as it eschews sentimental or emotional responses to the autonomous work of art in two significant ways: 1) the pure novel requires readers to suspend certain notions of affective engagement (again of a sentimental kind); and 2) readers must also suspend expectations about certain traditional, plot-based rewards for reading. In other words, Gide's conception of a pure novel both institutes a change in the work of art and requires a different kind of work from readers. The pure novel's assertion of difficult autonomy is thus informed both by novelty and an almost-stoic aesthetics: readers, if they want to encounter a new kind of novel and a new kind of reading, will have to forgo the old and familiar pleasures in order to attain a higher, "purer" aesthetic contemplation. Here, the notion of difficulty associated with the pure novel seems very similar to "macho pleasure" that Diepeveen associates with modernist arguments in favor of difficulty.

At the same time, there remains an absolute difference between the aesthetics of the pure novel and those of Gide's actual novel. For all of its many recursions and the inclusion of material from Edouard's diary, *The Counterfeiters* can in no way be considered a pure novel based on the criteria Edouard describes. This is so because the novel, like *Tarr*, absolutely relies on recognizable aspects of the novelistic tradition—including characters and plot—that the pure novel rejects. The novel's culminating dramatic event—which occurs with the suicide of a boy named Boris in front of his class—testifies to its reliance on surprising plot developments that reward readerly engagement in largely traditional ways. The difference between Edouard's unfinished novel and Gide's completed novel of the same name suggests that the pure novel itself is an aesthetic ideal that cannot be materially realized, since any real novel must, to some degree, involve these traditional aspects of the novel. Once again, the claim of autonomous difficulty here seems to operate dialogically: the notion of the pure novel, rather than describing the aesthetics of *The Counterfeiters*, both frames the work by emphasizing its difference from earlier novelistic forms and brings into sharp relief a series of dramatic tensions.

It is worth further underscoring that the notions of difficulty attached to deadness and the pure novel are not the same, and are even opposed in many ways. Gide's valorization of "purity" suggests a nigh-religious function for the work of art, which has often been associated with romanticism and nineteenth-century aestheticism. Lewis's rejection of depth and, indeed, the *soul*, seems to explicitly repudiate such connections. While the pure novel draws on a Flaubertian conception of the novel (albeit in an even more radical form), the concept of deadness seems more recognizably avant-garde, clearly informed by the rhetoric and poses of such movements as Futurism and, of course, Vorticism. Nonetheless, the pure novel and deadness are linked by what they implicitly reject, which is an older mode of sentimentalized aesthetic contemplation that relies on a post-Enlightenment notion of humanism as represented within the tradition of the realist novel. It is not that Lewis's and Gide's accounts refuse all affect: the concept of deadness relies on affect insofar as it seeks to present an aesthetics that is variously alien, uncomfortable, and inhuman, while the pure novel relies on the notion of style to create extended experiences of aesthetic contemplation that are still, at heart, affective. These gestures resonate with the aesthetics of defamiliarization which have typically been viewed as a key aspect of modernist aesthetics.

But both novels depict fictional aesthetic programs that are far more radical than the aesthetics of the works that they actually appear in. Rather than being objective descriptions of their authors' aesthetics or statements of intent, they are confrontational rhetorical assertions meant to provoke a response. In this respect, they share many qualities with avant-garde manifestos (and, indeed, both arguably *are* fictionalized avant-garde manifestos), and like such manifestos they possess a hyperbolic rhetorical character that presents challenges for interpretation. But these local rhetorical ambiguities and uncertainties are further complicated by the novelistic contexts in which these claims of difficult autonomy appear. These claims of autonomous difficulty function dialogically within their respective texts in several ways. On the one hand, they serve traditional novelistic ends by highlighting differences between characters and creating tensions between different modes of thinking, feeling, and artistic creation. But they also do something else: the appearance of the radical notions of autonomous difficulty, and what appears to be the tacit or partial endorsement of the same, mark both of these novels out as *modernist* texts by highlighting their oppositions to an earlier tradition of realism. Both of the modernist autonomy claims in these novels serve as framing devices: they signal the importance of aesthetics as a topic of discussion and flag the ways in which the aesthetics of these modernist works differ from earlier forms of realism. But the modernist autonomy claims within these novels and their accompanying hyperbolic rhetoric make them seem to break more decisively with the traditions of realism than is actually the case.

Acknowledging this does support, in certain ways, Diepeveen's claims about the rhetorical nature of modernism's valorization of difficulty, which was typically brashly asserted rather than advocated in a clear and logical way. That literary modernism relied on emotive articulations of this kind is not surprising given that literature and fiction by their nature tend to privilege rhetoric and emotion over logic and rational argument (which are traditionally the province of philosophy and scholarship). More importantly, however, these rhetorical arguments—understood within their proper dialogic context—cease to be as naïve or even as problematic as Diepeveen sometimes implies. Both *Tarr* and *The Counterfeiters* tacitly satirize their protagonists and their radical aesthetic claims—particularly in the suggestion that their aesthetic programs are not really able to be realized. My claim is that these rhetorical gestures were purposive insofar as they enabled 1) the creation of a dialogic novelistic framework that could explore questions around traditional and modernist aesthetics, and 2) enabled modernist writers like Lewis and Gide to establish their difference from the traditions they were drawing on. In a sense, it is not their fault that subsequent critics have often taken their fictionalized, highly ironic, and contextually ambiguous claims of difficult autonomy at face value.

Ultimately, understanding the complex and often disjunctive relationship between modernist autonomy claims and their relationship to the works produced by modernists is important insofar as it clarifies a series of important factors. It serves as a reminder not to take modernists claims to have enacted a rupture with tradition at face value. Examining these specific autonomy claims also helps to clarify in what ways specific modernists sought to differentiate their work from certain traditions, and clarifies to what degree this differentiation was either substantive or successful. Moreover, it problematizes the notion that modernism was always difficult or that it gave no quarter to readers, since the claims that modernists often made about the difficulty of their works overlooked their continuing allegiances to traditions of realism. Understanding this disjuncture also clarifies yet again that the modernists took an active role in framing their own works in relation to tradition and actively sought to emphasize these differences in ways that might benefit them. Finally, it brings to light a very different conception of the *modernist work*, which is no longer an austere and monolithic work that seeks to stand apart from the social, but a provocative and self-reflexive work that places absurd and hyperbolic autonomy claims within a dialogic structure.

Notes

1. Fredric Jameson, "Postmodernism, or the Cultural Logic of Late Capitalism," *New Left Review* 146 (July–August 1984), 53.
2. Jennifer Ashton, *From Modernism to Postmodernism: American Poetry and Theory in the Twentieth Century* (Cambridge: Cambridge University Press, 2006), 6.
3. Nicholas Brown, "The Work of Art in the Age of Its Real Subsumption Under Capital," *Nonsite*, March 13, 2012. Retrieved at http://nonsite.org/editorial/the-work-of-art-in-theage-of-its-real-subsumption-under-capital
4. Charles Altieri, "Why Modernist Autonomy Claims Matter," *Journal of Modern Literature* 32.3 (2009), 1–21.
5. Lisa Siraganian, *Modernism's Other Work: The Art Object's Political Life* (Oxford: Oxford University Press, 2012), 3.
6. Andrew Goldstone, *Fictions of Autonomy: Modernism from Wilde to de Man* (Oxford: Oxford University Press, 2013).
7. For an extended argument about the aporetic nature of modernist autonomy, see Emmett Stinson, *Satirizing Modernism: Aesthetic Autonomy, Romanticism, and the Avant-Garde* (New York: Bloomsbury, 2017).
8. André Gide, *The Counterfeiters,* trans. Dorothy Bussy and Justin O'Brien (New York: Vintage, 1973), 73–4. Emphasis Gide's.
9. Wyndham Lewis, *Tarr* (Oxford: Oxford University Press, 2010), 265.
10. Nathan Waddell, *Modernist Nowheres: Politics and Utopia in Early Modernist Writing, 1900–1920* (London: Palgrave Macmillan, 2012), 179.
11. George Steiner, "On Difficulty," *The Journal of Aesthetics and Art Criticism* 36:3 (Spring, 1978), 263.
12. Steiner, "On Difficulty," 267, 270.
13. Steiner, "On Difficulty," 272.
14. Steiner, "On Difficulty," 273.
15. Leonard Diepeveen, *The Difficulties of Modernism* (London and New York: Routledge, 2003), xi.
16. Diepeveen, *Difficulties of Modernism*, xi.
17. Diepeveen, *Difficulties of Modernism*, 48.
18. Diepeveen, *Difficulties of Modernism*, 170.

19 David Trotter, *Paranoid Modernism: Literary Experiment, Psychosis, and the Professionalization of English Society* (Oxford: Oxford University Press, 2001), 5–6.
20 Suzanne Clarke, *Sentimental Modernism: Women Writers and the Revolution of the Word* (Bloomington, IN: Indiana University Press, 1991). See also, Martin Hipsky, *Modernism and the Women's Popular Romance in Britain, 1885–1925* (Athens, OH: Ohio University Press, 2011), 17.
21 Hipsky, *Modernism and the Women's Popular Romance*, 219. For Hipsky, however, both difficult modernist literature and popular present "consolatory or compensatory resources" that are essentially escapist or affirmative in character (219).
22 Here, Lewis anticipates some of Greenberg's claims about modernist painting and flatness. Clement Greenberg (1959), "Modernist Painting," in *Clement Greenberg: The Collected Essays and Criticism*, Vol. 4, ed. John O'Brian (Chicago: University of Chicago Press, 1993), 85–93.
23 Lewis's focus on the outside of the statue also anticipates Sontag's valorization of surfaces and her rejection of a depth model of hermeneutics. Susan Sontag (1966), "Against Interpretation," in *Against Interpretation and Other Essays* (New York: Picador, 2001), 3–14.
24 Hipsky, *Modernism and the Women's Popular Romance*, 220.
25 Andrzej Gasiorek, "Wyndham Lewis's *Tarr*," in *A Companion to Modernist Literature & Culture*, ed. David Bradshaw and Kevin J. H. Dettmar (Malden, MA: Blackwell Publishing, 2006), 406.
26 Michael Levenson, "Form's Body: Wyndham Lewis's *Tarr*," *Modern Language Quarterly* 45:3 (1984), 259 (241–62). See also, Toby Avard-Foshay, *Wyndham Lewis and the Avant-Garde: The Politics of the Intellect* (Montreal and Kingston: McGill-Queen's University Press, 1992), 44–78.
27 Levenson, "Form's Body," 241.
28 Fredric Jameson, *A Singular Modernity: Essay on the Ontology of the Present* (London: Verso, 2002), 176.

Chapter 3

MIMESIS AND THE TASK OF THE WRITER FOR LAWRENCE AND WOOLF

Helen Rydstrand

Questions surrounding the nature of art's relation to the world have occupied Western aesthetics for centuries. The modernists of the early twentieth century are often thought to have abandoned the concerns that had long been considered central to art—representing the world and teaching us about it, and ourselves— in favor of the exploration of abstract material form. This essay challenges this conception, by considering the parallels between two major modernist writers' divergent attitudes towards the relationship between the work of art (especially literature) and the world. D. H. Lawrence presents a transcendental vision of human work as the mimicry of the original energetic rhythms of universal creation; in Virginia Woolf's more secular, and perhaps more radical, conception, the universe manifests as a spontaneous and collaboratively developed "pattern"—as both the process and product of (art)work.[1] Yet each of these theories is reducible to the idea that this relation between world and work has a repetitious quality, so that Lawrence's and Woolf's aesthetics are each grounded in a conception of mimesis that foregrounds rhythm. A paradox at the heart of the concept of repetition allows for a nuanced understanding of this relation: absolute repetition is impossible, so that any repetition (whether rhythm or imitation) simultaneously creates difference—the new.[2] Thus, for both Lawrence and Woolf, whose thinking is grounded in rhythm, art is an organic outgrowth of the world, *as well as* being an artificial replication of it. This point of connection between two such different figures suggests that the rumor that mimesis was dead is, even at the center of British modernism, an exaggeration.

Attending to these rhythmic theories of mimesis also offers a route into comparing Lawrence's and Woolf's attitudes towards the task of the writer, or the social function of literature, and this is where they again diverge. For Lawrence, who sees the universe as inherently rhythmic, the task of the writer is to use literary rhythm to help bring readers into accordance with this cosmic rhythm. I begin this essay by tracing rhythm and mimesis through Lawrence's writing on metaphysics and aesthetics, before investigating how these are developed in "The Man Who Loved Islands" (1926), a cautionary fable about creative work centered on the fate of a man who attempts to make a world of his own. This didactic leaning in Lawrence's work is at odds with Woolf's idea of the task of the writer, which is more concerned with the epistemological work of understanding the world, via mimesis. Woolf's work expresses a tension between mimetic representation and self-conscious artistry: she demolishes the distinction between mimetic aesthetics and formalist ones, by claiming that the core truth of reality is aesthetic. After mapping Woolf's ideas on rhythm and mimesis, I turn to "Kew Gardens" (1919), one of her most overt presentations of the world as formally and aesthetically unified, and a text which has more in common with the modern form of the essay than it does with the ancient moral tale. While both these authors remain best known as novelists, the brevity and consequent speed of production of the short story makes it one of modernism's most flexible forms, and Lawrence and Woolf's contrasting and productive generic experimentation with it in the texts chosen demonstrates its significance in any nuanced consideration of how mimesis features in modernist concepts of the *work* of art.

Lawrence: (art)work imitates life

Lawrence saw human work in general as a replication of cosmogenesis. In his early "Study of Thomas Hardy" (finished late 1914, but unpublished until after his death), he represents human production or creation, and more generally, all work, as the repeated imitation of the original, energetic generation of life. He argues that humanity

> can at will reproduce the movement life made in its initial passage, the movement life still makes, and will continue to make, as a habit, the movement already made so unthinkably often, that rather than a movement, it has become a state, a condition of all life; it has become matter, or the force of gravity, or cohesion, or heat, or light.[3]

With this focus on inhuman and apparently unliving examples of "life," Lawrence blends the rhythms studied by science into his own vitalist metaphysical theories. These concepts largely share a rhythmic basis though, defined by laws of attraction and repulsion, or characterized by wave forms. In this account, the most fundamental of rhythmic physical forces in our universe are affiliated with work. Indeed, for Lawrence, "work is the repetition of some one of those re-discovered movements, the enacting of some part imitated from life, the attaining of a similar result as life attained."[4] This understanding of work as a repetition or imitation of some higher movement can be seen as the fulfillment of a mimetic drive.

The idea of human work as a mimetic replication of cosmogenesis fits into Lawrence's broader metaphysical vision of a progressive, rhythmic cosmos, and the moral goal of individual development in line with that cosmos. Lawrence consistently portrayed the universe as a whole as rhythmic. Most memorably, in "The Reality of Peace" (1917), he claimed the existence of a "systole diastole of the universe.... At all times it is, like the beating of the everlasting heart." People have a subordinate role within this rhythmic universe:

> We are like the blood that travels. We are like the shuttle that flies from never to forever, from forever back to never. We are the subject of the eternal systole diastole. We fly according to the perfect impulse, and we have peace. We resist, and we have the gnawing misery of nullification which we have known previously.[5]

While the viscerally biological quality of this image is certainly striking, the emphasis on a rhythmic basis for the universe is also remarkable. This juxtaposition of the organic materiality of the human body with the massive, impersonal scale of the universe brings our mundane existence into direct relation with the religious. And, Lawrence's moral stance on this cosmic rhythm is overt: he suggests a link between a person's existential state and their relative concordance with the natural rhythm of the universe.

To understand the complexity and contradiction of Lawrence's metaphysics, it is important to recognize that he also saw this underlying cosmic rhythm as evolutionary, and in some senses, progressive. He considered humanity to be engaged in an intertwined evolution of biology, culture, and consciousness. Rather than conceiving this act of imitation as collaborating to a cyclical pattern, solely reinforcing a "natural" norm for the individual and society, Lawrence insists on a model of progression: an evolution of life, of which he sees humanity as the pinnacle. He posits that a progressive differentiation of life forms is a "condition" of life, and perhaps its "Purpose," imagining life beginning as an amorphous singularity, "a great Mass." In this primordial vision, the initial "movement" of life led to its evolving "ever more distinct and definite forms... as if it were working always to the production of the infinite number of perfect individuals," until, extraordinarily, these "wonderful, distinct individuals, like angels, move about, each one being himself, perfect as a complete melody or a pure colour."[6] This means that change, growth, and indeed progress are essential for both individuals and society to continue to "fly according to the perfect impulse" of the universal heart.

This romanticist belief in humanity's capacity, even its destiny, for development is at the heart of the didactic aims that Lawrence had for his fiction. The importance of rhythm to Lawrence's metaphysics, and especially to the connection that he makes between this cosmic vision and human work, means that the rhythm of the work of art takes on a special significance. That is, the rhythm of Lawrence's writing is underpinned by the rhythmic character of his notion of cosmic development, and he also makes use of literary rhythm to teach his readers how to live in accordance with the universal rhythm. In "Why the Novel Matters" (1925), Lawrence explicitly identifies prose fiction as having the capacity to rhythmically capture the essence of life itself, and to connect the reader to it: "The novel is the one bright book of life. Books are not life. They are only tremulations in the ether. But the novel as a tremulation can make the whole man-alive tremble."[7] In this, Lawrence insists on the novel's capacity to physically, as well as emotionally, move the reader, to communicate life in rhythmic terms, as a "tremulation" that causes a corresponding vibration in the receiver (that is, the reader of the novel). A common understanding of this aspect of Lawrence's aesthetics is expressed in Donald Gutierrez's description of it as organicist, as opposed to mimeticist, viewing art "not as modelled on or mirrored in life, but as being itself life, vitality, aliveness raised to the highest pitch registrable."[8] There is much truth in this, except that it ignores Lawrence's statement, above, that "books are not life." Their capacity for mimetic communication is deeply important for him though, because, he argues, "to be alive, to be man alive, to be whole man alive: that is the point. And at its best, the novel, and the novel supremely can help you. It can help you not to be dead man in life."[9] Lawrence's certainty of the moral role of literature is evident in this, as is, by extension, his sense of the novelists' obligation to use literature to help their readers.[10]

This notion that literature should concern itself with the individual's development has ramifications for Lawrence's ideas on style and form. This is apparent in his 1919 argument that it is essential that literature record the individual's "passionate struggle into conscious being," because it is a "very great part of life."[11] On the one hand, Lawrence's use of the term "struggle" here acknowledges the difficulty of aligning one's rhythms with those of the cosmos—that is, that the task of the dedicated writer is an onerous one. He also explicitly links this struggle to his stylistic rhythms, arguing that the "continual, slightly modified repetition" often found in his writing is "natural to the author," and also that "every natural crisis in emotion or passion or understanding comes from this pulsing, frictional to-and-fro, which works up to culmination."[12] There is good reason to see this as a deliberate modeling of such existential and creative "struggle". While Anna Grmelová describes this part of Lawrence's style as a "permanent striving for the most accurate signifier," and suggests that it is "a consequence of his effort to verbalise what he feels cannot be verbalized,"[13] in this passage Lawrence actually emphasizes that this is an authentic registration of his particular voice, and more generally, that this style mimics how thought and feeling work. That is, his "continual, slightly modified repetition" is itself the medium of expression, rather than its by-product.

The son of a coal miner, Lawrence positions writing as physical labor, so that his "struggle" also aligns the work of the hands with that of the mind. For him, the work of inscription makes the human body a mimetic medium between these cosmic rhythms of "life," and the literary rhythms on the page. Lawrence's veneration of the corporeal is undoubtedly one of the most striking aspects of all his work, and this includes his writing on writing. It is plain in a 1913 review essay in which he reflects on the body's involvement in creativity:

> I look at my hands as they write and I know they are mine, with red blood running its way, sleuthing out Truth and pursuing it into eternity, and I am full of awe for this flesh and blood that holds this pen.[14]

Here, the work of writing and the materiality of the body are the instruments of art's higher ambitions, and align with his image of the universe as modeled on human biology in "The Reality of Peace" discussed above. Anne Fernihough identifies this aspect of Lawrence's art criticism as a point of contrast to the transcendent ideal of the autonomous work of art, as represented by Clive Bell's "significant form," which is most often affiliated with modernist aesthetics. She argues that Lawrence instead privileges "the ('feminine'?) viscosity and contingency of day-to-day living ... the material and the bodily."[15] On the other hand, Lawrence's ardent language above clearly illustrates why Fernihough would also observe that although "he never ceases to denounce idealism and 'the ideal', Lawrence constantly risks reifying the body into what is merely another transcendental category."[16] However, this quotation also signals Lawrence's alertness to the problematic role of subjectivity in creativity, which is one of the main themes of the short story to which I turn now.

"The Man Who Loved Islands" is a late tale that dramatizes Lawrence's idea of work, especially creative work, as mimicry of cosmogenesis. At the same time, the story can be understood to act on his notion of the didactic task of the writer: that is, to help the reader to be "man-alive."[17] It is the cautionary tale of a man—quite closely based on Lawrence's friend and fellow writer, Sir Compton Mackenzie—who dreams of having "an island all of his own: not necessarily to be alone on it, but to make it a world of his own."[18] Lawrence felt that "The Man who loved islands has a philosophy behind him, and a real significance."[19] What Lawrence means by this "philosophy" is not clear, but the tale is easily read as a parable centered on the figure of the artist, and exploring the nature of the relationship between world and (art)work. Viewed in this light, the story indicates the longevity of Lawrence's notion from "Study of Thomas Hardy" that human work revolves around imitating, or even simply repeating, the creation of the universe. Its cautionary tone and plot make it equally clear that this "philosophy" is intended to be instructive to the reader. "The Man Who Loved Islands" therefore serves as an important case study for understanding Lawrence's attitudes towards both the nature of creative work as process and product, and the social role of art.

The form of this story supports the idea that the islander's endeavor should be considered as allegory for creative work's fluid relationship to the world, via its close alignment with the islands. Broadly, we can understand the islands within the story as both imitations of the existing world that the islander wishes to escape, and also new creations (a relationship mirroring that between Mackenzie's real islands and Lawrence's fictional ones). But the island worlds are positioned as works of art not just by the mere fact that they are "made" by the islander, but through the rhythmic-aesthetic form of the story. The text is comprised of three sections, each describing distinct phases in the islander's deteriorating situation, and progressively reducing in total length, reflecting his moves to successively smaller islands. Each of these sections is distinguished by significant differences in tone, style, and theme, and the islander is even given a different epithet in each. The story does, however, retain a rhythmic unity through the very fact of the various repetitions that run throughout it: the series of islands, which shrink progressively in tandem with the islander's capital, and his gradual reduction of connections to society and the world as a whole. This is set against the backdrop of a range of natural rhythms, such as the patterns of weather, plant and bird life, and most notably the cycle of the seasons. This host of rhythms combines into one polyrhythm of contraction and decline, so that the islander's gradually intensifying rejection of human society and culture is equated with a repudiation of life in general, until he reaches the "misery of nullification" Lawrence warns of elsewhere.[20]

While the tale is not unsympathetic to the islander's disillusionment with modern society, he is presented as having made significant errors as an artist. His first island venture is the most idealistic, and it is based on a dream of a wholesome, bucolic life that balances the physical labor of farming—thus being in tune with the seasons and the earth—with the intellectual and creative labor of writing a book. However, the islander is really disconnected from both of these types of work, and this disconnection mirrors that of his relationships with the people around him. The actual physical labor of farming, and of maintaining his home and lifestyle on the island, is outsourced to a large group of staff brought with him "from the world," and his knowledge of farming and land management gleaned from books rather than experience (153, 157). His staff call him "the Master" throughout this section, and his hopeful new world is doomed by this reproduction of the class stratification of mainstream society. Instead of creating a collaborative work of art, the islander is single-minded and micro-managerial, with the result that his relationships with these people are inauthentic, his staff regarding him "quite without sympathy," as "a queer, alien animal" (157). This disconnection from others extends into the intimate relationship he forms with one of his staff on the second island, despite the fact that this results in a child, and their marriage (164–6). In fact, these events precipitate the islander's complete withdrawal from the world, to the third island.

Moreover, the islander's intellectual work—"compiling a book of reference to all the flowers mentioned in the Greek and Latin authors"—is of little serious worth to him or the world: "He was not a great classical scholar: the usual public-school equipment. But there are such excellent translations nowadays. And it was so lovely, tracing flower after flower as it blossomed in the ancient world" (156). This approach to intellectual or creative work, dilettantish from the start, is further attenuated with each successive island. On the second island, he spends "long, silent hours in his study, working not very fast, nor very importantly, letting the writing spin softly from him as if it were drowsy gossamer. He no longer fretted whether it were good or not" (163). By the final, tiny island, where he lives entirely alone aside from, at first, a cat, he "no longer worked at his book. The interest had gone" (167). In fact, after being on this island for a period, he finds both speech and writing "obscene" and in consequence "[tears] the brass label from his paraffin stove. He obliterate[s] any bit of lettering in his cabin" (170). His eschewal of occupation and human interaction are thus pathologically intertwined.

It is in this closing section of the story that we most clearly see Lawrence acting on his sense of the writer's moral task, as the text's function as a cautionary tale comes sharply into focus. His retreat from society results in the cessation of thought, and the islander increasingly loses hold of his very humanity, which includes attending to his physical well-being. When winter arrives in earnest, his tiny island is covered in huge snowdrifts. It is not until he realizes that he is doomed because he lacks the strength to dig his boat out to escape, that he acknowledges at last his own subordinate place in the "systole diastole" of the universe: "The elements! The elements! His mind repeated the word dumbly. You can't win against the elements" (173). This dramatic resolution positions the islander's rejection of human society, and especially of being a productive member of a social group, as arrogance, in assuming his capacity for total self-sufficiency and control. This personal failing can be traced back to both the islander's dabbling approach to work and his avoidance of genuine, equal interpersonal connections on the very first island—his failure to really "struggle" with the things that matter most.

Woolf: life imitates art(work)

While sharply differing from Lawrence's aesthetics, and lacking his particular moral views and didactic aims, Woolf is similarly engaged with a conception of the relation between world and art that is defined by repetition. She envisioned the world that surrounds us as itself a dynamic work of art: as having art-like features that underlie the apparent randomness of everyday life. As with Lawrence, this aesthetic principle directly informed Woolf's conception of the task of the writer and the function of art. Her idea of the world as a work of art is apparent in one of her earliest pieces of published writing, an essay titled "Street Music," which appeared in the *National Review* in 1905. In this, Woolf makes a direct link between a kind of cosmic music, and that made by people:

> We all know that the voices of friends are discordant after listening to beautiful music because they disturb the echo of rhythmic harmony, which

for the moment makes of life a united and musical whole; and it seems probable considering this that there is a music in the air for which we are always straining our ears and which is only partially made audible to us by the transcripts which the great musicians are able to preserve. In forests and solitary places an attentive ear can detect something very like a vast pulsation, and if our ears were educated we might hear the music also which accompanies this.[21]

In this passage, Woolf refers to human music as an audible echo of an all-but intangible universal rhythm or "vast pulsation"; that is, she explicitly presents artistic rhythm as the transcription of a natural or cosmic rhythm. There is a tension here, even a potential contradiction, between two understandings of art's function in the world. On the one hand, Woolf suggests that art, in this case music, can make the world a united whole: it can make it coherent and meaningful. But she follows this with the conclusion that this means that beautiful human music is an echo, a link to a pre-existing "music in the air," that is, an artistic quality that is inherent in the world itself. This suggests that art's task is both to interpret the world, which we might also describe as applying a pattern to it, and also to reflect the patterns that already exist.

Woolf's vision of a cosmically unifying aesthetic phenomenon is more famously expressed over thirty years later, in her memoir "A Sketch of the Past" (written 1939–40, published 1976). In this piece, she explains her "constant idea ... that behind the cotton wool is hidden a pattern; that we—I mean all human beings—are connected with this; that the whole world is a work of art; that we are parts of the work of art." Again, Woolf parallels the idea of an aesthetic order existing beyond the "cotton wool" of daily life with human creative endeavor: "*Hamlet* or a Beethoven quartet is the truth about this vast mass that we call the world."[22] Not only is the world itself a complex and beautiful work of art, but these exemplary works are considered intrinsically, indeed formally, to represent the true aesthetic quality of the universe. The fact that this later vision is of an underlying "pattern" could be seen to emphasize the artificial constructedness of Woolf's universal "work of art." However, she insists that where the world is concerned, "there is no Shakespeare, there is no Beethoven; certainly and emphatically there is no God; we are the words, we are the music; we are the thing itself" (72). The notion of humanity as a whole collaboratively forming a work of art implies natural, spontaneous generation, which in turn links human-made works of art directly to life itself, since life is, itself, artistic. This indicates that for Woolf, mimetic results may be achieved through formal experimentation.

In one sense, acknowledging the mimetic dimension of Woolf's aesthetics implies that creativity is secondary to the artist's role—rather, it is simply to reflect an existing reality. Yet she also gives precedence to the work of the writer: it is this sense of the "pattern hid behind the cotton wool" that motivates her vocation for writing. As she puts it, she demonstrates the significance of this conception for her "by spending the morning writing, when I might be walking, running a shop, or learning to do something that will be useful if war comes. I feel that by writing I am doing what is far more necessary than anything else" (73). She thereby elevates the value of writing as a form of useful labor, rather than an idle pastime. This sense of the importance of writing permeates her mimetic ideals, too: her aesthetically unified universe is created through artistic expression. She describes her first realization of her aesthetic metaphysics as "a sudden violent shock" out of the "cotton wool," or "non-being," of everyday life, experienced when looking at a flower-bed as a child and realizing that "the flower itself was a part of the earth" (71). Woolf explains that this shock gave her a feeling of satisfaction at having understood something important about the world, and she links this glimpse of understanding, this "moment of being," explicitly with the creative act. For her, such an experience "is a token of some real thing behind appearances; and I make it real by putting it into words. It is only by putting it into words that I make it whole" (72). In other words, it is the process of art making, in Woolf's case capturing an experience in words, that reifies "reality" and in particular, her sense of the world as a unified whole.

This question remains an animating one for Woolf's entire oeuvre: that is, whether a work of art creates or proposes a pattern, vision, or interpretation of the world, or whether it simply reflects that which does exist. Her interest in this problem is, for example, apparent in her representation of artists throughout her fiction. One example of this is John, the collector–artist in her 1920 short story, "Solid Objects," which describes his increasingly obsessive hunt for random objects—a lump of glass, a star-shaped shard of china, a globular piece of iron—that satisfy some aesthetic need in him.[23] John recognizes the artfulness of the world: the relations and contrasts between these things forming a kind of pattern for him. The best known of Woolf's artists, however, is the abstract painter Lily Briscoe in *To the Lighthouse* (1927), whose painting is not "of" Mrs. Ramsay, and does not attempt a likeness, but is instead an intensely sought "tribute" to mother and child through a heightened sense of mass, light, and shapes, and whose sudden clarity of "vision" concludes the book.[24] In the work of each of these artist characters, there is a tension between some kind of fidelity to and appreciation for the world, and an attempt to achieve a new, personal vision. For John, it is simply in placing unusual and unrelated found objects together and contemplating their form. For Lily, this lies in the balancing of abstract shapes on her canvas. This tension is also present throughout Woolf's writing itself, and the following reading of "Kew Gardens" seeks to tease it out, as part of the problem of the relation between the work of art and the world, in both aesthetic and social senses.

As can be seen from "Street Music" and "A Sketch of the Past," for Woolf, art is an aesthetic ordering, a holistic coherence (even if that coherence includes radical fragmentation and disjunction), or a unified theory about the world. Perhaps more than any other of her fictional works, "Kew Gardens" may be seen as an illustration of Woolf's vision of "life itself" as a unifying aesthetic phenomenon, a pattern that is hidden behind everyday appearances. One of her best-known short stories, it was first published by Hogarth Press in May 1919, illustrated with woodcuts by Vanessa Bell.[25] It does not tell a story in the traditional sense as "The Man Who Loved Islands" does. Instead, it presents a representative sample of life on a summer's day in the botanical gardens of London, composed of the plants and wildlife that live in a particular flower-bed, and brief snatches of the conversation of four pairs of human characters as they pass it. Woolf's idea "that the whole world is a work of art,"[26] or a "vast pulsation,"[27] is present in the story's rhythmic structural and linguistic forms, which are used to evoke a polyrhythmia of human voices, and a broader interweaving of human and natural rhythms.[28] In its employment of textual rhythms to evoke an aesthetically unified world, "Kew Gardens" investigates a tension between mimetic and formalist aesthetics.

The thematic fabric of "Kew Gardens," its evocation of Woolf's idea of the hidden pattern, is woven in large part from the series of distinctive voices that pass near the flower-bed. This series illustrates the enormous differences in human experiences of the world, even between those who live in the same city and at the same point in history. The four pairs of characters are conscientiously balanced in terms of gender, age, class, and relationship, with two heterosexual couples and two pairs of same-sex companions passing through. The first we meet are a married couple, accompanied by their children, who are thinking about and discussing the past romantic and erotic experiences that led them to this moment in their lives. Mirroring the first couple, the last characters to pass the flower-bed are young people at the beginning of their courtship. This last couple signifies an unknown future, as they exit the story and are "dissolved in the green-blue atmosphere."[29] Woolf's succession of voices forms an alternating rhythm pointing indefinitely into both past and future, making these eight characters representative of humanity as a whole. This alternating and expanding rhythmic structure is more important to the story overall than any details about the lives or personalities of the individual characters who own those voices.

The story embeds its aesthetic question in the social world by overlaying explorations of everyday work with that of creative production. Each pair of characters is sketched via distinctive vocal and dialogic rhythms, which as a group forms the story's polyrhythmia of voices. Most strikingly, the conversation of a pair of "elderly women of the lower middle class" is introduced as a rhythmic collaboration:

> After they had scrutinized the old man's back in silence for a moment and given each other a queer, sly look, they went on energetically piecing together their very complicated dialogue:
> "Nell, Bert, Lot, Cess, Phil, Pa, he says, I says, she says, I says, I says, I says –"
> "My Bert, Sis, Bill, Grandad, the old man, sugar,
>   Sugar, flour, kippers, greens
>   Sugar, sugar, sugar." (87)

The presentation of the women's conversation as something that they cooperatively "piece together" identifies it as a collaborative creative work, and as Lorraine Sim observes, this exchange's "rhythmic and repetitive qualities recall a domestic ditty, chant or song."[30] The overtly selective narration of the women's conversation adumbrates their everyday routines and their positions in social networks ranging in scale from family groups to class structures, and more basically, foregrounds their linguistic patterns. The second speaker's words are divided into lines resembling verse, further emphasizing the rhythmic aspects of ordinary speech. Here, Woolf puts vernacular speech into direct conversation with poetic convention, thus attaching to the women's gossipy, collaborative dialog the aesthetic significance of a work of art. Furthermore, this links domestic labor to creative work. This framework may also be applied to Woolf's approach to vocal rhythms in the story overall, in illustration of her idea that in the art work that is the world, "we are the words; we are the music; we are the thing itself."[31]

"Kew Gardens" as a whole has an already much-noted affinity with poetry, and this too can be understood as part of a strategy for the mimesis of an artistic world. Many critics stress the lyrical and unifying quality of the story's imagery, which includes a "mechanical bird" and a "shattered marble column" of butterflies,[32] and Woolf's heightened linguistic rhythms also contribute to this unifying effect, by invoking affinities between rhythms. This is evident from the first sentence of the story:

> From the oval-shaped flower-bed there rose perhaps a hundred stalks spreading into heart-shaped or tongue-shaped leaves half way up and unfurling at the tip red or blue or yellow petals marked with spots of colour raised upon the surface; and from the red, blue or yellow gloom of the throat emerged a straight bar, rough with gold dust and slightly clubbed at the end.[33]

Rhythmically, there is a lot going on in this long, very Woolfian sentence. Perhaps most conspicuously, rhythm is used to evoke the energy of growth in the flowers of the garden. But also, the syntactic repetition expresses a sense of connection between parts of the flower-bed: the unbroken rhythm created by the lack of punctuation within its first clause further accentuates the coherence both of the individual plants, and of the garden bed as a whole. This recalls Woolf's anecdote about her childhood realization "that the flower itself was a part of the earth,"[34] so that the vibrant, highly wrought beauty of her prose has an epistemological function, in reflecting an important insight about the world.

Its narrative structure, too, serves to point up the artificiality of the text. Dominic Head observes that the story contains "four passages of natural description to balance the appearance of the four couples, and the human (H) and natural (N) elements are symmetrically arranged (N-H-N-H-H-N-H-N)."[35] The narration of "Kew Gardens" also turns repeatedly from the speaking human characters to describe the silent and deliberate progress of a snail as it negotiates the obstacles of dead leaves, loose earth, and other insects in its path. While this snail's-eye-view in itself presents a radically Other perspective on the world, it also adds another rhythmic dimension to the story's polyrhythmia. The snail's personal rhythm is on a completely different scale from that of humans, as it both moves at a snail's pace, and its life-cycle is much shorter than ours. This meticulous rhythmic construction is crystallized in the final image of the story, where the human voices, the snail's journey, and the contained world of the gardens are reframed as individually insignificant within the city, another microcosm of the world. London is imagined here principally as a place of unceasing and interrelated rhythms of mechanical movement and sound:

> But there was no silence; all the time the motor omnibuses were turning their wheels and changing their gear; like a vast nest of Chinese boxes all of wrought steel turning ceaselessly one within another the city murmured; on the top of which the voices cried aloud and the petals of myriads of flowers flashed their colours into the air.[36]

The summative image of the modern world here is one of a complex intermingling of rhythms—natural, human, and mechanical. Above all, it is an image of pattern, order, and coherence, if not of unadulterated beauty, within apparent chaos. It is an image of the world as work of art.

This kind of finely tuned construction, imbued as it is with the traces of Woolf's writerly labor, leads us back to the question of her idea of the task of the writer. Unlike Lawrence's, Woolf's story does not impart an instructive message about how to live in the world. Rather, it might be understood, as Woolf's other best-known short story, "The Mark on the Wall" (1917) often is, as a kind of essay in narrative form. It presents a theory, an attempt at understanding or explaining something—an exploration of Woolf's vision of the world as an aesthetically ordered whole.

This essay has, in turn, presented its own theory—about the place of mimesis and rhythm in modernist literary aesthetics. Comparing the aesthetic theories and short fiction of two otherwise very different authors illuminates a shared fundamental definition of the relation between world and artwork as rhythmical. While both Lawrence and Woolf prove to be concerned with the mimesis of a rhythmic world, where they differ is in their particular visions of the world around them, and their understandings of the task of the writer in representing it. Lawrence's pulsing cosmos is a fairly distant cousin of Woolf's artful universe, and his didactic, religious aims have little in common with her drive for epistemological exploration. Yet their very divergence hints at a widespread fascination with rhythm, and also that mimetic concepts remained more central to modernist understandings of the relation between the work of art (both as process and product) and the world around us than is often thought. The examples of Lawrence and Woolf further suggest the power of the idea that the writers' task was to discern the rhythms of the world, and to take them up in their work.

Notes

1. Lawrence and Woolf have long seemed an unusual pairing among modernist studies, but recently scholars have begun to consider their points of connection. See for example Beatrice Monaco, *Machinic Modernism: The Deleuzian Literary Machines of Woolf, Lawrence and Joyce* (Basingstoke: Palgrave Macmillan, 2008); Kirsty Martin, *Modernism and the Rhythms of Sympathy: Vernon Lee, Virginia Woolf, D.H. Lawrence* (Oxford: Oxford University Press, 2013); Petar Penda, *Aesthetics and Ideology of D.H. Lawrence, Virginia Woolf, and T.S. Eliot* (Lanham: Lexington Books, 2017). For further discussion of Lawrence's and Woolf's engagements with rhythm and mimesis, including an expanded version of my reading of Woolf's "Kew Gardens", see Helen Rydstrand, *Rhythmic Modernism: Mimesis and the Short Story* (New York: Bloomsbury, 2019).
2. Henri Lefebvre, *Rhythmanalysis: Space, Time and Everyday Life*, trans. Stuart Elden and Gerald Moore (New York: Continuum, 2004), 8.
3. D. H. Lawrence, *Study of Thomas Hardy and Other Essays* (Cambridge: Cambridge University Press, 1985), 40.
4. Lawrence, *Study of Thomas Hardy*, 41.
5. D. H. Lawrence, "The Reality of Peace," in *Reflections on the Death of a Porcupine and Other Essays* (Cambridge: Cambridge University Press, 1988), 27.
6. Lawrence, *Study of Thomas Hardy*, 42–3.
7. Lawrence, *Study of Thomas Hardy*, 195.
8. Donald Gutierrez, "Vitalism in D. H. Lawrence's Theory of Fiction," *Essays in Arts and Sciences* 16 (1987), 70.
9. Lawrence, *Study of Thomas Hardy*, 197.
10. While this kind of attitude may seem at odds with what are considered typical modernist aesthetic ideals, Omri Moses makes it clear that a significant number of modernist writers aimed to bring people "into greater continuity with the mutable world of which they are a part." Omri Moses, *Out of Character: Modernism, Vitalism, Psychic Life* (Stanford: Stanford University Press, 2014), 8.
11. D. H. Lawrence, *Women in Love* (Cambridge: Cambridge University Press, 1987), 486.
12. Lawrence, *Women in Love*, 486.
13. Anna Grmelová, *The Worlds of D.H. Lawrence's Short Fiction, 1907–1923* (Prague: Charles University, The Karolinum Press, 2001), 36.
14. D. H. Lawrence, *Introductions and Reviews* (Cambridge: Cambridge University Press, 2004), 203.
15. Anne Fernihough, *D. H. Lawrence: Aesthetics and Ideology* (Oxford: Oxford University Press, 1993), 4–5.
16. Fernihough, *D. H. Lawrence*, 3.
17. Lawrence, *Study of Thomas Hardy*, 197.
18. D. H. Lawrence, *The Woman Who Rode Away and Other Stories* (Cambridge: Cambridge University Press, 2002), 151. Subsequent references are given in text.

19 Lawrence to Secker, November 16, 1927, 6:218–19.
20 Lawrence, "The Reality of Peace," 27.
21 Virginia Woolf, "Street Music," in *The Essays of Virginia Woolf*, ed. Andrew McNeillie, vol. 1 (London: Hogarth Press, 1986), 31.
22 Virginia Woolf, "A Sketch of the Past," in *Moments of Being: A Collection of Autobiographical Writing*, ed. Jeanne Schulkind (San Diego: Harcourt, 1985), 72.
23 Virginia Woolf, "Solid Objects," in *A Haunted House: The Complete Shorter Fiction*, ed. Susan Dick, 2nd ed. (London: Vintage, 2003) 96–101.
24 Virginia Woolf, *To the Lighthouse*, ed. Stella McNichol and Hermione Lee (London: Penguin, 2000), 226.
25 Dick, "Notes: Kew Gardens," in *Haunted House*, 291.
26 Woolf, "Sketch of the Past," 72.
27 Woolf, "Street Music," 1:31.
28 "Polyrhythmia? It suffices to consult one's body; there the everyday reveals itself to be a polyrhythmia from the first listening." Lefebvre, *Rhythmanalysis*, 16.
29 Woolf, "Kew Gardens," in *Haunted House*, 89.
30 Lorraine Sim, *Virginia Woolf: The Patterns of Ordinary Experience* (Farnham: Ashgate, 2010), 56, 57.
31 Woolf, "Sketch of the Past," 72.
32 Woolf, "Kew Gardens," 89.
33 Woolf, "Kew Gardens," 84.
34 Woolf, "Sketch of the Past," 71.
35 Dominic Head, *The Modernist Short Story: A Study in Theory and Practice* (Cambridge: Cambridge University Press, 1992), 99.
36 Woolf, "Kew Gardens," 89.

Part II

ARTISTIC LABOR

Chapter 4

RICHARD STRAUSS AT WORK IN HIS WORKS

David Larkin

Were one to compare the life and career of Richard Strauss with the nineteenth-century composers he listed as his chief inspirations (the line runs from Beethoven through Berlioz and Liszt and culminates in Wagner), his would be sorely lacking in the dramatic elements that preponderate in those of his idols.[1] Beethoven's life-story is famously shaped by his encroaching deafness and his struggles to cope with this disability; Berlioz, disappointed in love, once set off from Florence to Paris dressed as a woman on a mission of homicidal vengeance, although he abandoned his plans of triple murder and suicide by the time he reached Nice;[2] Liszt's legendary pianism and equally legendary love life gave rise to a host of true and exaggerated stories, with at least two former paramours featuring him in scandalous *romans à clef*; and Wagner's biography includes a night flight from creditors in Riga evading armed Russian border guards en route, as well as a decade-long ban from Germany for his involvement in the Dresden Revolution in 1849. By their side, Richard Strauss comes across as a dull dog. Aside from a misunderstanding which temporarily led his wife to think he was having an affair (a domestic squabble comically memorialized in his much later *opera à clef, Intermezzo*), there is precious little that is anecdote-worthy about him when set alongside his precursors' lives. He had the gift of taking the drama out of a situation—for instance, the seismic political upheaval of November 9, 1918 was recounted in his diary as incidental to the personal disruption it caused his travel plans: "To Munich; events decided otherwise: no train, abdication of Kaiser, republic . . ., revolution; luggage packed; one hour at the zoo [station]; evening playing Skat at Levins."[3] Even the controversies of Strauss's involvement in musical life during the Third Reich—including his brief tenure as President of the *Reichsmusikkammer*, and his precipitate fall from grace in 1935 thanks to the interception of a letter containing unguarded critiques of official policy—are hardly sensational by the standards of that turbulent era.

For the most part, then, Strauss lived a humdrum life. His time was divided between artistic creation, conducting duties, and the domestic sphere. In private life, his pastimes of choice were reading, hill-walking and the card-game Skat, and he had the name of being a devoted husband and father. Like many another composer of the era, his creative work was subsidized by other professional musical activities, in his case conducting.[4] Strauss held an increasingly prestigious series of appointments (in chronological order, at Meiningen–Munich–Weimar–Munich [second stint]–Berlin–Vienna) and his list of guest appearances on the podium took him all over Europe and on tours of North and South America. A model of professionalism in this area, the same is also true of his approach to composition, which was industrious, even industrial. Not for him titanic struggles with his material (à la Beethoven), or decades-long gestations (à la Wagner); rather, for the most part he worked to an orderly schedule. Strauss would undertake his main compositional activities during the summer months, typically when on vacation in the Alps or Italy, during which time his earlier sketches would be worked up into a continuous draft in short score. This, in his eyes, was the main act of composition, and the most difficult part. Rendering this draft in full prismatic orchestral colors was for him a more mechanical activity, and as such could be undertaken during the winter season, in the intervals of conducting operas and symphony concerts.[5] In these months he would "work very coldly, without haste, even without any emotion."[6]

Such cold, methodical procedures in the studio were, in Strauss's view, a necessary precondition for producing works that were pulsating with passion. He even inferred (wrongly) that one of his greatest heroes, Wagner, worked in a similar fashion: "[t]he mind which composed *Tristan* had to be cold as marble."[7] Strauss's own works certainly belie their systematic production and are as sensational as their creator wasn't. The hypertrophic masculinity and libidinous energy of *Don Juan* (1888) launched a series of orchestral tone poems full of chaotic beauties, daring feats of representation and imaginative orchestral textures.[8] Adorno saw in the "lavishness" of the finished scores something new: "the gesture of the idealized big industrialist. He does not need to scrimp; his means are highly expendable."[9] Strauss's first two successful operas—*Salome* (1905) and *Elektra* (1909)—took these means and used them in the service of plots exploring the exotic and the degenerate. Both tone poems and early operas were hugely controversial, and roused a litany of critical rebukes for the formlessness, dissonance, and unmelodiousness of these noisy, nerve-destroying musical obscenities.[10] And yet, it was these same controversies which ensured his success, both artistic (by the early twentieth century he was widely recognized as the "leader of modernism"[11]) and financial (he was one of the best remunerated composers of the day). He had recognized the link between shock value and success from early on, commenting proudly after the divided reception of his symphonic fantasy *Aus Italien* in 1888 that it was "the first work to have met with the opposition of the multitude; that means it cannot be insignificant."[12]

So quick was his ascent, and so high were the fees that his works commanded from his publishers by the turn of the century that accusations of commercialism naturally followed. To his friends, Strauss was open about his desire speedily "to acquire a capital which will allow him to live without holding any official post and devote himself to composition and literature."[13] Adorno paid a backhanded compliment to this openness: "The fact that he utilized his scores as capital can be held against him only by the envious. What they so readily labeled his 'materialism' was his willingness to acknowledge, without ideological embellishment, the situation which applies to all music under capitalism."[14] Strauss's cozy accommodation with the capitalist system was most notoriously evinced when he put on two concerts of his symphonic music in Wanamaker's Store in New York in 1904. He attempted to deflect the ensuing scandal with the justification that "[e]arning money for his wife and child is no disgrace, even for an artist!"[15] The justification that he was doing it for his family is also one Strauss trotted out when explaining his hectic schedule to his wife Pauline: "Simply money: money, so that I can be at peace, and live quietly with you and Bubi and my noteheads, surrounded by beautiful nature, sunlight, and healthy air."[16] He was as good as his word: the profits from the scandalous *Salome* were used to build a villa in the southern Bavarian town of Garmisch, which became a regular place of retreat for the family, even when Strauss's career required them all to relocate elsewhere during the opera season. The goal of becoming financially independent from conducting was seemingly within his grasp when the outbreak of the First World War wrecked those aspirations.[17]

Adorno notes that in this era "[t]he bourgeois slogan *épater le bourgeois* becomes universally accepted."[18] *Qua* artist, Strauss clearly rode this wave with works calculated to titillate and shock just the right amount; *qua* man, he (shockingly?) refused to conform to the stereotypes about anti-conformist artists, and demonstrated not just the acumen of a business man but also the regular working practices of an artisan. In an interview about his compositional methods, he drily distanced himself from clichés associated with the disorderly genius trope that fit a figure like Berlioz so well: "I'm never feverishly stimulated, and my hair is close-cropped."[19] Nonetheless he followed the Frenchman by making himself the subject of his compositions. In fact, he went further than Berlioz did in the *Symphonie Fantastique* in terms of self-referentiality: not only did he openly use the circumstances of his life as creative stimulus, but he included references to earlier compositions in his works, and even represented the very act of composing itself. This essay will explore the tensions inherent in these acts of self-representation, the mixture of aggrandizement and romanticization on the one hand, while highlighting the composer as bourgeois artisan on the other—Strauss *at work* in his works.

The obvious place to focus such an enquiry in the orchestral sphere is on the tone poems *Ein Heldenleben* (A Hero's Life, 1899) and *Symphonia Domestica* (Domestic Symphony, 1904). The autobiographical dimension of both works was recognized from the start, despite the lack of specificity in the titles. The article in the first (*A Hero's Life*) suggests a generalized heroic archetype, as does Strauss's earlier working title *Held und Welt* (Hero and World), and the official "explanatory guide" [*Erläuterungsführer*] published by Wilhelm Klatte again propagated the view that "human heroism in general is what appears to be characterized here through the medium of musical language."[20] Nonetheless, based on certain features of the score to be discussed below, Strauss was quickly identified with the hero of his own work. Some found this distasteful: "The composer indulges in self-glorification of the most barefaced kind," fumed Otto Floersheim shortly after the premiere.[21] The autobiographical element was more openly formative in the case of *Symphonia Domestica*, as witness the title of the initial scenario: "My home: A symphonic self- and family-portrait."[22] The personal dimension to *Domestica* was all but openly conceded by Alfred Schattmann in the program booklet for the work: "it is admittedly not about the domestic life of an ordinary everyday man; rather it's about one who spends the evening hours in 'creating and thinking' ... [T]he poetic idea rises beyond the bounds of the purely personal and grows to a more encompassing meaning even if, as in every true artwork, the personality of the creator with its individual subjective traits naturally comes into the foreground."[23] The parallels between Strauss's family situation and a work featuring a father, mother, and child were unmissable, and (again) unwelcome in many quarters. Even someone as close to Strauss as Romain Rolland initially regarded *Symphonia Domestica* as "one of the most daring challenges which he has so far offered to taste and common sense.... Above all, I do not like this display of all that is most secret in a man. There is a lack of privacy in this *Sinfonia* [sic] *Domestica*. The home, the living-room, the bed-chamber are open to all comers.... I confess that the first time I heard this work it shocked me for purely moral reasons, in spite of the affection I have for its author."[24]

While I will pursue an autobiographical reading here, it should be understood that I am not thereby claiming that either of these tone poems is a transparent representation of Strauss and his private life. As the objectivity of any written autobiography will be colored by the agenda of the writer—if not through direct falsehood, then through omissions and emphases—so too Strauss's works are selective acts of self-representation. Moreover, the gap between the man and his music is not bridged by these apparently frank musical revelations. Leon Botstein has argued that the "enigma" that is Richard Strauss is only exacerbated by these works:

> *Ein Heldenleben*, the *Symphonia Domestica* and [the later opera] *Intermezzo* may be directly illustrative of Strauss's life, but they are neither intimate nor revelatory.... The Sixth symphony of Gustav Mahler ... and Wagner's *Tristan und Isolde* suggest to the listener more about their composers than perhaps all of Strauss's explicitly autobiographical works combined tell us about Strauss.[25]

The relationship between the composer as represented in the two works ("Hero-Strauss" and "Domestic-Strauss" respectively) and Strauss the man resembles that between the protagonist of a work of autofiction and the author herself. In other words, I'm using the term "autobiography" in a loose fashion, as a convenient shorthand for works which are presented as depictions of aspects of their creator's life. Foucault's reflections on novels which employ a first-person perspective are helpful:

> Everyone knows that, in a novel offered as a narrator's account, neither the first-person pronoun nor the present indicative refers exactly to the writer or to the moment in which he writes, but rather, to an alter ego whose distance from the author varies, often changing in the course of the work.[26]

Reflecting on this type of self-reflexive novel, Adam Mars-Jones drily notes that "Readers can cope with the contrivances that don't quite hang together, as long as the story is strong and the level of self-congratulation low."[27] It was on this last point that *Heldenleben* arguably came unstuck—the grandiosity of the opening tone portrait of the "hero" smacks of self-serving vainglory. In what follows, I will attempt to rescue Strauss from the charge of blatant narcissism, without thereby suggesting that there was no ego at all involved in the project. Since it is presented as a comedy, *Domestica* provides a prima facie defense against accusations of authorial arrogance, but it still offended on other grounds: the very banality of the subject matter coupled with its hyperbolic treatment sat ill with fin-de-siècle critics, invested as they were in the elevated ideals of symphonic music as the repository of metaphysical truth. A deeper look at Strauss's motivations and values around this time is needed, if we are fairly to evaluate these works as art and as autobiography.

Wife, child, music: Strauss's values

On a vacation on the Isle of Wight in 1902, Strauss first conceived of writing the "family scherzo," which would become *Symphonia Domestica*. This motivated him to indulge in a little doggerel:

> My wife, my child and my music
> Nature and sunshine, these are my joy.
> A little serenity and lots of humour,
> Then the devil himself can't beat me![28]

Only a few months before this was written, Strauss's frequent absences from home had led things to deteriorate to such an extent that preliminary plans for a divorce were drawn up in autumn 1901, even before the mistaken supposition that Strauss was having an affair led to a fresh marital crisis in 1902.[29] Consequently, we might conclude that there is more aspiration than actuality in this paean to domesticity. Nonetheless, the personal value he ascribed to family, his art, and nature was certainly genuine. A decade later in 1911, the death of Gustav Mahler prompted Strauss to indulge in a deeper bout of soul searching. He rejected the Christian moral compass to which (in his view) Mahler and Wagner had relapsed, and outlined an alternative basis for morality which was to be exemplified in the tone poem he was composing at the time:

> It is clear to me that the German nation will achieve new creative energy only by liberating itself from Christianity.... I shall call my alpine symphony: Der Antichrist, since it represents moral purification through one's own strength, liberation through work, [and] worship of eternal, magnificent nature.[30]

The importance of nature as a source of value in a post-Christian world is shown by its presence in both the 1902 quatrain and the 1911 diary entry, and finds its most obvious outlet in the aforementioned *Alpensinfonie* (Strauss ultimately backed away from appropriating Nietzsche's title for the work). The notion of self-reliance and the importance of work, however, shed light on the two pieces under scrutiny here. The notion of making oneself and not some external body or code the sole moral arbiter of one's actions wasn't a new idea for Strauss in 1911. It first found a voice in his earliest opera, *Guntram* (1893), when the title character proclaims his emancipation from the judgment of the artistic brotherhood to which he belonged: "The law of my spirit determines my life; / my God speaks through me only to me."[31] The link between this type of spiritual autonomy and immersion in one's work can be inferred through the negative example of Guntram, who ultimately destroys his lyre and gives up music (his vocation) to expiate his sins through contemplation. As Charles Youmans has argued, this makes the character the embodiment of Schopenhauerian morality, since in Volume 4 of *Die Welt als Wille und Vorstellung* the philosopher concludes that the true path to achieving the desired "will-less state" is ascetic, not aesthetic.[32] Strauss himself would take the contrary path, giving up Schopenhauerian philosophy with its denial of the will, and embracing a contrary set of values, which included dedication to his craft. To a friend, he emphasized: "*I am not giving up art, and I'm not Guntram either.*"[33] Strauss had always been a diligent, methodical composer, but after he parted company from Schopenhauer, work provided a moral pillar for his existence. The final revelation of Zarathustra—"My suffering and my pity—what do they matter! Do I strive for *happiness*? I strive for my *work*!"—might well have cemented this value for him, given how receptive he was to Nietzsche's ideas around this time.[34]

Strauss's heroic avatar

Your work shall be a struggle, your peace shall be a victory![35]

That Strauss was a serious student of both Schopenhauer and Nietzsche has been foregrounded in recent Anglophone scholarship on the composer. The sophistication of his creative responses to the German intellectual tradition is now more fully appreciated.[36] Where his decision to compose an instrumental work based on *Also sprach Zarathustra* might previously have been construed as opportunistic, a way of increasing his own notoriety by tapping into the Nietzsche vogue of the 1890s, nowadays it is recognized as consonant with the composer's philosophical position at the time.[37] The embrace of the physical, the natural, and the sensual in *Zarathustra* and the works which followed can be seen as an antidote to the metaphysical mania that dominated instrumental music of the era.

More generally, the "superficiality" of Strauss's tone poems, in particular their concrete programmaticism, has been recast as evidence of a deliberately anti-metaphysical stance.[38] An orchestral work exploring heroism in the abstract was sanctified by a tradition going back at least as far as Beethoven's 1804 *Eroica* Symphony (a work which Strauss acknowledged as a model for *Ein Heldenleben*). It continued to be a viable subject even at the end of the nineteenth century (cf. Dvořák's last symphonic poem *A hero's song*, 1897). But when the monumental gestures are anchored to a specific scenario in which the hero is understood to be the composer himself, and the hero's enemies his hostile critics, music loses its lofty pretensions. *Ein Heldenleben*, insofar as it is heard autobiographically, is deliberately desacralizing. And the critics responded in kind: Strauss reported after the premiere that with two exceptions, "the rest spew gall and venom, principally because they have read the analysis as meaning that the hideously portrayed 'fault-finders and adversaries' are supposed to be themselves, and the Hero me, which is only partly true."[39]

From Strauss's sketchbooks it is clear that the composer-vs-critics angle did indeed occupy him during the creation phase.[40] In the finished work, however, the only inducement for seeing Strauss as the protagonist is provided in the fifth of the six sections, entitled "The hero's deeds of peace."[41] This consists of a smorgasbord of quotations from Strauss's earlier tone poems and operas, the sonic equivalent of a nineteenth-century book frontispiece showing an author surrounded by characters of his creation.[42] Extrapolating from this, it becomes easy to read "The hero's adversaries" as the composer cocking a satirical snook at his hostile critics, "The hero's companion" as a vivid portrait of the capricious Pauline Strauss, and so on. However, this is only one potential layer of meaning, even within the autobiographical paradigm. In one sketchbook entry, the enemies are not just those external to the protagonist, but also those echt-Nietzschean interior voices of "doubt, disgust."[43] Youmans chooses to focus on the latter, and consequently sees the work as a kind of authorial psychodrama.[44]

Given Strauss's sardonic Bavarian sense of humor, the mismatch between his unheroic real-life persona and his avatar in *Heldenleben* was probably a source of amusement to him. But is there any incentive for the listener to find the saving grace of irony in the bombastic self-portrait, as opposed to hearing it simply as wish-fulfillment? This, strangely, has not been much probed by musicologists. There are various reasons why a straight reading has been preferred, the most important of which is the relationship in which the work stands to *Don Quixote*, another Straussian tone poem which appeared the previous year. Strauss conceived the two as companion pieces,[45] and called *Don Quixote* a "satyr play."[46] The implication, therefore, is that *Quixote* is "parodistic/critical," while *Heldenleben* is by default treated as its serious counterpart.[47] James Hepokoski is one of the few to appreciate the double nature of the later tone poem. On the one hand, it "parodied another cherished aspect of the romantic hero stereotype: . . . the image of the masculine artist-creator . . . as a Promethean figure: the *Eroica*-propelled, Beethoven-through-Wagner legacy." At the same time, "in this self-aggrandizing display one may perceive a performative act of personal affirmation, a quasi-Nietzschean heroic deed promulgated under the aegis of a new aesthetic regime."[48]

One example will have to suffice to establish this double perspective. The opening section entitled the "the hero" is all thrills and testosterone, a hypertrophic rewriting of Beethoven's *Eroica* via Strauss's own *Don Juan*. Beethoven's cello fanfare, which swings back and forth within the span of an octave, is reimagined as a soaring lower-string cello arpeggio, which rises over two octaves before it is checked, just like the opening rush in *Don Juan*. This air of swaggering confidence runs through the whole of the first section, containing gestures associated in that era with an uncomplicated, romantic portrayal of heroism: major-mode themes that boldly stride forward, pulsating accompaniments, strong cadential gestures, rich orchestration with prominent brass, and so forth. Read on this level, it supplies ammunition to those who would charge Strauss with megalomania. However, Strauss undercuts his own bombast: the tremendous final dominant chord of this first section, which should discharge its energy by resolving onto the expected tonic chord of E♭ major, instead is diverted into spiky wind themes in a different tonality (g minor). No matter which way one interprets this next section ("The hero's adversaries"), the most important thing is the way it derails the momentum and punctures the importance of the opening. Strauss's heroism has been inside quotation marks, and we've just realized it; or, to offer a different metaphor, it is as if the director has called "cut," and we become aware we have been experiencing a filmed unreality, a performance of heroism.

Whether the work is considered as a satirical hit at the conservative press, or a portrayal of a creative figure struggling with his inner demons, the function of the "deeds of peace" section remains the same: it demonstrates that creativity follows the successful overcoming of conflict. Strauss's compositional processes were described above as methodical rather than manic, so it is appropriate that the ingenious display of themes from his earlier works would occur within an oasis of calm. But the storm before the calm was a necessary precursor. In a late essay on the nature of inspiration, Strauss acknowledged that the provenance of the initial melodic idea was mysterious: it "appears in the imagination immediately, unconsciously, uninfluenced by reason. It is the greatest gift of the divinity."[49] In his experience, such inspirations often followed "excitements of a completely different nature entirely unconnected with art." Later, he clarified that his "artistic imagination is particularly stimulated by excitement and annoyance—and not, as is frequently supposed, by sensual impressions, by the beauty of nature, or by solemn moods evoked by poetic landscapes."[50] (Within his marriage, Pauline provided plenty of stimulus through her erratic behavior, captured with humorous fidelity in the "Hero's companion" section of this work.[51]) Again, if we dig down, this is actually not all that different from a love-sick Berlioz channeling his frustrations into the composition of the *Symphonie Fantastique*; but where Berlioz elevates and dramatizes, Strauss embraces the humdrum.

In *Ein Heldenleben*, we are given snippets from finished works in a context which demonstrates afresh the composer's craft. By this I'm referring to the way in which dissimilar ideas from heterogeneous sources are ingeniously woven together and contrapuntally combined. For instance, in bar 743 the ideal theme from *Tod und Verklärung* and the nature fanfare from *Also sprach Zarathustra* are pitted against a theme associated with the title character in *Guntram*. But masterful though this whole passage may be, all we hear is the frictionless end result, rather than the process by which this was reached. It is only in *Symphonia Domestica* that Strauss to some extent lifts the veil on the act of composition itself. The difference between the sorts of self-representation in the two works might be characterized as follows: Strauss the composer is partly allegorized in *Heldenleben*, whereas Strauss engaged in composing is represented in *Domestica*.

Strauss's domestic persona

[A]t bottom one loves only one's own child and work; and where there is great love for oneself it is the hallmark of pregnancy.[52]

If *Heldenleben* was a provocation, then the still greater realism of *Domestica* was an outrage to those who believed in the sacredness of art. When a vast symphonic apparatus, quintessentially associated with the most public form of music making, is used to represent the composer's home life, the charge of bathos cannot be evaded. One might be tempted to speak of a bourgeoisification of art, were it not for the fact that the bourgeoisie themselves, through their appointed representatives, the critics, responded with a large dose of skepticism and hostility. Brahms's biographer, Max Kalbeck, poked fun at the vanity of the project:

[I]f a man like the tone poet of the "heroic symphony" becomes a happy father, then this is really no longer a simple family matter, but rather the fact becomes an event of world-wide importance, and the nations must hurry to congratulate the sovereign of Western music, in whose realm the sun of fame never sets, on his [new] heir.[53]

Others disliked the mismatch between the end and the means. This was the burden of Romain Rolland's complaints about the work quoted earlier, and another contemporary critic, Heinrich Welti, noted that "a romantic interlude between a married couple is augmented into a scene of worldly passionate bliss, and a 'jolly' family dispute degenerates into a roaring and heroic battle."[54] Most memorable of all was the quip attributed to Hans Richter, the first conductor of Wagner's *Ring* Cycle: "All the cataclysms of the downfall of the gods in burning Walhalla do not make a quarter of the noise of one Bavarian baby in his bath."[55] If unsettling bourgeois listeners by desacralizing symphonic music was Strauss's aim, he succeeded admirably. He was unapologetic, arguing "What could be more serious than married life? Marriage is the most profound event in life and the spiritual joy of such a union is heightened by the arrival of a child. [Married] life naturally has its humour, which I also injected into this work, in order to enliven it."[56] This defense of the quotidian clearly ties in with the personal values he articulated at the start of work on this project. However, Strauss was not above stoking the flames of controversy, such as with his tongue-in-cheek remark to Rolland: "I don't see why I shouldn't write a symphony about myself. I consider myself just as interesting as Napoleon or Alexander."[57] Were that meant even semi-seriously (and I suggest that there is a grain of truth beneath the hyperbole), it would bear out Gilliam's assessment of the work as evincing "an anti-metaphysical stance taken to a level that even Nietzsche might not have recognised."[58]

In a work of such apparent egoism, it is fitting that we open with a tone portrait of the paterfamilias himself. Through appropriate expression marks, Strauss indicates the facets of the father's personality that are on display, with different motifs on the first page marked "Leisurely," "Dreamily," "Grumpily," and "Fierily." For my purposes, the music associated with the second of these is the most interesting. The good-humored first four bars have set up certain expectations in terms of mood and rhythm, and without warning these are derailed: the jaunty rhythms cease, and the oboe melody is heard above a static g-minor harmony. This feeling of temporal suspension ends with the resumption of more active rhythms in the passage which follows, marking it as an atypical oasis amid the general liveliness of the opening.

Needless to say, there was specific referential intent behind all this. There are additional textual clues in the complete draft score of the work (i.e., the version written on two staves, before orchestration), the first page of which bears the title "Daheim: ein sinfonisches Familienpotpourri u. Selbstporträt" (At home: a symphonic family potpourri and self-portrait). In the top corner of the page, above this same oboe melody, Strauss scribbled: "through it all Richard works constantly on a melody. In its waxing and waning this melody amounts to something like a cantus firmus, which runs through the whole."[59] At the place

Figure 4.1 Strauss, *Symphonia Domestica*, transcribed for piano by Otto Singer (Berlin: Bote & Bock, 1907), bars 1–22.

marked with the double asterisk in Figure 4.1, an additional note indicates "es geht nicht weiter" (it doesn't go any further).[60] The inference, confirmed later on, is that this oboe motif is the germ of the melody, but the composer is stuck at this stage in terms of how to build on it, and hence he "grumpily" moves on to other things. That he continues to brood on it is clear by the return of this figure in the French horn at bar 415 (see the middle staff in Figure 4.2), a moment's daydreaming in the middle of the Scherzo section in which Papa and Mama are playing with the child and answering its questions. Again, it is backed by very slow-moving chords, but still nothing further comes of it, and Papa's attention is soon taken up with the "little monster's bath." Of future relevance is the descending melodic line in the solo violin which occurs in counterpoint with the "germ" idea (shown in the dotted box in Figure 4.2).

Figure 4.2 Strauss, *Symphonia Domestica* (Berlin: Bote & Bock, 1904), bars 410–422 (reduced score).

Figure 4.3 Strauss, *Symphonia Domestica* (Berlin: Bote & Bock, 1904), bars 559–570.

The third significant appearance of this motif occurs after the child has been put to bed with a lullaby, and there is now an opportunity to work. Again, the draft score is helpfully annotated with "Papa componiert" (Papa composes).[61]

Even more revealing is an earlier sketch of this passage, with the penciled comment: "Here (alone in the evening) the melody which was being worked on for the whole afternoon is <u>completed</u>."[62] The completion involves pairing the initial motif (in the unbroken box) with the idea which in Figure 4.2 occurred in conjunction with it (in the broken-line box). On the earlier occasion, they were vertically set against each other, but here the one flows linearly into the other. Strauss thereafter sequences this composite idea, initially in the flutes, and derives new material from inverting the opening leap. These and similar techniques are used to build the germ theme into a complete musical paragraph with satisfying cadential closure. Late in life, Strauss confirmed that this was how he worked in practice.

> To judge from my own experience of creative work, a motif or a melodic phrase of two or four bars occurs to me immediately. I put this down on paper and then expand it straight away into a phrase of eight, sixteen or thirty-two bars which is not of course left unaltered, but after a longer or shorter period of "rest" is slowly fashioned into its final form, which must hold its own against the severest and most detached self-criticism. Now this operation is carried out in such a manner that what is most important is to wait for the moment when the imagination is most willing and ready to serve me further.[63]

This essay, which remained in manuscript until after his death, no more than confirms what *Symphonia Domestica* had illustrated: the combination of initial inspiration, subsequent frustration, and eventual systematic/critical expansion. That Strauss would feature his creative process alongside his family members in this tone poem shows how important the wife–child–music triad was to him then and indeed throughout his life. It also undercuts the common association of the act of composition with excited states, mythologized settings, and the rest of the romantic paraphernalia: Strauss's hyper-romantic sound-worlds originated instead in mundane domesticity.

In 1949, Strauss's last notebook entry complained that critics had misunderstood one of the most important qualities running through his oeuvre:

> Why do they not see what is new in my works, how the individual becomes visible in the composition as only in Beethoven—this begins already in the third act of *Guntram* (rejection of collectivism), *Heldenleben*, *Don Quixote*, *Domestica*—and in *Feuersnot* the deliberate tone of mockery, of irony, the protest against the typical libretto represent individual novelty.[64]

The works cited all stem from a single decade (1893–1903), but Strauss's self-representations are not limited to this period (as the 1924 opera *Intermezzo* demonstrates), nor even necessarily to these few works within this decade (Youmans, for instance, sees Till Eulenspiegel and Zarathustra as alter egos of the composer[65]). What distinguishes the two works which were the focus of this essay from the other three is the virtual absence of any pretense that they are other than autobiographical: Guntram, Quixote and Kunrad (the hero of *Feuersnot*) may in some respects be paper-thin allegories for Strauss the artist, but there still is a gap between the characters and their creator which isn't present in *Ein Heldenleben* and *Symphonia Domestica*. Moreover, the aspects which unambiguously link these two tone poems to Strauss are the sections where, respectively, his works and working methods are on show. The hero might have been an abstraction, were it not for the cornucopia of self-quotations which ties it back to Strauss himself. Even *Domestica* might have featured an abstract family, were it not for the sections where "Papa" is revealed to be a composer. Thus, for all his apparent prominence in these works, Strauss the man ultimately dissolves back into his creative persona. What remains, and what was important to him, is the craftsman. In his final decade, he produced two Sonatinas for wind ensemble whose titles emphasize the artisanal (*Aus der Werkstatt eines Invaliden* (From the workshop of an invalid) (1943), and *Fröhliche Werkstatt* (The happy workshop) (1944–5)). More generally, his self-deprecating description for the entirety of his instrumental output from these years as "wrist exercises" frames these as low-level handiwork, rather than Art with a capital A. That he felt he needed to continue to compose even after he thought his true life's work was finished speaks volumes.[66] Strauss clearly took justifiable pride in his works, but it was in work itself that he saw his personal salvation.

Notes

1 This lineage is set out diagrammatically in a letter from Strauss to Roland Tenschert, December 17, 1944; facsimile in David Larkin, "The Unbroken Career of Richard Strauss, Symphonic Dramatist," *Richard Strauss-Jahrbuch 2016*, ed. Günter Brosche and Oswald Panagl (Vienna: Hollitzer, 2017), 45.

2 This almost incredible story is told by Berlioz himself; see *The Memoirs of Hector Berlioz*, trans. and ed. David Cairns (London: Panther, 1970), 181–7.

3 "Nach München; die Ereignisse entschieden anders; kein Zug, Abdankung des Kaisers, Republik . . ., Revolution; Koffer gepackt; 1 Stunde im Tiergarten; abends bei Levin und Skat." Franz Trenner, *Richard Strauss: Chronik zu Leben und Werk*, ed. Florian Trenner (Vienna: Verlag Dr. Richard Strauss, 2003), 402; see also Bryan Gilliam, *Richard Strauss* (Cambridge: Cambridge University Press, 1999), 109. Unless otherwise indicated, all translations are my own.

4 This aspect of his career is the primary focus of Raymond Holden, *Richard Strauss: A Musical Life* (New Haven: Yale University Press, 2011).

5 In one interview (*c.* 1914), he is reported to have said: "The preliminary sketches are then turned into sketches. These are written out and worked out, often up to four times. This is the hard part of the labour. I write the score in my room straightaway and without trouble, working without pain for up to twelve hours in the day." [Die Vorskizzen werden dann zu Skizzen. Diese werden ausgeschrieben, ausgearbeitet, oft bis zu vier Malen. Dies ist der harte Teil der Arbeit. Die Partitur schreibe ich in meinem Studienzimmer geradewegs und ohne Mühe bis zu zwölf Stunden am Tage arbeitend]. Richard Strauss, *Dokumente*, ed. Ernst Krause (Leipzig: Reclam, 1980), 64–5.

6 "Im Winter, vom November bis zum April, arbeite ich sehr kühl, ohne jedes Hasten, ja sogar ohne jede Emotion." Interview excerpt from 1914, in Krause, *Dokumente*: 65.

7 "Der Kopf, der 'Tristan' komponiert hat, mußte kalt sein wie Marmor." Ibid.

8 *Don Juan* is normally regarded as the second tone poem, although it was the first to be premiered (in 1889). *Macbeth* was written earlier, but was substantially revised after its 1890 first performance.

9 Theodor W. Adorno, "Richard Strauss: Born June 11, 1864," trans. Samuel and Shierry Weber, *Perspectives of New Music* Vol. 3 (1964), 14. The epithet "industrialist" might refer, *inter alia*, to the total control Strauss exerted over his musical material (in Adorno's eyes), as opposed to the less coercive thematic processes he observed in Mahler's work, which "escape the hand of the composer who was chiselling them to their definite shape." See Richard Wattenbarger, "A 'Very German Process': The Contexts of Adorno's Strauss Critique," *19th-Century Music* Vol. 25/2-3 (Fall/Spring 2001-2), 325.

10 A sample of negative responses to Strauss's music found in the press and from noteworthy individuals is given in Nicolas Slonimsky, *Lexicon of Musical Invective* (New York: Norton, 2000), 180–95.

11 This title "Führer der Moderne" was one Strauss himself cited, and affected to despise. Richard Strauss, "Gibt es für die Musik eine Fortschrittspartei?" in *Betrachtungen und Erinnerungen*, 2nd enlarged edition (Zurich: Atlantis, 1957), 14.

12 "Das erste Werk, das auf die Opposition des großen Haufens gestoßen ist; da muß es doch nicht unbedeutend sein." Letter from Strauss to Lotti Speyer, June 23, 1887;

quoted in Willi Schuh, *Richard Strauss: Jugend und frühe Meisterjahre—Lebenschronik 1864-1898* (Zurich: Atlantis, 1976), 143.
13 Alfred Kalisch, "Richard Strauss: The Man," in Ernest Newman, *Richard Strauss* (London: John Lane, 1908), xviii.
14 Adorno, "Richard Strauss," 15.
15 Kurt Wilhelm, *Richard Strauss: An Intimate Portrait*, trans. Mary Whittall (London: Thames & Hudson, 1999), 98.
16 "Nur Geld, Geld, damit ich bald zur Ruhe komme u. ganz still dir u. dem lieben Bubi, u. den Notenköpfen leben kann in schöner Natur, Sonnenschein u. kräftiger Luft." Letter from Strauss to Pauline Strauss, December 4, 1901, quoted in Bryan Gilliam, *Richard Strauss: Magier der Töne* (Munich: C.H. Beck, 2014), 85.
17 Strauss claimed to have lost £37,000, the savings of thirty years, when his British bank accounts were confiscated. This equates to *c*. £1.5 million today. Richard Strauss, *Späte Aufzeichnungen*, ed. Marion Beyer, Jürgen May, and Walter Werbeck (Mainz: Schott, 2016), 69.
18 Adorno, "Richard Strauss," 14.
19 "Ich bin niemals fieberhaft erregt und trage mein Haar kurz geschoren." Krause, *Dokumente*: 65.
20 "Menschliches Heldentum im allgemeinen ist es, was hier durch das Mittel der Tonsprache charakterisiert erscheint." Wilhelm Klatte, "*Ein Heldenleben*: Tondichtung für großes Orchester op. 40" [1899] in Herwarth Walden (ed.), *Richard Strauss: Symphonien und Tondichtungen*, Meisterführer 6 (Berlin: Schlesinger, n.d. [*c*. 1908]), 150. This was in fact one of two guides produced for the work; the other was by Friedrich Rösch (*Ein Heldenleben: Tondichtung für grosses Orchester von Richard Strauss. Erläuterungsschrift*. Leipzig: Leuckart, 1899).
21 Otto Floersheim, Review in the *Musical Courier*, New York (April 19, 1899), in Slonimsky, *Lexicon*, 185. This was probably a response to the performance on April 18, 1899 in Cologne, the third German city to mount the work after the March 3, 1899 premiere in Frankfurt. See Mark-Daniel Schmid, "The Tone Poems of Richard Strauss and their Reception History from 1887-1908" (PhD Dissertation: Northwestern University, 1997), 371, 373, 376–7.
22 "Mein Heim: Ein sinfonisches Selbst- und Familienporträt." Trenner, *Richard Strauss: Chronik*, 223 (May 25, 1902).
23 "Es ist freilich nicht das häusliche Leben eines Alltagsmenschen, um das es sich handelt, sondern eines solchen, der abendliche Stunden gar oft mit 'Schaffen und Schauen' [the original title for one section of the work] zu verbringen pflegt, ... dadurch erhebt sich die poetische Idee über das Maß des rein Persönlichkeit des Schaffenden mit einzelnen subjektiven Zügen auch bei diesem Werke leitend im Hintergrunde steht." Alfred Schattmann, "Sinfonia domestica, Op. 53," in Walden, *Richard Strauss: Symphonien und Tondichtungen*, 166.
24 *Richard Strauss & Romain Rolland: Correspondence, Diary & Essays*, ed. Rollo Myers (London: Calder & Boyars, 1968), 211.
25 Leon Botstein, "The Enigmas of Richard Strauss: A Revisionist View," in *Richard Strauss: New Perspectives on the Composer and His Work*, ed. Bryan Gilliam (Durham, NC: Duke University Press, 1992), 7.
26 Michel Foucault, "What is an author?" in *Aesthetics, Method and Epistemology*, trans. Robert Hurley et al., ed. James D. Faubion (New York: The New Press, 1998), 215.

27 Adam Mars-Jones, "V2 into Space" [a review of Michael Chabon's *Moonglow*], *London Review of Books* Vol. 39/5 (March 2, 2017), 15.
28 "Mein Weib, mein Kind und meine Musik / Natur und Sonne, die sind mein Glück. / Ein wenig Gleichmut und viel Humor / Drin thut mir's der Teufel selbst nicht vor!" Transcribed from the rear flyleaf of Sketchbook 9 in Walter Werbeck, *Die Tondichtungen von Richard Strauss* (Tutzing: Hans Schneider, 1996), 173.
29 Gilliam, *Richard Strauss*, 78–9.
30 "Mir ist es absolut deutlich, daß die deutsche Nation nur durch die Befreiung vom Christentum neue Tatkraft gewinnen kann. . . . Ich will meine Alpensinfonie: den Antichrist nennen, als da ist: sittliche Reinigung aus eigener Kraft, Befreiung durch die Arbeit, Anbetung der ewigen herrlichen Natur." Quoted with facsimile in Stephan Kohler, Foreword to *Eine Alpensinfonie*, Op. 64 (London: Eulenberg, 1996), iv, translated in Gilliam, *Richard Strauss*, 93.
31 "Mein Leben bestimmt meines Geistes Gesetz; / mein Gott spricht durch mich selbst nur zu mir." *Guntram* Act III.
32 Charles Youmans, *Richard Strauss's Orchestral Music and the German Intellectual Tradition: The Philosophical Roots of Musical Modernism* (Bloomington: Indiana University Press, 2005), 69.
33 Letter from Strauss to Alexander Ritter, February 3–4, 1893; quoted in translation in Willi Schuh, *Richard Strauss: A Chronicle of the Early Years*, trans. Mary Whittall (Cambridge: Cambridge University Press, 1982), 285.
34 Friedrich Nietzsche, *Thus Spoke Zarathustra: A Book for All and None*, trans. Adrian del Caro, ed. Adrian Del Caro and Robert B. Pippin (Cambridge: Cambridge University Press, 2006), 266.
35 Nietzsche, *Thus Spoke Zarathustra*, 33.
36 The most detailed exposition of this view is found in Youmans, *Richard Strauss's Orchestral Music*, but see also Gilliam, *Richard Strauss*, and James Hepokoski, "The Second Cycle of Tone Poems," in *The Cambridge Companion to Richard Strauss*, ed. Charles Youmans (Cambridge: Cambridge University Press, 2010), 78–104.
37 Eduard Hanslick, the most famous music critic of his day, suspected that Strauss had seized on the "fashionable" Nietzsche and picked his "most peculiar, unpopular book." "E-moll-Symphonie und 'Der Wassermann' von A. Dvorak," in *Am Ende des Jahrhunderts* (Berlin: Allgemeine Verein für deutsche Literatur, 1899), 218.
38 Youmans, *Richard Strauss's Orchestral Music*, 14–15.
39 "[D]ie übrigen spucken Gift und Galle, hauptsächlich weil sie aus der Analyse zu ersehen glaubten, das mit den recht häßlich geschilderten 'Nörglern und Widersachen' sie selbst gemeint seien und der Held ich selbst sein soll, was letzteres jedoch nur teilweise zutrifft." Letter from Strauss to his parents, March 24, 1899; Richard Strauss, *Briefe an die Eltern 1882-1906*, ed. Willi Schuh (Zurich: Atlantis, 1954), 221. Trans. modified from Schuh, *Richard Strauss: A Chronicle*, 481, which includes a parenthetical identification of Rösch as the author of the analysis in question. However, it is more likely to have been Klatte's guide, as Rösch's publication probably didn't appear until the second half of 1899, according to Werbeck (*Die Tondichtungen von Richard Strauss*, 264).
40 See one of his earliest sketches of the opening, which is followed by the words "dann die Kritiker Gmoll" [Then the critics in G minor]. Sketchbook 4: 7 (in the Richard Strauss Archiv, Garmisch-Partenkirchen, hereafter "RSA"), also transcribed in Franz Trenner, *Die Skizzenbücher von Richard Strauss: aus dem Richard-Strauss-Archiv in*

Garmisch (Tutzing: Hans Schneider, 1977), 7. Further links to individual critics in the final score are listed in Max Steinitzer, *Richard Strauss*, 1st to 4th editions (Berlin: Schuster & Loeffler, 1911), 239–40; and Roswitha Schlötterer-Traimer, *Richard Strauss: Sein Leben und Werk im Spiegel der zeitgenössischen Karikatur*, ed. Roswitha Schlötterer-Traimer (Mainz: Schott, 2009), 30.

41 The score itself has no paratextual indications beyond the title. Even the six section titles, now universally known, were a late addition prompted by Wilhelm Klatte, who together with the author of the other explanatory guide (Friedrich Rösch) aided Strauss in coming up with them. Wilhelm Klatte, "Aus Richard Strauss' Werkstatt," *Die Musik* Vol. 16/9 (June 1924), 641.

42 Cf. Robert William Buss, "Dickens' Dream" (1875), or Cruikshank's illustration of Richard Barham in *The Ingoldsby Legends* (London: R. Bentley & Son, 1874).

43 Sketchbook 5: 40, also transcribed in Trenner, *Die Skizzenbücher von Richard Strauss*, 10.

44 Youmans, *Richard Strauss's Orchestral Music*, 206–9.

45 See Strauss's letter to Gustav Kogel, November 10, 1898, quoted in Werbeck, *Die Tondichtungen von Richard Strauss*, 158, translated in Schuh, *Richard Strauss: A Chronicle*, 461.

46 "Symphonic poem *Held und Welt* begins to take shape; as satyr play to accompany it—*Don Quixote*" [sinfonische Dichtung Held u. Welt beginnt Gestalt zu bekommen; dazu als Satyrspiel—Don Quixote]. Schreibkalendar entry for April 16, 1897 (RSA), translated in Schuh, *Richard Strauss: A Chronicle*, 460 (where he mistakenly uses Strauss's earlier spelling *Quichote*).

47 Cf. Youmans, *Richard Strauss's Orchestral Music*, 182–3.

48 Hepokoski, "The Second Cycle of Tone Poems," 82.

49 "Der melodische Einfall ... erscheint in der Phantasie unmittelbar, unbewußt, ohne Einfluß des Verstandes. Es ist das höchste Geschenk der Gottheit". The essay title in German is "Vom melodischen Einfall" (On melodic inspiration, *c*. 1940), which is inaccurately rendered as "On inspiration in music" in the 1953 translation. Richard Strauss, *Betrachtungen und Erinnerungen*, 2nd enlarged edition (Zurich: Atlantis, 1957), 161; translated in Strauss, *Recollections and Reflections*, trans. L. J. Lawrence (London: Boosey and Hawkes, 1953), 112.

50 "[E]ine seelische Emotion ... wie ich es bei Aufregungen ganz anderer, nicht künstlerischer Art oft an mir selbst erfahren habe"; "Nach meiner eigenen Erfahrung, daß bei großen Erregungen, Ärger, eine besonders lebhafte Tätigkeit der künstlerischen Phantasie einsetzt—bei mir nicht, wie oft geglaubt wird, nach sinnlichen Eindrücken, Anschauung von großen Naturschönheiten, feierlichen Stimmungen in poetischer Landshaft." Strauss, *Betrachtungen und Erinnerungen*, 161, 162–3, trans. *Recollections and Reflections*, 112, 113.

51 Romain Rolland quizzed Strauss about the "wife" in *Heldenleben*, who had been taken by some to be "a depraved woman, others a flirt. He [Strauss] says: 'Neither the one nor the other. It's my wife that I wanted to portray. She is very complex, very much a woman, a little depraved, something of a flirt, never twice alike, every minute different to what she was the minute before.'" Rolland, Diary entry March 9, 1900, in Myers, *Richard Strauss & Romain Rolland*, 133.

52 Nietzsche, *Thus Spoke Zarathustra*, 128.

53 Quoted in translation in Schmid, "The Tone Poems of Richard Strauss," 444.

54 Quoted in translation in Schmid, "The Tone Poems of Richard Strauss," 418.

55 Quoted in translation in Norman Del Mar, *Richard Strauss: a critical commentary on his life and works* Vol. I (London: Barrie & Rockliff, 1962), 188–9.
56 Quoted in translation in Gilliam, *Richard Strauss*, 81.
57 Myers, *Richard Strauss and Romain Rolland*, 211.
58 Gilliam, *Richard Strauss*, 81.
59 "Zwischen allem arbeitet Richard immer an einer Melodie. Diese Melodie in ihrem Werden u. Wachsen bildet quasi den Cantus Firmus, der durch das Ganze zieht." Sketchbook 8: 26 (RSA), also transcribed in Trenner, *Die Skizzenbücher von Richard Strauss*, 17.
60 Sketchbook 8: 26 (RSA), untranscribed in Trenner, *Die Skizzenbücher von Richard Strauss*.
61 Sketchbook 8: 36, also transcribed in Trenner, *Die Skizzenbücher von Richard Strauss*, 17.
62 "Hier ist sie (Abends beim Alleinsein) <u>fertig</u> geworden die Melodie, an der den ganzen Nachmittag gearbeitet worden." Sketchbook 8: 6, also transcribed in Trenner, *Die Skizzenbücher von Richard Strauss*, 17.
63 "Nach meiner eigenen Erfahrung bei schöpferischer Tätigkeit zu urteilen, fällt mir ein Motiv oder eine zwei- bis viertaktige melodische Phrase unmittelbar ein. Ich bringe sie zu Papier und erweitere sie gleich zur 8- 16- oder 32 täktigen Phrase, die selbstverständlich nicht unverändert bleibt, sondern nach kürzerem oder längerem 'Abliegen' allmählich zu der endgültigen Gestalt ausgearbeitet wird, die auch der strengsten, blasiertesten Selbstkritik standhält. Diese Arbeit geht nun in der Weise vor sich, daß es in erster Linie darauf ankommt, den Zeitpunkt abzuwarten, in welchem die Phantasie fähig und bereit ist, mir weiter zu dienen." Strauss, *Betrachtungen und Erinnerungen*, 165, trans. *Recollections and Reflections*, 115.
64 "[W]arum sieht man nicht das Neue an meinen Werken, wie in ihnen, wie nur noch bei Beethoven der Mensch sichtbar in das Werk spielt—dies beginnt im 3. Akt Guntram schon (Absage an den Collektivismus), Heldenleben, Don Quixote, Domestica—und in der 'Feuersnot' ist bewußt der Ton des Spottes, der Ironie, der Protest gegen den landläufigen Operntext das individuelle Neue." Strauss, "Letzte Aufzeichnung," in *Betrachtungen und Erinnerungen*, 182, translated in Morten Kristiansen, "Richard Strauss's *Feuersnot* in its aesthetic and Cultural Context: A Modernist Critique of Musical Idealism" (PhD Dissertation: Yale University, 2000), 13.
65 Youmans, *Richard Strauss's Orchestral Music*, 183.
66 "With *Capriccio* my life's work is finished, and the musical pieces which as a wrist exercise . . . I still scribble for my estate, have no musico-historical meaning" [Mit Capriccio ist mein Lebenswerk beendet und die Noten, die ich als Handgelenksübung . . . jetzt noch für den Nachlaß zusammenschmiere, haben keinerlei musikgeschichtliche Bedeutung]. Letter from Strauss to Willi Schuh, October 8, 1943; Richard Strauss, *Briefwechsel mit Willi Schuh* (Zurich: Atlantis, 1969), 50–1.

Chapter 5

STEIN'S IMMATERIAL LABORS

Kristin Grogan

In a May 1934 profile of Gertrude Stein published in *The New York Times*, Lansing Warren describes visiting Stein in her Left Bank apartment. "A visit to Miss Gertrude Stein in her studio in the Rue de Fleurus," he writes, "is like consulting a Grecian sibyl."[1] In the short piece, Warren describes Stein three times as a "sibyl," and we can detect a note of disappointment when he finds in her studio not the paint, easels, and elegant chaos that might indicate a dissolute artistic life, but "quiet comfort, neatness and order" accompanied by a "feeling of order and sanity."[2] Stein had acquired a reputation as a bohemian, had been modeled in clay as a Buddha by Jo Davidson, and had been described as a "priestess," in Michael Gold's words, "of a cult with strange literary rites, with mystical secrets."[3] The regularity of her home, the dusty books and paintings that Warren encounters, sit at odds with her mystical public image. If Parisian artistic genius is associated with the outrageous, the eccentric, and the unknowable, then work as we know it is everyday, repetitive, and regular. It is much harder to imagine Stein laboring at a desk than lounging in a chaise longue.[4]

Warren's sibyl, Davidson's Buddha, Gold's priestess: these characterizations of Stein are, I think, telling. Stein frustrates our ability to easily characterize her writing as work and her as a worker. In addition to these characterizations, rather than work, her writing has been described by almost all her critics as *play*. To cite just a handful, Dana Cairns Watson writes that Stein documents "the playful human mind."[5] For Sharon J. Kirsch, Stein's "Portraits and Repetition" from her *Lectures in America* is "playful and instructive."[6] Karen Leick describes Stein's "playful use of Alice as a subjective narrator" in *The Autobiography of Alice B. Toklas*; for Barbara Will that narrative choice was "playful, camp, self-fracturing," while Janet Malcolm lingers on how Stein's "playful egomania" drives the narrative of the book.[7] While work and play are by no means so easily divorced—the pleasure and experiment of play is embedded in some of our best experiences of work—Stein is considered primarily playful, and rarely if ever working or hardworking. If this is partly due to Stein's class and wealth, and certainly class is the basis of Gold's critique, my sense is that it has more to do with the fact that Stein sits uneasily within our dominant orthodoxies for describing modernist labor.

It is customary to think of modernist work in terms of craft and object-making, and of the modernist poet as an artisanal worker, carving forms out of a resistant material. Ezra Pound, perhaps the most notorious proponent of this craft ethos, found his aesthetic coordinates in artisanal work of various kinds, such as the medieval guild model of labor he absorbed while writing for the guild socialist magazine *The New Age* in the 1910s. Pound also took his theories of labor from artistic objects, including the carved marble of the *Tempio Malatestiano* on which he based his early Malatesta cantos; and, perhaps most enduringly, the Chinese character, in which he found a structural mode for a poetics of diverse particulars united into an elegant and painterly whole. This was a view cultivated well into the twentieth century by Pound's inheritors, especially in the Objectivist poetry of Louis Zukofsky and George Oppen, which emphasized "the appearance of the art form as an object."[8] "The objectivist," Zukofsky made clear in his 1968 interview with L. S. Dembo, "is interested in living with things as they exist, and as a 'wordsman,' he is a craftsman who puts words together into an object."[9] In Jasper Bernes's words, Pound, Oppen, and Zukofsky cultivated an ethos which "vouchsafed an artisanal dignity, where the made thing bore witness to the distinct hand of its maker" and which "proposes, against the mercenary and technocratic barbarization of matter and bodies, an artisanal grammar of tool, matter, environment, a grammar of the dignity of materials and makers, and a potential reciprocity between bodies and objects not possible in fully industrialized capitalism."[10]

How then can we understand and describe the labors of Gertrude Stein, a writer whose work clearly does not fit into the frame of craft? In this essay, I suggest that Stein's work frustrates the craft model of poetic labor because it primarily thinks of itself in immaterial terms, doing away with the vocabularies of craftsmanship, resistance, and elemental contact in favor of the "immaterial" products of intellectual and affective labor. I read this immateriality in two of Stein's early works: the "Objects" section of *Tender Buttons* and its focus on thought, and the intimacies and affects produced in Stein's long poem "Lifting Belly." My interest is in developing a language for thinking of labor that does not fall back upon descriptions of materiality or apply analogies of craftsmanship and object-making, and which might help us rethink some of our masculinist orthodoxies around what aesthetic work means.

The author of *Tender Buttons*, a book whose tripartite structure devotes an entire section to objects, would seem to be particularly aware of the physical things which populate and shape our lives. One of the enduring difficulties of Stein's 1914 prose-poem sequence is that it seems to deal only obliquely with its explicitly stated subject matter. Some of the "Objects" of the book's first section are the commodities we might find in a bourgeois interior: "A chair," "A box," "A plate," "Mildred's umbrella," "A shawl." Others are impressions, sensations, or prepositions: "Nothing elegant," "Careless water," "In between." I want to look first at one of the prose poems that takes as its subject a single object:

A SELTZER BOTTLE

Any neglect of many particles to a cracking, any neglect of this makes around it what is lead in color and certainly discolor in silver. The use of this is manifold. Supposing a certain time selected is assured, suppose it is even necessary, suppose no other extract is permitted and no more handling is needed, suppose the rest of the message is mixed with a very long slender needle and even if it could be any black border, supposing all this altogether made a dress and suppose it was actual, suppose the mean way to state it was occasional, if you suppose this in August and even more melodiously, if you suppose this even in the necessary incident of there certainly being no middle in summer and winter, suppose this and an elegant settlement a very elegant settlement is more than of consequence, it is not final and sufficient and substituted. This which was so kindly a present was constant.[11]

The first verb to appear in this piece is "makes." It signals from the very beginning its central concern, and a preoccupation of much of the book, with making and that which is made. But what is made is not an object but a state. Particles, cracking, lead, color and discolor, for the first two sentences we are in the chemistry laboratory—or inside the seltzer bottle itself—witness to the process of making still water carbonated. If the "neglect" of the first sentence (and the "cracking") position us momentarily within a negative mode, the first transformative verb, "makes," moves us from the negative to the positive, to the visible color and discolor. With the second sentence, "the use of this is manifold," we move into the subject of use. But *Tender Buttons* often feels only indirectly a volume about use. Stein offers to unveil the manifold uses of the seltzer bottle (a use which is, presumably, singular: the seltzer bottle makes carbonated water) yet what she gives us is not an answer at all, but rather a series of prompts and suggestions ("suppose this"). One of the animating contradictions of *Tender Buttons* is the opposition between the stable, solid form of the objects, and their unsettled and unsettling descriptions. The promise of stability in the titles ("A Seltzer Bottle") is left unfulfilled by the gnomic or aphoristic descriptions. The stability we are promised is never granted.

The seltzer bottle contains within it a chemical reaction that takes place on a daily basis and on a small, almost unsaid scale. The portrait's real subject is, I think, not the bottle itself, but the peculiarity of carbonated water, where a liquid is injected with a gas (carbon dioxide), resulting in the particular effervescent fizzing that marks this meeting of two states. We end in "a present" which was also "constant"—foregrounding what Stein would term the "continuous present"—a state that will not settle into something stable or solid. That lack of solidity has a great deal to do with the disjunction between the expected solidity of the objects and the malleability of language and vision.

Tender Buttons is as much about the labor of writing as anything else, but it suggests this only by implication. Within the manifold uses of the seltzer bottle we find encoded the language of writing. The water in the bottle is a "message," the "border" might be a page, we hear a pun on address in "a dress," the piece ponders "the mean way to state it" (and supposes that way might be "occasional"), and, after wondering whether this statement will be melodious, we alight twice on the word "elegant." This gives a new shape to Stein's arguments about the bottle's use: it is as if the use of the bottle can be measured not by function or practical, household usefulness, but according to the intellectual work that the chemistry of carbonation suggests. And this makes an implicit argument about the similarity of the fizzing carbonated water and the fizzing, unsettled, active writing mind.

Tender Buttons performs a kind of bait-and-switch: where Stein seems to offer us studies in the shapes, forms, and uses of household objects, she is significantly more attentive to our perception and understanding of them. Nowhere does this come out more clearly than in *Tender Buttons*' color paragraphs, such as "A Red Hat":

> A dark grey, a very dark grey, a quite dark grey is monstrous ordinarily, it is so monstrous because there is no red in it. If red is in everything it is not necessary. Is that not an argument for any use of it and even so is there any place that is better, is there any place that has so much stretched out.[12]

This is part of a series of color studies, followed by a blue coat and an achromatic piano. We begin not with red but with a gray that gradually intensifies into something "monstrous." Gray, the achromatic halfway point between white and black, contains neither red nor any other color, "there is no red in it." If red is in everything, we are told, if it is present, common, or available, then it is not "necessary," not required. Red is valuable and necessary, the passage seems to suggest, precisely because it is not contained in gray, it is not present everywhere. Only in the "any place" of the final sentence do we seem to move towards the hat itself, which is perhaps made of the "stretched out" red fabric. The paragraph circles around the redness of the hat, describing not the thing itself, but the presence and use of a color. The next section, "A Blue Coat", describes color in similarly unsettled terms. "A blue coat is guided guided away," we are told, "guided and guided away," in a description which calls to mind a shadow, a coat disappearing around the corner, or something—a balloon, perhaps—drifting off into the air.[13] Or the coat might be a metonym for its wearer: "A [child in a] blue coat is guided guided away," we might read the section as suggesting. This small section describes an ungraspable form, a blue coat that remains beyond our grip, that is being led away, that we can never quite pin down. *Tender Buttons* is Stein's first significant foray into abstraction, her first real move away from the figurative description of her early prose. Abstraction can also signify a sort of more attentive materiality, as if to decenter the subject or signified in order to bring out the particularities of the material, medium, or signifier more clearly—Kandinsky's non-figurative forms, to take an obvious example, mean that his distinctive use of color, as well as the distinctiveness of any one particular color, of blue or yellow or red, are made more obvious. A similar argument has been made about Stein. Writing about *Tender Buttons*, Nicola Pitchford has argued that Stein's repetitions "make the signified (substance) seem vague while the sound and shape of the signifier (covering) gain increasing prominence."[14] While I see this at work in the wordplay that populates poems like "Yet Dish," which is something of a companion piece to the prose poems of *Tender Buttons*, in pieces such as "A Red Hat" and "A Blue Coat" we are left with little clearer sense of what "red" or "blue" mean as words, as signifiers, than as substances or signifieds. We are left instead with thoughts that are ungraspable, barely able to be held at all, slipping away from us just as the blue coat is guided and guided away.

In his book on skill and deskilling in modern art, John Roberts compares Louis Zukofsky's poetics to Marcel Duchamp's ready-mades, arguing that both artists "make open mockery of certain kinds of deliberative, metaphysical, artistic labor, in favour of a craft of the intellectual, the craft of reproducibility," the end-point of which is to defy "the separation of craft and intellectual labour of the labour process."[15] Stein's most successful book, *The Autobiography of Alice B. Toklas*, is in part an extended mockery of the craft model: it does away completely with the image of the artist as artisanal worker and with the artist's unique "signature," at the same time that it emphasizes the regularity of Stein's writing practice. Stein insists that her sentence making occurs mainly during her long walks around Paris after sitting for Picasso's portrait in his Montmartre studio. "During those long poses and these long walks," we are told, "Gertrude Stein meditated and made sentences."[16] And then over the page: "She had come to like posing, the long still hours followed by a long dark walk intensified the concentration with which she was creating her sentences."[17] Thus for many critics, such as Ulla E. Dydo, reading Stein is an encounter with unmediated and unrevised thinking. "What Stein called composition is the written process of meditation," writes Dydo. "Meditating does not precede composing but is composing. Reading Gertrude Stein is reading the 'written writing process.'"[18] *Tender Buttons* is one of Stein's least "meditative" works, unlike the long streams of *The Making of Americans* or the explicitly intellectual *Stanzas in Meditation*. But it does make a similar mockery of the vocabulary of craft, not, like Duchamp and Zukofsky, by reattaching it to the intellect, but by severing the two almost entirely and focusing on the latter. What we are witnessing is something like an intellectual labor that has been let off its tether, as it drifts ever further from the stability of the object or the finished product.

What do we find, then, if not a poetics of craft? Several of Stein's critics have suggested that her writing owes much to mechanical reproduction and the Fordist assembly line. Wyndham Lewis famously and bitingly described her writing as "a cold suet-roll of fabulously-reptilian length" which is "of the sausage, by-the-yard variety."[19] Michael Davidson and Barrett Watten both read Stein in relation to Fordism, and Watten writes that "Stein saw in Ford's modern poetics of repetition a mode of production that was, in explicitly literary terms, analogous to her modernist one."[20] Others have thought of her writing not as mechanical, but as quasi-digital, and Stein holds a perhaps unsurprising place in studies of computer and information aesthetics.[21] My sympathy lies more with the immaterial leanings of the latter camp, though I want to approach this "immaterial labor" from a somewhat different direction. Here I am drawing on a term made famous in the mid-1990s by the Italian labor theorist Maurizio Lazzarato, which refers to labor which "produces the information and cultural content of the commodity," rather than producing a physical object.[22] Stein's poetry taps into and anticipates a kind of immaterial labor that is primarily of an affective kind. As it is theorized by Michael Hardt, affective labor is an aspect of immaterial labor within economic postmodernization (or informatization); specifically, it is the human face of the reproduction of services (in contrast to the computerization or cybernetics discussed by Lazzarato). Health services rely on caring and affective labor, the entertainment and culture industries rely on the manipulation of affects, so too do all aspects of the service industries, from waiters through to bank tellers and workers in financial services, and many of these workers are women. "This labor is immaterial," Hardt writes, "even if it is corporeal and affective, in the sense that its products are intangible: a feeling of ease, well-being, satisfaction, excitement, passion— even a sense of connectedness or community."[23] This labor involves the manipulation of affects through contact, which can be either virtual or actual. The products of this labor are "social networks, forms of community, biopower."[24] Affective, reproductive, and emotional labor have been key terms for feminist understandings of work. Silvia Federici articulates an important critique of affective labor, preferring the term "reproductive labor" and arguing that affective labor "describes only a limited part of the work that the reproduction of human beings requires and erases the subversive potential of the feminist concept of reproductive work."[25] In the remainder of this essay I focus not on reproductive labor in general but on the affective aspects of Stein's poetry.

Stein's most interesting suggestions of immaterial labor come out in the context of her erotic and love poetry. Between 1915 and 1917, as the First World War raged on, Stein composed a poem written about and for Toklas which was given the bodily title of "Lifting Belly." The war enters the poem only occasionally and obliquely; for the most part, "Lifting Belly" traces the contours of a romantic relationship in the form of a loose and repetitive dialog between two voices.[26] Often it slips into a fairly conventional love poem: "I fly to thee," Stein writes, "I love cherish idolise adore and worship you. You are so sweet so tender and so perfect."[27] All of this takes place against the backdrop of a home. "We like linen. Linen is ordered," we are told, "We are going to order linen" (65). Encoded in that ordering is the suggestion of folding sheets, the fabric of the bed, the daily labor of domestic life. But household labor is not the focus of the poem, and for the most part it describes "Kissing and singing" (87), "Laughing together" (90), moving through the regular activities and affections of a relationship, all of which revolves around the repeated phrase "lifting belly."

Like *Tender Buttons*, the poem is anchored in the vocabulary of composition, frequently reflecting back, if obliquely, on the fact of its own making. On its first page, we encounter "Bed of coals made out of wood" which, we are told, "may be an expression. We can understand heating and burning composition" (65). The coals are made from wood—the compacted plant matter that forms coal—and they "may be an expression," which moves us into the language of writing and composition. Like the seltzer bottle, the burning coal suggests a state of transformation. The emphasis is on something made: as coal is made from wood, which is then burned to make heat, so is the poem a made and transforming thing. "Lifting Belly" props the language of physical embodiment, sex, and bodily immediacy against the language of thought. Or, to put it another way, like *Tender Buttons* its interest lies just as much in the physical thing—the object, the body—as in the act of writing. "Lifting belly is an expression," Stein informs us (77). "Lifting belly is a language," we are told soon after, and on the same page, "Lifting belly is a repetition. Lifting belly means me" (78). In an important early critical intervention, Catharine R. Stimpson points out that "in Stein's more abstract writing, the body disappears into language utterly, or becomes an example of a linguistic category."[28] When Stein refers to "kisses" in "Lifting Belly," Stimpson suggests, they illustrate "not the body in action, but a problematical grammatical class: the noun."[29] I am less convinced that Stein is drawing attention to the grammatical particularities of the noun, and I read this more as emphasizing the fact that the poem is both a constructed thing, and that it is constructing its own language of composition and expression with its own system of terms and values.

"Lifting Belly is a repetition": where *Tender Buttons* works with singular perceptions of distinct objects, "Lifting Belly" thinks in duration, length, and repetition, presenting us with the dailiness of love and the maintenance of a relationship. "Lifting belly is so consecutive" (74), we are told, in a reminder that the action described takes place over time, that these days are consecutive and repeated. In this sense "Lifting Belly" is a more mimetic work than *Tender Buttons*. The poem makes use of a limited vocabulary and verbal structures which are repeated at length and give the impression of time passing as it is lived. Stimpson suggests that the phrase "lifting belly" becomes "both a repetitive synecdoche for a repeated, repeatable sexual act and a generalized metonymy for Stein's life at large."[30] I read it as a synecdoche too for a particular aspect of Stein's life, namely her writing life. "Lifting Belly's" self-referential language, where "lifting belly" means both "me" and "a repetition," makes an implicit case for the similarity between the repetitive work of writing and the daily intimate scenes that this writing describes. What I am describing, then, is an explicitly queer view of the connection between intimacy and labor, and an alternative to the heterosexual sex that, as feminists point out, places women in a position of duty and submission and obliges them to perform the work of giving pleasure.[31] In Stein we find a sort of productive intellectual intimacy, one which aligns with Michael Snediker's reading of queer literature that thinks outside narratives of self-destruction, dissolution, and shame, and one in which intimacy and intellectual labor are mutually generative.[32]

In addition to its measures of duration—"Lifting belly is so consecutive"—the poem thinks in weight. In its title, "Lifting Belly" implies heft and effort. The poem constantly returns to the effort of lifting and the strength we are repeatedly told Lifting Belly possesses. One of the efforts that the poem suggests is care. Sometimes that care is physical, made manifest by the making and giving of objects: "I knit woollen stockings for you. And I understand and I am very grateful" (90). We hear two voices within this single line, one makes, gives, and cares, the other receives and is cared for. Where the carer offers something physical and made, the receiver responds affectively: with gratitude. Both voices sit on the same line, and this makes a kind of equivalence between them and undoes any easy distinction between a giver and receiver. Objects—the woolen socks—are less important than affects, the understanding and gratitude that is expressed. This immaterial work is embedded into the poem's dynamics of power, pleasure, and withholding. "Lifting belly is so careful. Full of care for me," we are told (74). But then, immediately after, "Lifting belly is mean." The erotic dynamics of "Lifting Belly" are based around managing power. One way power is established is by praise, how it is given and received. Lifting belly "is so kind. So very kind" (74), "Lifting belly is so warm" (74), "Lifting belly is kind and good and beautiful. Lifting belly is my joy" (75). There is another kind of work embedded in the poem, and that is the work of pleasing another person. Take for example the following lines:

> I said that I was very glad.
> Why are you very glad
> Because that pleased me.
> Baby love. (69)

One voice is glad, having been pleased, and "Baby love" resolves these lines into a kind of satisfaction. By the third line something has been produced: pleasure. In "Lifting Belly," pleasure does not emerge *ex nihilo* but is something that must be produced. The poem works to produce certain states, to submerge us through its repetitions in the various tonal and emotional shifts of the lovers. One result of all of this is that the poem collapses the differences between work as effort and difficulty and work as pleasure; it operates in precisely that gray area in which affective labor lives and intimacy thrives. If in *Tender Buttons* Stein divorced the intellect from craft, here she marries the intellect to our intimate and affective lives, letting the two occupy the same space rather than divorcing them along the lines of work–life balance.

Part of what is at stake in reading Stein in this way is how we describe and attach value to poetic labor. The craft ethos of labor constructs and implies a hierarchy of values and achievement. In comparing himself to Sigismondo Malatesta, for example, Pound is able to inhabit a position of power and autonomy which positions himself less as worker than as overseer, and it is unsurprising that he would eventually praise Mussolini not only as a leader, but as a worker. When Yeats suggests

> Better go down upon your marrow-bones
> And scrub a kitchen pavement, or break stones
> Like an old pauper, in all kinds of weather;
> For to articulate sweet sounds together
> Is to work harder than all these, and yet
> Be thought an idler by the noisy set[33]

he is making an argument for the hierarchical superiority of aesthetic labor, a practice based in the careful manufacture—"stitching and unstitching"—of an appearance of spontaneity.[34] Craft is also a kind of bravado, which allows the artist to take on the stance of an embattled and unappreciated marginal figure laboring in the shadows, or worse, a prophet removed from the social relations of labor but nevertheless able to speak in general and unimpeachable truths. If Stein herself was insulated from those social relations by virtue of her class, her work nevertheless offers us a differently gendered hierarchy of values. Natalia Cecire reads Stein's poetics of repetition as centralizing "feminized, typically unwaged labor, especially repetitive labor including housework and information work" and, further, suggests that Stein "insists on the value of repetitive labors without presupposing that that value must come on capital's gendered terms (as wage-eligible 'hard work')."[35] Stein does this and more, I think, for she reminds us that the effort of work is not divisible from our intimate experiences, that the divisions of the work society—that ubiquitous phrase "work–life balance"—are artificial, and that work does not exist in the positivism of craft alone, but in the gestures, efforts, and thoughts that so often go unnoticed and unspoken because their forms are not solid or easily quantifiable, but primarily immaterial.

In *Solid Objects*, his study of modernism's conflicted relationship with the object world, Douglas Mao describes the strange intimacy between Sigmund Freud, H. D., and a handful of objects—some of Freud's figurines of divinities—as a kind of loving bond: "a bond that cannot be love in one sense, since these pieces of brute matter are clearly incapable of loving back, and yet which clearly must be something like love, since no other term can be invoked without seeming to impoverish description."[36] Mao is describing a kind of love embedded in the regard that modernists held for the indelible otherness of the object, "as not-self, as not-subject, as most helpless and will-less of entities, but also as a fragment of Being, as solidity, as otherness in its most resilient opacity."[37] I quote this paragraph not because Stein has the same respect for the object's otherness but because, like Freud and H. D., Stein sees the subject of her labors—the seltzer bottle, a red hat, the strong body of "lifting belly," some knitted socks—not as neutral objects, but as loved things to be treated with care.[38] If in the craft model careful composition is evidenced primarily in finely sculpted poetic forms, in Stein's writing we can see care in precisely this lack of fine sculpting, and we can detect in her repetition an attempt to capture a thing in its living wholeness. This, then, is an affective kind of work: Stein reminds us that writing is also a loving and attentive act, and that poetic work at its best can attend to the unspoken intimacies of our intellectual lives.

Notes

1. Lansing Warren, "Gertrude Stein Views Life and Politics," *The New York Times* (New York, NY) May 6, 1934.
2. Warren, "Gertrude Stein Views Life and Politics."
3. Michael Gold, "Gertrude Stein: A Literary Idiot," *Change the World!* (London: Lawrence and Wishart, 1937), 25.
4. Jeff Solomon has traced this perception of Stein, writing that "from the 1910s until the 1930s, many pictured Gertrude Stein lounging on a divan that drew from fin-de-siècle clichés as well as tropes of silent films of the next generation." Solomon vigorously denies the accuracy of this representation, suggesting that "while Stein did many things in her long and eventful life, she never lolled on chaise longue": Jeff Solomon, "Gertrude Stein, Opium Queen: Notes on a Mistaken Embrace," *Journal of Lesbian Studies* 17, no. 1 (2013), 17.
5. Dana Cairns Watson, *Gertrude Stein and the Essence of What Happens* (Nashville: Vanderbilt University Press, 2005), 110.
6. Sharon J. Kirsch, *Gertrude Stein and the Reinvention of Rhetoric* (Tuscaloosa: University of Alabama Press, 2014), 89.
7. Karen Leick, *Gertrude Stein and the Making of an American Celebrity* (New York: Routledge, 2009), 154; Barbara Will, *Gertrude Stein, Modernism, and the Problem of "Genius"* (Edinburgh: Edinburgh University Press, 2000), 161; Janet Malcolm, *Two Lives: Gertrude and Alice* (New Haven and London: Yale University Press, 2007), 13.
8. Louis Zukofsky, "Sincerity and Objectification: With Special Reference to the Work of Charles Reznikoff," *Poetry* 37, no. 5 (February, 1931), 273.
9. Louis Zukofksy, Interview with L. S. Dembo, in *Prepositions+: the collected critical essays of Louis Zukofsky* (Hanover, NH: University Press of New England, 2000), 232.
10. Jasper Bernes, *The Work of Art in the Age of Deindustrialization* (Stanford: Stanford University Press, 2017), 67–8.
11. Gertrude Stein, *Tender Buttons* (New York: Claire Marie, 1914), 16–17.
12. Stein, *Tender Buttons*, 17.
13. Stein, *Tender Buttons*, 17.
14. Nicola Pitchford, "Unlikely Modernism, Unlikely Postmodernism," *American Literary History* 11, no. 4 (1999), 647.
15. John Roberts, *The Intangibilities of Form: Skill and Deskilling in Art After the Readymade* (London and New York: Verso, 2007), 70–1. Stein too has occasionally been compared to Duchamp. Marjorie Perloff suggests that Stein's compositions

"resemble Duchamp's 'objects' in their wholesale rejection of the mimetic contract" and that "Duchamp's dismissal of the 'retinal' is also hers." Marjorie Perloff, "'A Cessation of Resemblances': Stein/Picasso/Duchamp," *Moving Modernisms*, ed. David Bradshaw, Laura Marcus, and Rebecca Roach (Oxford: Oxford University Press, 2016), 129.

16 Gertrude Stein, *The Autobiography of Alice B. Toklas* (London: Penguin, 2001), 56.
17 Stein, *Autobiography*, 57.
18 Ulla E. Dydo, "Composition as Meditation," in *Gertrude Stein and the Making of Literature*, ed. Shirley Neuman and Ira B. Nadel (London: Macmillan, 1988), 42.
19 Wyndham Lewis, *Time and Western Man* (London: Chatto & Windus, 1927), 61.
20 Barrett Watten, *The Constructivist Moment: From Material Text to Cultural Poetics* (Middletown, Connecticut: Wesleyan University Press, 2003), 124. See also Michael Davidson, *Ghostlier Demarcations: Modern Poetry and the Material Word* (Berkeley: University of California Press, 1997).
21 For Stein and the gendered history of computing and information work, see Natalia Cecire, "Ways of Not Reading Gertrude Stein," *ELH* 82, no. 1 (2015), 281–312. Cecire begins her article with a discussion of Tanya E. Clement's essay, "'A Thing Not Beginning and Not Ending': Using Digital Tools to Distant-read Stein's *The Making of Americans*," *Lit Linguist Computing* 23, no. 3 (2008), 361–81. See also Paul Stephens, *Poetics of Information Overload: From Gertrude Stein to Conceptual Writing* (Minnesota: University of Minnesota Press, 2015).
22 Maurizio Lazzarato, "Immaterial Labor," trans. Paul Colilli and Ed Emery, *Radical Thought in Italy: A Potential Politics*, ed. Paolo Virno and Michael Hardt (Minneapolis: University of Minnesota Press, 1996), 133.
23 Michael Hardt, "Affective Labor," *Boundary 2* 26, no. 2 (Summer, 1999), 96.
24 Hardt, "Affective Labor," 96.
25 Federici continues "By highlighting its function in the production of labor power, and thus unveiling the contradictions inherent in this work, the concept of 'reproductive labor' recognizes the possibility of crucial alliances and forms of cooperation between producers and the reproduced: mothers and children, teachers and students, nurses and patients." Silvia Federici, *Revolution at Point Zero: Housework, Reproduction, and Feminist Struggle* (Oakland: PM Press, 2012), 100.
26 For the poem's relationship with the First World War, see David M. Owens, "Gertrude Stein's 'Lifting Belly' and the Great War," *Modern Fiction Studies* 44, no. 3 (1998), 608–18.
27 Gertrude Stein, "Lifting Belly," *Bee Time Vine: The Yale Edition of the Unpublished Writings of Gertrude Stein*, vol. 3 (New Haven: Yale University Press, 1953), 85, 80. Subsequent references will list page numbers parenthetically.
28 Catharine R. Stimpson, "The Somagrams of Gertrude Stein," *Poetics Today* 6, no. 1/2 (1985), 74.
29 Stimpson, "The Somagrams of Gertrude Stein," 74.
30 Stimpson, "The Somagrams of Gertrude Stein," 74.
31 See for example Silvia Federici, "Why Sexuality is Work," in *Revolution at Point Zero*, 23–7.
32 See Michael Snediker, *Queer Optimism: Lyric Personhood and Other Felicitous Persuasions* (Minneapolis: University of Minnesota Press, 2009).
33 William Butler Yeats, "Adam's Curse," *Collected Poems* (New York: Scribner, 1996), 83.

34 Yeats, "Adam's Curse," 83.
35 Cecire, "Ways of Not Reading Gertrude Stein," 303–4.
36 Douglas Mao, *Solid Objects: Modernism and the Test of Production* (Princeton: Princeton University Press, 1998), 4.
37 Mao, *Solid Objects*, 4.
38 In this sense, I disagree with Michael Davidson's suggestion that any feelings Stein might have for the objects described in *Tender Buttons* "are not an issue in their composition." Davidson, *Ghostlier Demarcations*, 42.

Chapter 6

TRACE AND FACTURE: LEGACIES OF THE "READY-MADE" IN CONTEMPORARY SOUTH AFRICAN ART

Alison Kearney

Introduction: From representation to re-presentation

Since the avant-garde experiments with collage and found objects in the first decades of the twentieth century, artists have continued experimenting with incorporating objects from everyday life into their artworks, in gestures that have been interpreted as a means to challenge the conventions, and later, the institutions of art. In line with contemporary international art-making praxis, a number of contemporary South African artists incorporate found objects in various ways in their artworks. Contemporary artists' use of found objects can, however, no longer be understood as a rupture from tradition as it was in the early decades of the twentieth century, because found objects are part of a longer genealogy in art making, and have become an accepted part of the artist's tool kit, unlike when first used by Picasso and later Duchamp.

The idea of the "found object" is built around the distinction between artworks and what Danto refers to as "mere things."[1] When artists select quotidian objects to be used in artworks these objects move from everyday social practices and are embedded in the discourses of art where different sets of cultural practices are at work. In this process, the objects (now distinguished from other objects like them that remain part of everyday social practices) become "found objects". A found object may be a whole object, or a fragment of an object that can be used as material, and is altered as it is joined to other objects when embedded in an artwork. Picasso's inclusion of an actual piece of rope and a piece of oil-cloth with a design of chair caning printed on it in his *Still Life with Chair Caning* (1912),[2] is arguably one of the first instances of the inclusion of found objects in Modern art. In including found objects in artworks, Picasso and Braque's praxis marked a shift from representations of elements from everyday life, to the inclusion of the actual object. In the process of becoming part of an assemblage, the newspaper cuttings and faux wood veneer were removed from everyday circulation, to become part of the *representation* of everyday life. The use of collaged fragments from everyday life could be interpreted as a representation of the increased mechanization of other forms of production in modern Europe, such as the invention of the lithographic printing processes, discussed by Walter Benjamin.[3]

While linked in their use of previously non-art materials and unorthodox methods, Marcel Duchamp's "ready-mades" nevertheless mark a significant shift from the way Picasso and Braque used found objects in their assemblages. The term "ready-made" was invented by Duchamp for an object from the outside world which is claimed or proposed as art.[4] Duchamp designated "whole" industrially produced objects, such as a bottle rack, a snow shovel and a urinal, that he did little to change, as art; by contrast Picasso and Braque included fragments of real things in their collages, reconstituting those things in the new environment of the artwork.[5]

Drawing on discussions of the implications of the found object for the nature of art-making, in this chapter I begin by exploring the ways in which the historical and neo-avant-gardes challenged notions of the artist's labor through their use of found objects. This is followed by an exploration of the manner in which contemporary South African artists Alan Alborough, Penny Siopis and Usha Seejarim engage with notions of the artist's labor through their choice of objects and the manner in which they work with those objects. I then consider the implications of their use of found objects for contemporary ideas of the artist's labor in order to move beyond an understanding of the use of found objects as it appears in the work of the historical and neo-avant-gardes. By focusing on the selected artists' choice of objects and the manner in which they work with those objects, I am able to investigate the ways in which their praxis can be understood as a continuation of, or challenge to, the avant-garde's exploration of the artist's labor. In exploring the historical use of found objects, and situating contemporary uses of found objects within the discourse of the avant-garde, this study addresses the need Foster identifies for new genealogies of the avant-garde that complicate its past and suggest possible futures.[6]

Some implications of the ready-made

Duchamp's designation of unaltered found objects as ready-mades in the early part of the twentieth century took Picasso and Braque's exploration of modes of representation further. The ready-mades challenged the nature of art, notions of authorship and the originality of art at the time in which they were made. Duchamp is thus credited with having opened the way for the varied use of found objects in art since his first ready-mades of the second decade of the twentieth century. Benjamin argues that before the age of mechanical reproduction, artworks were valued because of their "aura" of authenticity.[7]

Implied in the notion of the "aura" is that the authenticity, and therefore the value of the artwork, is contingent on its being an "original" artwork, with a unique existence in time and space, as evidenced in the traces of its history and facture. Before the possibility of mechanical reproduction, the trace of facture indicated the artist's hand, and thus implied the *presence* of the maker, distinguishing artworks from mass produced, machine made things, and mechanical reproductions of the artwork.

While Duchamp did little to the physical appearance of the unassisted ready-mades, he nevertheless changed the objects in three significant ways: he placed them in the field of exhibition, gave them titles and attributed their authorship to himself (by labelling them as his artworks). Therefore, Duchamp succeeded in *almost* removing the hand of the artist from the art-making process. Buskirk argues that a consequence of Duchamp's ready-mades is that "the removal of the artist's hand rather than lessening the importance of artistic authorship, makes the sure connection between work and artist that much more significant."[8] Further, the kind of object Duchamp selected was industrially produced, not the hand crafted unique object associated with works of art. In showing that anything the artist designates as art *is* art, Duchamp's ready-mades demonstrated that even when the artist does not physically manufacture the artwork, the artwork still has the quintessential "aura" of art described by Benjamin because the artwork is an index of the artist's conceptual labor. Thus, while artworks such as *Fountain* (1917)[9] call into question notions of what counts as the artist's labor as well as the value of an artwork, such works do not disrupt the conventions of art making. As Foster notes, Duchamp's ready-mades can be understood as a performance of the conventions of art making, which left the conventions themselves intact.

It was in showing that the artist's conceptual labor is an essential part of the art making process, that the ready-mades were able to challenge conceptions of art making, and by extension, conceptions of artists' labor. Roberts argues that the act of designating the ready-made as art object challenged the nature of the artist's labor in two ways. In one sense, this was an act of deskilling art—because the artist no longer had to physically make something.[10] In another sense, however, the ready-made involved re-skilling art, in that the choosing and assemblage of parts emerged as a new method of art making. The ready-mades therefore caused a shift in art-making praxis from processes such as manipulating materials on a surface, to selecting, arranging and manipulating objects in space. Roberts posits that the inclusion of mass-produced, prefabricated objects from the world outside of art was in keeping with artists' critical questioning of the social status quo, and industrial modes of production, like the mechanized production line, that were increasing in the early twentieth century.

Further explorations of the discourses of art were taken up by neo-avant-garde artists of the 1950s and 1960s, who critiqued the institutions of art, in part through their analysis of the successes and failures of the historical avant-gardes. Foster argues that in extending the historical avant-garde's critique of the institutions of art, the "neo-avant-garde has produced new aesthetic experiences, cognitive connections, and political interventions."[11] However, despite the clear connections between the practices of the historical and neo-avant-gardes, it is a mistake to think of this process as teleological, not least because the historical avant-garde's exposure of the conventions of the field of exhibition was only understood in hindsight by the broader art community.[12] Foster points out that "the status of Duchamp as well as *Les Demoiselles* is a retroactive effect of countless artistic responses and critical readings, and so it goes across the dialogical space-time of avant-garde practice and institutional reception."[13]

In his discussion of the relationship of the historical and neo-avant-gardes, Foster demonstrates that the discourse of the avant-garde is characterized by repetition, and reiteration. Foster argues that it was the iterative practices of the first wave of neo-avant-garde artists in 1950s America and Europe, such as Rauschenberg, who returned to the methods of the historical avant-garde, that enabled the art of the historical avant-garde to become part of the art-historical canon. For Foster repetition is the means through which the neo-avant-garde was able to address the issues that emerged in the historical avant-garde. Thus, the reiterative challenging of the institutions of art is a necessary strategy of the avant-garde's rhetoric of rupture. Furthermore, Foster suggests that each iteration can be thought of as a new articulation that cannot be understood in the same way as its predecessor, because such iterations are performed with knowledge of, and often in dialogue with, the former practices. Foster points out that contemporary iterations of the avant-garde have abandoned the historic and neo-avant-garde's grand claims to disrupt the conventions and institutions of art, in favor of subtle gestures that displace the center through focusing on the local and personal. It is to these local and personal investigations that I now turn in exploring selected contemporary South African artists' use of found objects, which can be understood as contemporary iterations of the avant-garde.

Trace and facture

Notions of trace, facture and value are interesting to consider in relation to Alan Alborough's art-making praxis. Alborough makes use of mass-produced, quotidian objects as readily available art-making materials, in a manner similar to that in which modern painters buy readily available tubes of paint to paint with. The plastic washing-line pegs, cable ties and coins Alborough used to create his *Beautiful Objects* series (Figure 6.1) have no "aura" in Benjamin's terms. At the time Alborough purchased them from the factories where they were made, or from hardware stores where they were sold, they were as yet unused. These new objects nevertheless have particular associations as useful objects common to the world outside of the field of art, as well as having distinct aesthetic and technical properties. The coins used were commonly available one pence coins, mass produced and of little value. Washing-line pegs, also mass produced, plastic, and disposable, have a particular design, and can be joined together in limited ways, all of which Alborough exploits, echoing the Minimalists' repetition of prefabricated industrial materials.[14] Alborough nevertheless subverts this reference through the multiplicity of objects and intricacy of construction. While the objects used to create the sculptures are recognizable, Alborough does not necessarily seem to make reference to the object's former life or possible banal associations in the work. The recognizability of the objects used by Alborough is however important, since it is through understanding their former quotidian status that we are able to understand their new significance as part of art, where they are displaced from everyday practices, and assigned a different value.

In works like *Beautiful Objects: Hyphen* (1997) (Figure 6.2) and *Beautiful Objects: Ellipses* (1997) (Figure 6.3) Alborough combines recognizable quotidian objects with a cool, calculated mathematical precision that seems to eradicate any signs of inconsistencies that arise in the hand-made. The spaces between the parts that make up the sculpture are uniform, creating intricate patterns.

Further allusions to language can be found in the subtitles of each sculpture in the *Beautiful Object* series: *Asterisk, Ellipses and Hyphen*. The subtitles of each of these works refer to punctuation marks that variously represent a pause,

Figure 6.1 Alan Alborough, *Beautiful Objects: Ellipses and Asterisk*, 1997. Installation view, University of the Witwatersrand Art Galleries, University of the Witwatersrand. Image courtesy of the artist.

Figure 6.2 Alan Alborough, *Beautiful Objects: Hyphen,* 1997. Plastic pegs, cable ties, coins, electric cable. Dimensions variable. Image courtesy of the artist.

Figure 6.3 Alan Alborough, *Beautiful Objects: Ellipses,* 1997. Detail. Plastic pegs, mixing bowls, cable ties, coins, electric cable. Image courtesy of the artist.

and ways of connecting ideas, as if the artist is asking viewers to pause and reflect on the artworks. In *Beautiful Objects: Hyphen* (1997) and *Beautiful Objects: Asterisk* (1997), a pattern is created from the repeated elements, as if the form develops out of the system of making the object. In the process of tying, joining, sewing—becoming art—the mundane is transformed into the extraordinary. Different combinations of the same materials across a range of works in the series suggest that, in the process of making these art works, the artist was exploring what the constraints and affordances of the materials were. These works could be understood as an exploration of the artwork as a semiotic field with its own internal logic and sign system.

Even though the use of found objects in artworks is historically a sign of the removal of the artists' labor, in this series of works, there is a paradox of the ready-made components being reworked into highly labor intensive, precisely engineered and utterly singular (although, possibly replicable) works of art. The manufactured elements thus stand in contrapuntal relationship with the painstaking labor and careful precision that the artist has used to make these sculptures. Therefore, in these works the banality of the mass-produced objects used to construct the artworks is juxtaposed with the idea of the completed sculptural installations as "*art*", as indexes of the artist's labor and, thus, as in some way exalted. Through contrasting the banality of the materials with the labor-intensive method of art making, Alborough engages with discourses of found objects in art, and challenges notions of artistic labor in a manner different from Duchamp. Duchamp did little to change both his unassisted and assisted ready-mades, thereby proposing that the artist's labor is conceptual. In contrast, the painstaking precision manner in which Alborough combines found objects to create artworks suggests that even when artists use found objects to create artworks, there is a link between the conceptual and the manual labor of the artist.

A perpetual state of becoming

The idea that the ready-made has shifted art-making praxis from manipulating materials on a surface to arranging and manipulating objects in space is tempting for a comparison of painting and installation. A shift from representations of objects to the use of actual objects can be seen when comparing Penny Siopis's *History Paintings* series with her installations. For example, in *Patience on a Monument: A History Painting* (1988) (Figure 6.4), a black African woman, swathed in fabric reminiscent of the carved folds of simulated fabric draped around marble statues of Greek goddesses, sits on a pedestal. The pedestal is made of a pile of things, including a skull, books, paint brushes, flowers and canvases. I interpret the woman on the pedestal as Patience—a personification of a virtue, and also, in a South African context, a reference to Apartheid naming practices. Names such as "Patience" were given to black African women by Apartheid officials who oversaw the creation of identity documents. Names such as Patience were crude English translations of given African names which were considered difficult for white English and Afrikaans-speaking employers to pronounce. The disregard for identity and heritage, and assuming the right to name another is symbolic of the denigration of black African people during Apartheid. Through foregrounding a seemingly ordinary woman who would have been left out of the grand narrative of history, Siopis subverts the genre of history paintings. The background is a vast space, made of scenes of ethnographic illustrations and fragments torn from Apartheid era textbooks of scenes such as African slaves in chain gangs, and the colonial wars between the British and the amaZulu which have been collaged onto the surface. Patience sits on her monument, peeling a lemon, seemingly waiting for a revolution or some kind of social justice from the disasters of war and pillage around her. Ironically, despite Siopis's inversion, the figure in this painting lacks

Figure 6.4 Penny Siopis, *Patience on a Monument: A History Painting*, 1988. (Detail). 180 × 200 cm, oil and collage on board. Collection: William Humphreys Art Gallery, Kimberley. Image courtesy of the artist.

agency; she sits peeling lemons, seemingly oblivious to the pile of wreckage around her. Siopis states that the image of Patience on her pile is in part a reference to Walter Benjamin's angel of history, who, looking back into history "sees one single catastrophe, which keeps piling wreckage upon wreckage."[15] As history progresses, the angel is helpless "while the pile of debris before him grows toward the sky."[16]

In 1994 Siopis made a shift from representing piles of things in paintings to creating installations. *Reconnaissance 1900–1997* (1997) (Figure 6.5) was the first installation she created using her personal collection of objects she inherited or salvaged from second-hand stores.[17] The banal and extraordinary co-exist in Siopis's collection, which consists of objects such as taxidermied animals, human and animal bones, her mother's wedding shoes, the skin of a popped balloon, ornaments, jewelry, family pictures, ethnographic pictures, sporting equipment, pangas, lace gloves, and plaster casts of hands. Most of the objects in Siopis's collection are used and bear the traces of their use. Many of them are her heirlooms, associated with a particular class, and linked to a particular time, in South African history. As such, the objects point to Siopis's everyday life, and are part of her biography.

In *Reconnaissance 1900–1997* (1997), the objects were grouped together and presented in discrete piles, rather than the piles of wreckage in the history paintings. The word "*reconnaissance*" has multiple referents. In French, "reconnaissance" comes from the root *reconnaître* meaning recognition but

Figure 6.5 Penny Siopis, *Reconnaissance 1900–1997*, 1997. Detail of installation at Goodman Gallery, Johannesburg. Image courtesy of the artist.

more specifically, gratitude, suggesting that the work could be interpreted as an homage to Siopis's ancestors and cultural heritage. In English the word "reconnaissance" points to processes of surveying, an inspection of a situation or resources. It is as if through sorting, categorizing and presenting the objects she inherited, Siopis surveys her familial legacy, and her place within broader social contexts. A survey is carried out in order to "prepare" for something; in this case an unnamed future event—perhaps the future installations, each of which explore different relationships for the objects on display, thereby constructing different possibilities of meaning. The English word "reconnaissance" also has an additional connotation: to survey the resources of the "enemy", suggesting conflict of some kind. The idea of conflict is emphasized through the deliberate juxtaposition of cricket bats next to a pile of pangas and ballet shoes next to a figurine of a black woman in handcuffs (figure 6.6). Such contrasts elicit associations of privilege and excess at the expense of the exploited classes. In choosing to draw on her personal history, Siopis reveals the ways in which her personal history was, and continues to be, entangled in broader social and political histories. This entanglement of personal and social histories is present in all of Siopis's installations made with her personal objects, because it is present in the materiality of the objects themselves.

Referring to the ways in which she constructs her installations, Siopis states that there are similarities between her painting process and the manner in

Figure 6.6 Penny Siopis, *Reconnaissance 1900–1997*, 1997. Detail of installation at Goodman Gallery, Johannesburg. Image courtesy of the artist.

which she works with objects.¹⁸ As she selects and places objects in her installations, she considers each in relation to the other as she would consider each new mark in relation to others when drawing or painting. Siopis adds that, because of her method of working in response to objects and contexts, it is important that she creates the installations herself. Her working methods enable her to reuse the objects, reinterpreting them in different situations. Siopis says:

> The method for constructing the installations is similar to making a painting. It's contingent, but there's logic to the way the objects are arranged—something that emerges through the making. The installations are created in the moment, in situ, and each one is different. . . . The objects are like an archive, which I use similarly to how I use film. . . . It's an ephemeral art really. The objects get taken down and become like paint tubes again.¹⁹

Here the artist makes a connection between the objects as medium, like paint, and the intellectual labor of painting and of creating installations. This resonates with Roberts's suggestion that the intellectual labor of selecting and arranging objects in space is not unlike the manipulation of paint on a surface.²⁰ While there may be similarities, I contend, however, that the use of a real object is different from painting because of the layers of meaning that accumulate around objects, and which they bring with them into the artwork. This is surely what Duchamp played on when he put the urinal on a plinth. The artist's labor here is to arrange objects in space in ways that help us to think about what the objects mean, how their meanings change in relation to other objects, as well as how forms of representation help us to reflect on ourselves.

Transforming the everyday

Like Siopis, contemporary South African artist Usha Seejarim makes use of a range of collected objects that bear the traces of their use. Used bus tickets, fragments of things collected while walking and discarded mops and brooms from family and friends are among the objects Seejarim uses. For *50 Stories* (1998) (Figure 6.7), Seejarim collected objects that could fit in her pocket, while waiting at bus stops, and walking around central Johannesburg.²¹

In walking the streets to collect objects for the work the artist positioned herself as a contemporary woman urban wanderer in contrast to Baudelaire's male *flâneur*. Through her process of collecting, Seejarim can be understood as exposing aspects of contemporary South African urban life, through holding up what has been discarded as the by-products of urban living, for a particular kind of looking.

There is a double meaning in the title of the work. First, *50 Stories* can be understood as an allusion to the site where the artwork was installed. *50 Stories*

Figure 6.7 Usha Seejarim, *50 Stories*, 1997. (Detail) Dimensions variable. Found objects, pigment, Perspex, steel. Image courtesy of the artist.

(1998) was exhibited as part of the *Urban Futures* exhibition curated by Storm van Rensberg and Tracey Rose, held at the "Top of Africa"—a viewing deck on the top floor of the Carlton Centre a fifty-floor-high sky scraper in the center of Johannesburg, which was completed in the 1970s. At the time it was the tallest building in the Southern Hemisphere and regarded as testament to South African Afrikaner ingenuity. Visitors to the "Top of Africa" have a bird's eye view of the tall buildings and bustling streets of the city, but the details are lost. The plastic containers on special plinths that Seejarim made for the objects she collected while walking the streets of Johannesburg were reminiscent of the small vitrines in which insect specimens used to be kept in entomological collections. In this context these makeshift vitrines signaled that even those objects which appear to be trash, are special, worthy of keeping, and worthy of display (Figure 6.8).

In a second reading, the title could refer to the hidden stories that the objects might tell. Appadurai argues that it is through the processes of circulation that things can be said to have "a social life" because their meaning is culturally embedded, and changes as they circulate.[22] As objects move in and out of different social fields, the meanings associated with the objects change. The kind of exchange also matters, because objects acquire layers of meaning as they are circulated in different ways, for example, through economic exchange or gifting. Therefore, Appadurai suggests that the meaning of things is inscribed "in their forms, their use, their trajectories" concluding that if one is trying to find meanings other than the use-meaning of objects one must look at "the things in motion."[23] One such motion is when objects are removed from

Figure 6.8 View from the "Top of Africa": the 50th floor of the Carlton Centre, looking west onto Johannesburg. Photo: Alison Kearney.

everyday circulation and re-contextualized into the field of art. The changing classification, and value attached to the objects in *50 Stories*—from trash, to art—provides a good example of the manner in which the meaning of objects changes as they circulate through social spaces. Implied in Appadurai's theory of "the social life of things" is that as objects are used and circulated, so they acquire richness of meaning. However, not all layers of meaning are recoverable, as some of the past layers of meaning are obscured by the newer ones layered over them, and some of the meanings inscribed in objects are personal and kept private. A question that emerges when thinking about the "social life of things" and the possible layers of meaning that objects acquire as they circulate through social fields, is how do outsiders have access to these layers of meanings? In his critique of Appadurai's theory of "the social life of things," Harré points out that "material things have magic powers only in the contexts of the narratives in which they are embedded."[24] Therefore, Harré suggests that most people largely ignore the objects around them until they insert them into a narrative that gives them meaning and a place.

The audience does not have access to the biographies of the objects that make up *50 Stories*, however, by singling these objects out from others that look like them, and making use of conventions of museum display, Seejarim adds a new layer their hidden histories. In this work, objects that had lost their value and which were discarded were found by the artist, then literally elevated fifty stories above the ground, and figuratively elevated as part of art. Exhibited in their little Perspex boxes, those seemingly worthless objects formed a microcosm of the metropolis below, bringing into view minute details of the everyday against the backdrop of the panorama.

Rupture/continuum

It is within the contemporary iterations of the avant-garde that Alborough, Siopis and Seejarim's use of found objects is situated. Just as the neo-avant-garde's reiteration of historical avant-garde practices brought new inflections to discourses of found objects in art, so do Seejarim, Siopis and Alborough's uses of found objects bring new inflections to discourses of found objects in contemporary art. These contemporary South African artists' particular contribution lies in the distinct ways in which they harness the expressive and performative qualities of objects as signifiers in their artworks. The specificity of the objects as part of the artists' life worlds brings local, particular meanings to the artworks.

I propose that Alborough, Siopis and Seejarim's use of found objects has shifted from the historical avant-gardes' challenging of the conventions of art-making, to working with the discourse of the avant-garde in order to make comment on everyday practices in their own particular contexts. Thus, to use found objects in art is not only an engagement with the discourse of art, but it is also a means through which artists engage with the meanings that accrue to objects, and construct new meanings for objects—giving them a new social life of sorts. To pay attention to the kinds of objects that artists use and the ways in which they work with the objects is also a means to shift the rhetoric from a focus on anti-art to a focus on the possible meanings of artworks. After 100 years of the use of found objects, the practice continues to pose new questions regarding the ontologies of art because the objects bring various associations that are bound up with their materiality and social biography in to the field of art.

Notes

1 Arthur Danto, *The Transfiguration of the Common Place* (Cambridge, MA: Harvard University Press, 1981), vi.
2 Pablo Picasso, *Still-life with Chair Caning*, 1912. Oil on oil-cloth over canvas edged with rope. 29 × 37 cm. Musée National Picasso, Paris.
3 Walter Benjamin, "The Work of Art in the Age of Mechanical Reproduction," in *Illuminations: Walter Benjamin Essays and Reflections* ed. Hannah Arendt (London: Random House, 1968), 217–238.
4 Alexander Alberro, "Reconsidering Conceptual Art, 1966–1977," in *Conceptual Art: A Critical Anthology*, eds. Alexander Alberro and Blake Stimson (Cambridge, Massachusetts: The MIT Press, 1999), xvi–xxxvii.
5 According to Alberro, Duchamp distinguished between "assisted" and "unassisted" ready-mades. An "unassisted ready-made" is an industrially produced object, that the artist has not *apparently* changed, but which has been designated as art, for example Duchamp's *Bottle Rack* (1914). Assisted ready-mades such as *L.H.O.O.Q.* (1919) were noticeably physically changed by the artist. For instance, *L.H.O.O.Q.* (1919) was a reproduction of the *Mona Lisa*, on which Duchamp drew a beard, a curly moustache, and added the title *L.H.O.O.Q.*
6 Hal Foster, *The Return of the Real* (Cambridge, MA: The MIT Press, 1996).
7 Benjamin, "Work of Art," 221.
8 Martha Buskirk, *The Contingent Object of Contemporary Art* (Cambridge, MA: The MIT Press, 2005), 2.
9 Marcel Duchamp, *Fountain*, 1950 (replica of 1917 original). Found object, 30.5 × 38.1 × 45.7 cm. Philadelphia Museum of Art.
10 John Roberts, *The Intangibilities of Form: Skill and Deskilling in Art After the Readymade* (London and New York: Verso, 2007).
11 Foster, *Return of the Real*, 14.
12 Duchamp's ready-mades were relatively unknown in the art world until after Duchamp made replicas of them for his *Boite en valise* (1934), and when he made "reproductions" of them in the 1960s with the help of Harold Szneemann. See Thierry de Duve, "Echoes of the Readymade: Critique of Pure Modernism," in *The Duchamp Effect: Essays, Interviews, Round-table*, ed. Martha Buskirk and Mignon Nixon (Cambridge, MA: An October Book, The MIT Press, 1996), 93–130.
13 Foster, *Return of the Real*, 8.
14 On Minimalism in this context, see Martha Buskirk, *The Contingent Object of Contemporary Art* (Cambridge, MA: The MIT Press, 2005).
15 Penny Siopis in conversation with Gerrit Olivier, "Cake Paintings, History Paintings," in *Penny Siopis: Time and Again*, ed. Gerrit Olivier (Johannesburg: Wits University Press, 2015), 53–69.
16 Walter Benjamin, "On the Concept of History," in *Walter Benjamin: Selected Writings Volume 4: 1938-1940*, ed. Howard Eiland and Michael W. Jennings (Cambridge, MA: Belknap Press, 2006), 392.
17 Penny Siopis in conversation with Gerrit Olivier, "Installation and Collection," in *Penny Siopis: Time and Again*, ed. Gerrit Olivier (Johannesburg: Wits University Press, 2015), 109–26
18 Siopis, "Installation and Collection," 116.
19 Siopis, "Installation and Collection," 211.

20 Roberts, *Intangibilities of Form*.
21 This method of collecting recalls Karsten Bott's (1996) *Trouser Pocket Collection*, in which Bott collected things that could fit in his pocket while walking the streets of Cologne. See James Putman, *Art and Artefact: the Museum as Medium* (London: Thames and Hudson, 2001).
22 Arjun Appadurai, "Introduction: Commodities and the Politics of Value," in *The Social Life of Things: Commodities in Cultural Perspective*, ed. Arjun Appadurai (Cambridge: Cambridge University Press, 1986) 3–63.
23 Appadurai, "Introduction," 5.
24 Rom Harré, "Material Objects in Social Worlds," *Theory, Culture & Society*, no. 19 (2002): 25.

Part III

REPRESENTING WORK AND WORKERS

Chapter 7

JOSEPH CONRAD'S *NOSTROMO*: WORK, INHERITANCE, AND DESERT IN THE MODERNIST NOVEL

Evelyn T. Y. Chan

That which you inherit from your fathers
You must earn in order to possess.[1]

This essay explores the relationship between ideas of work and of inheritance in Joseph Conrad's *Nostromo*, captured by the claim—described in the two lines in *Faust* quoted at the beginning of this essay and demonstrated in Nostromo's actions, as we will see—that one can work for and earn one's inheritance. It shows how this belief gives rise to Nostromo's identity conflicts, and how it allows the novel to critique assumptions of meritocratic desert underpinning both the ideologies of work and—surprisingly—of inheritance, a prominent trope in nineteenth-century fiction, but a relatively less explored topic in literary modernism. Kieran Dolin has written of the "persistence of inheritance plots in an era of industrial and urban expansion" in the nineteenth century, which "is indicative not only of the political strength of the landed classes, but of their ideological power."[2] John R. Reed calls inheritance an "over-worked device," often to mete out moral desert.[3] In nineteenth-century novels such as *Oliver Twist* "the hero's merit and birth . . . are two sides of the same coin," and Oliver's "inheritance at once sanctions his birth and rewards his merit."[4] In other words, external material inheritance reflects innate worth. Although nineteenth-century protagonists must also prove their worth through tribulations and trials, the two forms of inheritance of inborn merit and material legacy very often translate into each other, because they are really each other's corollaries. Self-discovery and self-growth parallel coming into one's inheritance. This is also the meritocratic premise (according to which rewards and resources are arranged according to ability and effort, which yield commensurate rewards) so one could say that the literary trope of inheritance and the meritocratic ideal go hand in hand in nineteenth-century fiction—that inheritance discourses accommodated new meritocratic ideals, although the exact term "meritocracy" was a later twentieth-century coinage. An example of this is the Victorian "science" of phrenology, where the assumption is "that people differed from each other in their innate abilities, that these innate abilities were open to assessment ... [which] would then dictate the proper—or, more to the point, natural—stations for individuals in society."[5] The entanglement of the meritocratic ideal and the inheritance trope in literature prevailed even as what Susan E. Colón has described as "a shift from traditional aristocratic hegemony to that of a professional meritocracy" was well underway.[6]

The predominant trope of inheritance and legacy in Victorian fiction, and its role in the construction and assumption of masculinity, would thus seem a slightly outdated lens to use to read modernist literature. This is reflected in Conrad's novels, where there is often a brief patrilineal description of male protagonists that seems to have limited bearing on the paths they try to forge for themselves, as befits a context where the construction of powerful masculinity became less focused on traditional modes of inheritance in the form of titles, estates and wealth. Yet a closer reading of *Nostromo* reveals that it explores the breakdown in the close correlation in earlier fiction between the trope of inheritance and meritocratic values. As this essay demonstrates, *Nostromo* explores the ramifications of inheritances that cannot be properly earned through the vehicle of work, that cannot become one's desert. In so doing Conrad refashions the nineteenth-century trope of inheritance in *Nostromo* so that it reflects later anxieties about the relationship between work and identity-creation.

The inheritance trope is relevant to *Nostromo* in both of the two senses in which it often appears in nineteenth-century literature: first inheritance that is owned in material form, for instance as a financial legacy and an estate; and second, that which is owned personally or morally, in the form of innate abilities and worth. The applicability of the first sense to Charles Gould, the inheritor of the mine, is apparent, and will be examined further on. But this first sense is also relevant to Nostromo because work proves an inadequate mediator between merit and rewards and an inadequate method of self-making, so that his anticipation of great expectations—which I will show he sees as his rightful "inheritance"—needs to come to the aid of his self-fashioning. Nostromo is officially an employee of the Oceanic Steam Navigation Company in Sulaco, a city in the fictional South American country of Costaguana. His supervisor Captain Mitchell says that Nostromo was appointed "the foreman of our lightermen, and caretaker of our jetty. That's all that he was."[7] But of course that is also *not* "all that he was": Mitchell adds that "without him Señor Ribiera would have been a dead man," and that Nostromo "became the terror of all the thieves in the town" (12). Although at first glance Nostromo seems the poster child of meritocratic ideals—he possesses ability and claims to desert in plenty—these exceed the bounds of his formal work, and do not end up in commensurate rewards.[8] Nostromo's more unofficial title is that of Capataz de Cargadores, and under that name he performs heroic deeds and maintains capitalist order against all odds. But when Martin Decoud says that "[Nostromo's] work is an exercise of personal powers; his leisure is spent in receiving the marks of extraordinary adulation" (138), we start to get the sense that although Nostromo's work is an excellent fit with his abilities, he misapplies it in his emphasis on its performativity, on receiving "extraordinary adulation."[9]

Nostromo does not exactly find himself through work, as Marlow's words in *Heart of Darkness*, of work as "the chance to find yourself," suggest is possible, with Nostromo's story instead becoming a radical, destabilizing narrative on the uncertain status of selfhood in modernity. Marlow's conception of work here resembles nineteenth-century idealizations of work as "intrinsically satisfying."[10] But they can also indicate a meritocratic vision of work: work can bring out and do justice to the self and its innate abilities. For Nostromo, work seems to take on these meritocratic possibilities, but upon closer scrutiny becomes merely part of performing a heroic, and inadequately remunerated, persona. His work is not so much "initially a creative activity that constituted true liberty and permitted him to realize his potential as a social individual," reflective of him as a "fully integrated social being," but rather the superficial hallmark of his persona.[11] Upon swimming back from the Isabel islands to the shore of the mainland after his mission to keep the silver from the mine in Sulaco out of the hands of the revolutionaries, Nostromo can then shed his previous social identity like mere clothes, thinking that "everything that had gone before for years appear[s] vain and foolish, like a flattering dream come suddenly to an end" (298).

The most obvious symptom of this misfit with his work, despite the thorough aptness of it on the surface, is the way in which Nostromo is paid. Nostromo may be an employee with the Company, but most of his work, his heroism, is not done for direct remuneration (he is, after all, just "the foreman of our lightermen" [12]); rather, it is performed to show that his persona is deserving of additional unofficial rewards, of which "extraordinary adulation" (138) is only the first step.[12] Nostromo expects not regular payments which are commensurate with the services that he renders, nor even irregular payments in the form of the people's adulation, but to "get something *great* for it some day" (179; my emphasis), as he tells Decoud later. His efforts seemingly comprise work and labor, therefore, but really are more about his great expectations, about coming into *his own* one day, and in saying so I have already partially explained why I would use the term "inheritance" to account for this excess beyond direct rewards. This excess comprises Nostromo's claims to his "inheritance," in both senses of the word: the inherent abilities and merit he possesses—what Jennifer Ruth, discussing Charlotte Brontë's *The Professor*, has called "embodied property"[13]—which, when properly demonstrated, will yield an inheritance in the form of social status and rewards. Nostromo's failure to earn his inheritance is used to express the deeply troubled relationship between work and identity in the modernist context.

Upon closer examination, Nostromo constantly invokes the trope of inheritance when he talks of the services he has rendered the rich Europeans in

Costaguana. So to Giorgio Viola he says: "The old Englishman who has enough money to pay for a railway?... I've guarded his bones all the way from the Entrada pass..., *as though he had been my own father*" (93; my emphasis). On yet another occasion, he says, "I have sat alone at night with my revolver in the Company's warehouse time and again by the side of that other Englishman's heap of silver, guarding it *as though it had been my own*" (93; my emphasis). The similes here indicate not only the scarcity and quality of his service, but also what he in fact expects: in treating the rich people as his family, he expects to be seen as family; in treating this silver as his own, he already acts as if it is his own. Capitalist terminology in the novel combines with the vocabulary of inheritance: so Decoud astutely calls Nostromo's charismatic, "picturesque" work his "investment," and Dr. Monygham observes that "[h]is prestige is his fortune" (230).

Nostromo's lack of significant parentage (he is a "Man of the People" with "no parentage to boast of" [410]), which seems to free him from the encumbrances of inheritance, becomes the very reason why Nostromo draws on the trope of inheritance. Nostromo needs a concrete inheritance precisely because he has none "to boast of"; he needs to remake the very notion for himself precisely because this is his vacuum. To turn charisma into great material rewards—certainly greater than what being the foreman of the lightermen can give him—Nostromo relies on the reasoning of adoption and inheritance through portraying himself as fully deserving.[14] Despite the apparent relationship of "filiation" between him and the Violas,[15] he rejects their unofficial adoption of him, considering neither Giorgio, who encourages him to perform the heroic actions that "my son would have" (*Nostromo*, 339), nor Teresa, who says that she "has been like a mother to him" (15), truly worthy of being his new parents. Nostromo seems instead to be holding out for unofficial adoption by the rich Europeans in Costaguana, to be seen as fully one of their own. When "protecting his own" (14) in saving Sulaco from the Monterist revolution, "his own" does not just refer to his job and his friends in this adopted home, but also his share in the "material interests" (188) of Sulaco, derived from the immense wealth of the San Tomé mine. Nostromo expects "that the Señor Administrador of San Tomé will reward me some day" (179), that the work he has rendered should mean that he should have "been taken into account" (302)—and in what way, what kind of "account," we start to see more fully once we read his narrative as one of coming into his great expectations, his well-earned inheritance.

Thus the second sense of inheritance I mentioned earlier, as innate abilities and worth, also applies because the idea of coming into one's own through work necessarily depends on the idea of a self that finds external expression, to refer back to Marlow's words—yet inherent abilities and worth, and their external expression, are far from certain, stable or reliable, rendering any such argument for desert similarly unstable. The tension between innateness and externality, and essentialism and constructionism, in Conrad's reworked notion of "inheritance" in the modern context emphasizes acute doubts about what one can, and what one cannot, become, and how much of oneself is already made, or made by oneself—some of the key issues driving literary modernism that we can see reflected in *Nostromo*.

Therefore, *Nostromo* shows that the concept of "inheritance," and the new emphases which it took on, became in some ways even more relevant in the identity crises and the anxieties of self-making wrought by fin-de-siècle and early twentieth-century modernity. Nostromo's path still shares some similarities with the Victorian inheritance plot. His great expectations of social status and wealth derive from the idea of a *deserved* (but deferred) inheritance, where one proves one is intrinsically worthy of obtaining these great rewards, of coming into one's own—just as in the Victorian novel, the inheritance trope often "function[ed] as the reward of virtue."[16] But the difference is that Nostromo's great expectations are an inheritance that he actively tries to forge for himself—the rewards themselves (first to be well-regarded, and then more concretely to get his fortune) are his goal. The idea of inheritance marries the idea of work, so that the one takes on the ideals and values of the other, creating a different mode of remuneration that combines both patterns of legacy and work. Coming into his own is self-fashioning through work, under the meritocratic terms of obtaining commensurate well-earned rewards for ability and effort. By showing how this process of claiming one's inheritance goes awry, *Nostromo* calls the meritocratic premise of these claims into question: merit evidenced through effective and exceptional work does not create concrete desert; it seems, to refer back to Goethe's words, that inheritances may not be able to be earned, in contrast to the morally positive form they so often take on in nineteenth-century fiction. In thwarting Nostromo's efforts to earn his inheritance, his great expectations, through work, Conrad critiques emergent meritocratic ideals, and the very shaky foundation they provide for constructing the heroic masculine identity Nostromo yearns for.

Thus *Nostromo* also addresses the conflict in the early twentieth century between work and inheritance, the latter of which in its most basic definition is a morally arbitrary form of non-work. The cultural reiteration of the work ethic, first, as Max Weber argued, as part of the religious mission under Protestantism to answer one's calling through work, and then subsequently as a secular form of vocation, expressly sees work as not morally arbitrary.[17] In its ideal conception, the rewards reaped from work are fair, just, and morally well-deserved, with input (in terms both of quality and quantity) proportional to earnings and rewards, whether earthly or heavenly. The problem is, of course, that work rarely attains this ideal state. One needs to look no further than Marx's critique of capitalist work as alienating workers from the products of their labor rather than achieving such commensurateness, and in a way Nostromo's appropriation of the Victorian inheritance trope can be read as attempts, ending up in failure, to redress the insufficiencies of alienated labor, which, rather than being individuating as he hopes his work can be, is abstract and interchangeable. Even Weber's argument on Calvinism points to the contradiction in the idea of *earning* one's inheritance, which Nostromo's ill-fated marrying of the ideals of inheritance and of work tries to attain. "[T]ireless labor in a calling" cannot be used to attain salvation, the relevant inheritance in this case, yet it is "the best possible means of attaining ... assurance of one's state of grace."[18] According to such impossible logic, then, one applies oneself in a calling as an indirect way of proving one possesses the inheritance of salvation and not as a direct way to earn salvation. In the novel too, the seemingly straightforward formula of meritocracy which should apply to work, of ability and effort translating into commensurate and morally deserved rewards, proves not at all that straightforward. The invocation of the inheritance trope in *Nostromo* reminds us of the limit to the possibilities of self-making that the meritocratic conception of work promises.

Anti-commercialism

Reading Nostromo's expectations as a figurative inheritance explains the seeming contradiction between Nostromo's carelessness with the monetary side of his service, his "disinterested[ness] with the unworldliness of a sailor" (297), and his desire for deferred rewards. He is uncaring about money because he implicitly expects it down the line. His vanity, from which all his actions derive, can then without conflict be simultaneously "materialistic and imaginative" and "an unpractical and warm sentiment" (297). But his claims are extremely precarious, because Nostromo's "investment" (160) into his worthy persona may not pay off: unlike being paid directly for one's work, one cannot exert much direct control using one's own actions over whether one attains these great expectations or not. After saving President Ribiera, one of the landed aristocracy, Nostromo asks Decoud "moodily," "And how much do I get for that, señor?" (164). The answer is, unfortunately, very little, because the rich do not ever think of Nostromo as one of their own. When Decoud says that Nostromo "promised me that if a riot took place for any reason ... his Cargadores, an important part of the populace, you will admit, should be found on the side of the Europeans," Mrs. Gould at first has trouble making sense of this: "He has promised you that? ... What made him make that promise to you?" (159). She cannot conceive that Nostromo considers himself one of the rich Europeans, or at least deserving of being one of them, and not merely their wage worker. Mrs. Gould's surprise indicates that the allegiance Nostromo imagines, which transcends commercialism and operates based on the in-group logic of inheritance, is not one that is reciprocated by the rich. Decoud on the other hand astutely observes that "[u]pon the whole ... I suppose he expects something to his advantage from it.... He told me ... that he had come here to make his fortune. I suppose he looks upon his prestige as a sort of investment. (159–60). This is an investment in a future inheritance, much like a character who acts in a certain way to ensure his rich relatives leaves him with their fortune might behave.

The new way of remuneration Nostromo seeks is then notably opposed to direct commerce, and in this way can be read as mirroring some of the anti-commercialist tactics of literary modernism that scholars such as Patrick Collier have analyzed.[19] Inheritances are not directly earned, unlike wages. From this derives the irony of Nostromo being repeatedly called "invaluable" (73), or essentially priceless. His services are so crucial, his achievements so great, that a price tag cannot really be put on them. This anti-commercialism has been read in different ways. For instance, Tamás Juhász reads Nostromo as gradually progressing from archaic to modern commerce, while also going back and forth between these modes, and Ursula Lord sees Nostromo as changing from a state of full being and social integration to one of alienation and slavery to material and commercial interests.[20] This is of course not a clear-cut change. Even prior to it, Nostromo's anti-commercialism is superficial, used to fulfill his great expectations. And after it, being paid directly for his heroic feats remains out of the question for Nostromo. This would make Nostromo not "invaluable for our work—a perfectly incorruptible fellow" (94), but potentially corruptible and partial, selling his services to the full no differently from other tradespeople. It would do away with the prospect of great expectations down the line which Nostromo keeps anticipating—until he becomes so disillusioned he purloins the silver he has been hired to guard, again not for any direct reward.

Nostromo's gradual disillusionment with the non-commercial reward of mere individuation (of being "the only man fit for [142] such heroic tasks as saving the silver), his diminishing hopes in "get[ting] something great . . . some day" for being the only man "that could have been even thought of for such a thing" as saving the silver becomes a source of bitterness that justifies his appropriation of it. The non-commercial act of saving the silver shows his individual worth—a worth that, ironically, he finally puts the money value of the worth of the silver on. His superficial rejection of direct market evaluation—even when he is finally fully cognizant of his desire for money, and finally fully fears the "poverty, misery, and starvation" (334) the dying Teresa has prophesied—is so perverse that although he heroically saves Sulaco from the Monterist revolution, and is asked by Gould "what he could do for him" (351), he does not name a price. The blighted inheritance of the silver must ironically be his covert fortune because that is part and parcel of the persona he wants: someone who does not do anything for personal gain, who will accept higher status if given it as reflective of his person but will not ask for it.

So Nostromo must pretend to do his heroic work for the sake of the work only, keeping up the semblance of "disinterested[ness]" (160) which Mrs. Gould is utterly convinced of, but of which Decoud is more doubtful. My position on Nostromo here pulls back somewhat from Lord's view that before Nostromo's revelation that "he has been betrayed by the owners of the silver," he was "the relic of a pre-monetary world of glamour, adventure, independence, and unquestioning loyalty"—in other words, that he is, in Mrs. Gould's view, "disinterested, and therefore trustworthy" (160).²¹ Although it is true, as the dying Teresa Viola observes, that the rich "have been paying [Nostromo] with words" (186), not money, they may be seen, in Decoud's words again, as "a sort of investment" (160). These words are promissory notes, to be redeemed for Nostromo's great expectations, a form of coming fully into his own, an expectation of greatness that Nostromo had even prior to his complete sense of betrayal by the rich, when he was not fully certain yet what he would get. Nostromo's corruption by the silver is thus less of a narrative break or a character change, and more a culmination and realization of the logic by which he has worked all along.²²

The silver epitomizes the conflicts between ideologies of work and inheritance that Nostromo has been trying to combine together throughout the novel by attempting to earn his great expectations. Thinking he deserves and has successfully obtained the inheritance of the silver for himself, he cannot nevertheless escape from having to continue to work for it, thus proving that he does not truly own his inheritance after all. Having embezzled it, Nostromo must take care to "grow rich very slowly" (360) as he puts it, so that others do not find out. He has to draw on the silver as if it is a salary, withdrawing small amounts from it at regular intervals. Yet at the same time he owns all of it, as a simultaneously well-deserved and yet also an illegitimate inheritance. It is his, but is also his paymaster: "the difficulty of converting it into a form in which it could become available" means bizarrely that he works it just as Gould works the mine, needing to take lengthy "voyages along the coast" in his schooner as "the ostensible source of his fortune" (375), while really using them to sell his silver piece by piece. So the original relationship between paymaster and laborer is reproduced; "the silver of San Tomé was provided now with a faithful and lifelong slave" (359). His desire to be equal to that which owns him, his "yearn[ing] to clasp, to embrace, absorb, subjugate in unquestioned possession this treasure" (379), ensures it.

Nostromo's failure to secure his great expectations is as much an existential study of thwarted desires and aspirations, as it is a critique of the meritocratic ideals on which idealized, romanticized notions of work are based in the modern context, the type Marlow suggests with his utterance. The tragedy of Nostromo's situation arises from his assumption that work can lead to commensurate rewards—even those of inherited social station that one was traditionally born into. But even fully demonstrated merit such as Nostromo's is not definitive enough of social identity in the context of Costaguana, nor as significant, or as stable, as traditional forms of inheritance. In the face of the recalcitrance of traditional inheritance, the case of Nostromo probes how much "chance" there really is to "find yourself" in work,²³ to find a self that is able to obtain the commensurate rewards one believes one is entitled to through one's work—and conversely, how much work, and any rewards or lack thereof, must also be tied to morally neutral forms of non-work, and have little to do with desert. Work under capitalism exploits Nostromo's abilities but does not reward him accordingly, no matter what meritocratic ideology implies is now possible. Nostromo remains merely "[a] most useful fellow" (*Nostromo* 34) to all the Europeans he is "lent" to by Captain Mitchell (34). Even Mitchell who calls Nostromo "*my* Capataz de Cargadores" (emphasis mine), "devoted to me, body and soul" (35) reiterates Nostromo's instrumental value as a "perfect handy man" (230). Nostromo becomes caught in an identity crisis: he creates an exceptional persona, but discovers the limits of self-making when he is not acknowledged by the rich as anything other than an exceptional servant. His nickname "Nostromo" sticks to him like the curse of the silver: meaning boatswain in Italian, also possibly derived from *nostro uomo* or "our man" (432), Nostromo as "man of the people" seems destined to be excluded from the ranks of the rich aristocrats, "the *hombres finos*—the gentlemen" (313)—the circles he thought himself worthy of entering as his great expectations. He only fully realizes his permanent outsider status in these circles, as merely "[t]he best dog of the rich" (337), upon returning from the Isabel islands after taking the silver there for safety: "Kings, ministers, aristocrats, the rich in general, kept the people in poverty and subjection; they kept them as they kept dogs, to fight and hunt for their service" (298), crucially without commensurate reward. "[T]he interest" (327) of the rich, Nostromo recognizes, is not his own. Birth still predetermines socioeconomic position; the meritocratic ideal is a farce. Finally, his hopes dashed, instead of waiting for the "great" inheritance of which he deems himself worthy, he ends up appropriating the silver he was supposed to save, in doing so taking the "curse" (187) of this silver upon him—itself the accursed inheritance of Gould, the owner of the mine, who received it as a legacy from his father who told him to stay well away from it.

With his aristocratic lineage and his inheritance of the Sulaco mine, Gould seems the opposite of Nostromo in his social position. Indeed, what sets them apart is their relationship to money: while Nostromo must obfuscate his desire to obtain financial rewards for his exceptional services, to maximize profit must be Gould's ostensible reason to all the investors for exploiting the mine, even while his real purpose is very far removed from "simple profit in the working of a silver mine" (51). Yet like Nostromo, Gould must still work his inheritance, one that is also an investment into uncertain future rewards from the mine, situated as it is in its politically explosive context. The San Tomé mine is the archetype of the inheritance that must be proven and earned,[24] occupying the simultaneous ontological status of an inheritance and not yet an inheritance, something which connects Gould to his father and yet separates them. Gould Senior, who "had been weak," "must be put completely in the wrong" (56). The mine must be described in new language: not that of exploitation and moral depravity, but stability, prosperity, and moral integrity. Whereas his father "knew nothing of mining," "had no means to put his concession on the European market" (42), and warns Gould "never to claim any part of his inheritance" in Costaguana because of the curse of the perpetually granted concession (44), Gould imbues the mine with "hope, vigour, and self-confidence" (45), makes it his express mission to find out everything he can about mining, in the end transforming it into "the Treasure House of the World" (374). His becoming the "King of Sulaco" (105) continues his family's legacy where it failed in the past: as the narrative repeatedly reminds the reader, Gould's uncle, declared President of Sulaco when Costaguana was a Federation, had been shot by the dictator Guzmán Bento; and Gould's father, "for a long time one of the most wealthy merchants of Costaguana" (41), lost the bulk of his wealth to subsequent political regimes.

Gould's fight to earn his inheritance is, like Nostromo's, a striving for a desired identity: "he felt that the worthiness of his life was bound up with success" (*Nostromo* 64). This is in contrast to the comparatively indifferent financial investors in the mine who put in capital but little effort and little personal attachment. Gould does not use the multinational corporate structure to obfuscate his ownership; rather, he *is* the mine. This is why Gould declares he could "never have disposed of the Concession as a speculator disposes of a valuable right to a company—for cash and shares, to grow rich eventually if possible" (55). Such an act would demonstrate legal and financial ownership, but not the personal or moral ownership that reflects his inner worth, "the almost mystic view he took of his right" (288). The former gives rise to mere institutional entitlement, whereas the latter creates an argument for moral desert (a distinction I will elaborate on in a moment), for deserving the parental legacy he both does and does not automatically come into. Both Gould and Nostromo therefore showcase the acute desire in modernity to avoid moral contingency in one's self-making via the vehicle of work—in their cases through actively demonstrating they deserve their inheritances instead of merely coming into them.

The fruits of work: inheritance as moral desert

Earning their inheritances would enable Nostromo and Gould to turn them from products of contingency to desert via their work. What is not really their own could then become properly their own. The two characters' efforts to make inheritance morally positive through effort and work, to *earn* it, adopts the moral vocabulary of modern meritocratic ideals. This reading looks beyond Conrad as "simply bypass[ing] the place of inheritance and hold[ing] economic matters in abeyance ..., not directly challeng[ing] them",[25] recognizing how Conrad addresses their resultant conflicts in a novel that reflects, in Paul Armstrong's words, "a paradigm which stands for the being of society and exemplifies its contradictions."[26]

But wanting to properly deserve one's inheritance poses a dilemma: the ontological status of inheritances on which claims to moral desert, including meritocratic claims and rewards, depend, is far from stable. This applies not just to material inheritances, but also to the idea of inherent abilities on which merit-based claims to desert often depend, a topic that would increasingly attract the attention of moral philosophy as the twentieth century went on, and that we can see *Nostromo* as looking ahead to. The innate abilities of the "self" that one can supposedly discover through work, as per Marlow's famous utterance, should be demonstrated externally not just through the materiality of the products of work (which in the cases of Nostromo and Gould is the prosperity of Sulaco, and is thus obvious), but also through due recognition and rewards accorded the worker himself. Without these, it is as if the person Nostromo thought himself to be never was, accounting for his crisis in identity when he swims back from the Isabel islands after his rescue mission to save the silver.

For no one in the novel are these issues more acute than Nostromo and Gould, although there are many examples of desert seeking and claiming in the novel. One could say *Nostromo* is about people desiring what they believe to be their due. General Montero stages a coup because "he only wanted his share" (132). Pedrito Montero sees "in the elevation of his brother" the means "to acquire a serious fortune for himself" because he "meant to have his share of [the] prosperity" of Sulaco (277–78). Decoud, "if successful" in the counter-revolution, expects "to receive my reward, which no one but Antonia can give me" (178). The emphasis on rewards and deserts from chapter ten onwards, which returns the narrative to the golden era of Sulaco prosperity after the failed Monterist revolution, is especially pronounced. Sulaco is now a stable, independent state, and a prosperous Captain Mitchell (re)counts the dues to every significant person who has helped defeat the Monterist revolution. Mitchell himself "hold[s] seventeen of the thousand-dollar shares in the Consolidated San Tomé mines" (341–42). Dr. Monygham opines that "we who played our part in it had our reward" (363). The success of his reward, the safety of Mrs. Gould and continued time spent with her, allows him to say that "I am rewarded beyond my deserts" (363). All this counting of rewards deliberately sets up the questions: has Nostromo received his desert? Does he deserve his great expectations, so that his purloining of the silver can be seen as a type of moral justice? Nostromo is not mentioned until well into the chapter, when Mitchell says that "He has done for Separation as much as anybody else, and ... has got less than many others by it" (346). Because of him "There are people on this Alameda that ride in their carriages, or even are alive at all today"; because of him "the 'Treasure House of the World' ... was saved intact for civilisation—for a great future" (347).

To address these questions is to return to the question that the essay started off with, on whether inheritances can be earned and thus made properly one's own and one's moral desert. Here a crucial distinction needs to be made first between entitlement and desert. Entitlements, as the moral philosopher John Rawls has pointed out, are institutional, and arise because "as persons and groups take part in just arrangements, they acquire claims on one another defined by the publicly recognized rules."[27] The goal of a "just scheme" of entitlements to be striven for is to "satisf[y] their legitimate expectations as founded upon social institutions."[28] The problem with entitlements, however, is that "what [people] are entitled to is not proportional to nor dependent upon their intrinsic worth."[29] "[I]ntrinsic worth" is instead the domain of desert, which is a moral concept. Dr. Monygham distinguishes between entitlement and desert when he comments on the capitalist institutions in Sulaco:

> There is no peace and rest in the development of material interests. They have their law and their justice. But it is founded on expediency, and is inhuman; it is without rectitude, without the continuity and the force that can be found only in a moral principle. (366)

Nostromo and Gould both feel they must earn their inheritances because both wish to prove their ability beyond mere entitlement (that is, Nostromo's wages and Gould's paternal legacy), to create their desert, which should reflect their intrinsic worth. That is why for Nostromo not getting what he sees as commensurate rewards for his efforts is a moral outrage. "They keep us and *encourage* us" (301; my emphasis), Nostromo complains, as if "work[ing] all day and rid[ing] about at night" (301) will finally bring just rewards beyond mere regular wages; but they do not. That is also why Gould thinks of appropriating his inheritance as a moral quest: "The mine had been the cause of an absurd moral disaster; its working must be made a serious and moral success" (50). The Goulds feel they are "morally bound to make good their vigorous view of life against the unnatural error of weariness and despair" (56) that marked Gould Senior's handling of the mine. Gould, as Decoud observes, "attaches a strange idea of justice" to the mine (177), with "justice" referring both to Gould's quest for justice as a public social institution in Sulaco, but also "justice" as private justice, as his just and moral desert. As Mrs. Gould thinks, their goal is "to keep their prosperity without a stain on its only real, on its immaterial side" (56), where the social institutions that create the stable environment for the creation and possession of wealth coming from the San Tomé mine and the integrity and morality of the Goulds are one. The creation of "[a] better justice" (63) in Sulaco simultaneously reflects the Goulds' moral status.

Meritocratic ideals—parodied later with the publication of the satirical *The Rise of the Meritocracy* by Michael Young, which declares that IQ + effort = MERIT)—equate entitlement and desert.[30] They claim rewards granted by institutions, which would normally be considered entitlements, are natural and thus *also* become moral desert if one has proven that one has earned them through meritocratic principles, and that moral desert can be ensconced in and reflected in institutional entitlement.[31] This becomes the false promise that drives the plot of both characters: that to be rewarded for one's inherent merit, or to earn one's inheritance, is both natural and institutional. As Daniel Cottom has written, "the meritocratic illusion [is] the belief that one can isolate merit within a society by means of a neutral rationality and thus promote a society that stratifies itself according to the laws of nature", so that "a rational organization of society would result in a natural stratification of individuals according to their innate deserts."[32] These "natural endowments are [seen as] somehow more essentially *his*, more deeply constitutive of his identity than his socially-conditioned attributes."[33] Yet that certain ways of treating others' characteristics or conduct seem "'natural' or 'conventional' methods of expressing our attitudes is hardly sufficient justification for instituting practices in which we respond to persons in these ways."[34] What we think of as desert is not given or natural, although we may often mistake it as such.

Rawls' critique of the meritocratic principle goes further. His argument in *A Theory of Justice* is that since natural abilities are a product of contingency, they do not lead to desert. Not even material "distribution according to effort," "which seems intuitively to come closest to rewarding moral desert," reflects desert:

> the effort a person is willing to make is influenced by his natural ability and skills and the alternatives open to him. The better endowed are more likely, other things equal, to strive conscientiously, and there seems to be no way to discount for their greater good fortune. *The idea of rewarding desert is impracticable.*[35]

This means that "it is incorrect to say that just distributive shares reward individuals according to their moral worth." The only claim that can be made is institutional: "a just scheme gives each person his due: that is, it allots to each what he is entitled to as defined by the scheme itself."[36]

Reading the novel alongside Rawls's perspective, Nostromo's efforts to earn his inheritance, his overreaching desire to escape "the scheme itself," to prove extra-institutional desert as the source of deeper, more thorough self-making, seems even more misguided than before. We have already seen how inherited class and wealth positions prove too intractable to overcome, leading finally to his sense that "He had been betrayed!" But in addition, similar to Rawls and in what can be seen as part of Conrad's destabilizing modernist narrative, Conrad highlights the constructedness of recognized merit, and of the nature and moral status of these so-called inherent abilities. For instance, Nostromo says that he is "going to *make* [the removal of the silver] the most famous and desperate affair of my life" (191, my emphasis). The affair *is* not such, but will be *constructed* as such so that Nostromo can forge his own desired merit. Nostromo's

> success in the work he found on shore enlarged [his conceptions of himself] in the direction of personal magnificence.... And who can say that it was not genuine distinction? It was genuine because it was based on something that was in him—his overweening vanity.... *Without it he would have been nothing.* It called out his recklessness, his industry, his ingenuity, and that disdain of the natives which helped him so much in the line of his work and *resembled an inborn capacity for command*. It made him *appear* incorruptible and fierce" (297; my emphases).

Language that points to inherency jostles with language that suggests dissemblance. His qualities reflect "genuine distinction" which is "based on [the vanity] in him," or inherent in him. All the other qualities which in others' eyes make up his heroic identity are merely a façade, "resembling" but not truly constituting "an inborn capacity," attached to this inherent vanity "[w]ithout [which] he would have been nothing." This passage twists Marlow's words on work as a way to find yourself, questioning the idea of work as self-discovery.[37] It also foregrounds the arbitrariness of the notion of merit, and as a result its morally positive status under a meritocratic scheme. A little later, Conrad deconstructs even the most basic and inborn quality of vanity: "even that had been simply sensuous and picturesque, and could not exist apart from outward show" (*Nostromo* 300). What others consider Nostromo's innate abilities are built on a shaky foundation. So in the boat with Decoud in their joint mission to save the silver, in their fraught situation and with no other onlookers, "Something deeper, something unsuspected by everyone, had come to the surface" (203). Nostromo's qualities depend on external observation and recognition, on what "outward show" to put on, on what counts as "picturesque" (300), which guides his actions and behavior. Thus, the defense put forward for the meritocratic principle that natural inequalities "are intractable in a way that" social inequalities are not is flawed, as "those qualities most plausibly regarded as essential to a person's identity ... are often heavily influenced by social and cultural factors."[38] What society recognizes as meritorious can be an "outward show" (*Nostromo* 300) even when it is based on "genuine distinction" (297). Since so-called inborn traits are little without external recognition, "[e]ven if the vast majority of differences between persons turned out to be genetic rather than cultural, it would still remain for society to determine *which* of these differences, if any, should properly be made the basis for differential distributive shares."[39] The necessity of recognition in the creation and evaluation of meritorious ability renders any claims of certain rewards as morally deserved weak.

But Nostromo's misguidedness is precisely Conrad's novelistic premise. Had Nostromo only taken the path of steady work, he would likely have ended up like Captain Mitchell; had he literally been the son of one of the rich families, he would likely have ended up like the other aristocrats in Sulaco. Nostromo's attempts to earn his inheritance drive his worthiness as a novelistic hero. This also reveals a crucial limit to the extent to which we can read Conrad, the modernist author, and Rawls, the moral philosopher, together. Rawls's suggestions to redress this arbitrariness and move towards greater egalitarianism using mainly social mechanisms and rules is the opposite of Conrad's characters' impulse. Although Conrad questions Nostromo's claims to desert, showing the limits of human autonomy and the arbitrariness of rewards, he does so while taking fully into account the human yearning for self-making through earning and creating desert, rendering its failure into a tragedy. Despite the fact that Nostromo gets nothing in the end, Conrad views Nostromo's claims sympathetically, as injudicious yet utterly meaningful.

No matter what Nostromo does, he cannot earn his right to be adopted by the great families he serves and saves into a better position, those same families whose fortunes depend so much on his effort. Exceptional work, with Nostromo "not 'one in a thousand,'" but "absolutely the only one" (*Nostromo* 325), does not yield dependable rewards, the great expectations he yearns for. Work cannot be the perfect mediator between oneself and one's self-perceived desert, cannot be used to come into his own. Nostromo's eventual refusal of paid work, when he rejects Mitchell's suggestion that he take up his old post as the Capataz de Cargadores again by stating that "I am too tired to work just yet" (350), finally turns definitively away from Marlow's claim that one can find oneself through work. His case sets up the radical refusal of paid work by the Professor in Conrad's next novel, *The Secret Agent*. It also looks ahead to the continuing troubled relationship between literary modernism and work as both an essential identity-maker in modernity, and an identity-effacer when its fruits are relegated to mere functions of the socioeconomic structures of capitalism.

Notes

1 Johann Wolfgang von Goethe, *Goethe's Faust, Part I*, trans. Randall Jarrell (1808; New York: Farrar, Straus & Giroux, 1976), 35. The work for this essay was supported by the Research Grants Council of Hong Kong (General Research Fund project code 14615715).
2 Kieran Dolin, *Fiction and the Law: Legal Discourse in Victorian and Modernist Literature* (Cambridge: Cambridge University Press, 1999), 34.
3 John R. Reed, *Victorian Conventions* (Athens: Ohio University Press, 1975), 268–88.
4 Anny Sadrin, *Parentage and Inheritance in the Novels of Charles Dickens* (Cambridge: Cambridge University Press, 1994), 39, 42.
5 Ruth, *Novel Professions*, 47.
6 Colón, *Professional Ideal*, 76–77.
7 Joseph Conrad, *Nostromo*, ed. Jacques Berthoud and Mara Kalnins (1904; Oxford: Oxford University Press, 2007), 12. Subsequent references are given parenthetically in text.
8 Susan E. Colón has related the rise of meritocratic ideals with the ascendency of the professional classes in the nineteenth century. Susan E. Colón, *The Professional Ideal in the Victorian Novel: The Works of Disraeli, Trollope, Gaskell, and Eliot* (New York: Palgrave Macmillan, 2007).
9 As Jeremy Hawthorn has pointed out, "[w]hereas at the start of the novel Nostromo *was* the role he played, by the end of the novel his public self is separate from his private self." *Joseph Conrad: Language and Fictional Self-Consciousness*. (London: Edward Arnold, 1979), 69.
10 Rob Breton, *Gospels and Grit: Work and Labour in Carlyle, Conrad, and Orwell* (Toronto: University of Toronto Press, 2005), 20. For Marx, for example, in *The Economic Manuscripts of 1844*, labor fulfils man's "species being", while for Carlyle in "Past and Present", "the whole soul of man is composed into a kind of real harmony the instant he sets himself to work". Quoted in Morag Shiach, *Modernism,*

Labour and Selfhood in British Literature and Culture, 1890–1930 (Cambridge: Cambridge University Press, 2004), 32, 35.
11 Ursula Lord, *Solitude versus Solidarity in the Novels of Joseph Conrad: Political and Epistemological Implications of Narrative Innovation* (Montreal: McGill-Queen's Press, 1998), 209, 208.
12 For other interpretations of Nostromo's unconventional approach to work, see, for example, Joshua Gooch, "'The shape of credit': imagination, speculation, and language in *Nostromo*," *Texas Studies in Literature and Language* 52, no. 3 (2010): 270 and Timothy J. Wager, "'There is meaning in endeavour': Conrad's artistic labor," *Conradiana* 30, no. 3 (1998): 220. This aspect of Nostromo's character could also be read in terms of what Fredric Jameson calls the "feudal ideology of honour" in Conrad's fiction. *The Political Unconscious: Narrative as a Socially Symbolic Act* (London: Routledge, 1981; 2002), 205.
13 Jennifer Ruth, *Novel Professions: Interested Disinterest and the Making of the Professional in the Victorian Novel* (Columbus: The Ohio State University Press, 2006), 41.
14 Josiane Paccaud-Huguet sees Nostromo as part of a series of Conradian characters "whose symbolic alienation from family continuity must be understood as a liberation from the dependency of parentage and conventions." "Nostromo: Conrad's Man of No Parentage," *The Conradian* 18, no. 2 (1994): 65. For a discussion of symbolic parentage in the novel, see Bernard Constant Meyer, *Joseph Conrad: A Psychoanalytic Biography* (Princeton: Princeton University Press, 1967).
15 Jameson, *Political Unconscious*, 263.
16 Dolin, *Fiction and the Law*, 117.
17 On Weber's account of work as having "a morally positive character" in modern capitalist societies, see John A. Hughes, Wes Sharrock, and Peter J. Martin, *Understanding Classical Sociology: Marx, Weber, Durkheim* (London: Sage, 2003), 95.
18 Max Weber, *The Protestant Ethic and the Spirit of Capitalism and Other Writings*, ed. and trans. Peter Baehr and Gordon C. Wells (1905; London: Penguin, 2002), 77–78.
19 Patrick Collier, *Modernism on Fleet Street* (Burlington: Ashgate, 2006).
20 Tamás Juhász, *Conradian Contracts: Exchange and Identity in the Immigrant Imagination* (Plymouth: Lexington Books, 2011), 166–74; Lord, *Solitude versus Solidarity*, 207–09.
21 Lord, *Solitude versus Solidarity*, 207.
22 Gooch explains how Nostromo has often been read as "a failed character" because of this change. Gooch, "'The shape of credit,'" 286.
23 Conrad, *Heart of Darkness*, 35.
24 To become "mine," in wordplay suggested by Aaron Fogel, *Coercion to Speak: Conrad's Poetics of Dialogue.* (Cambridge, MA: Harvard University Press, 1985), 114.
25 Breton, *Gospels and Grit*, 111.
26 Paul B. Armstrong, "Conrad's Contradictory Politics: The Ontology of Society in *Nostromo*," *Twentieth-Century Literature* 31, no. 1 (1985): 4.
27 John Rawls, *A Theory of Justice* (Cambridge, MA: Harvard University Press, 1999), 273.
28 Rawls, *Theory of Justice*, 273.
29 Rawls, *Theory of Justice*, 273.
30 Michael Young, *The Rise of the Meritocracy, 1870–2033: An Essay on Education and Equality* (Baltimore, MD: Penguin, 1961).

31 Amartya Sen, "Merit and Justice," in *Meritocracy and Economic Inequality*, ed. Kenneth Joseph Arrow, Samuel Bowles, and Steven N. Durlauf (Princeton: Princeton University Press, 2000), 13.
32 Daniel Cottom, *Social Figures: George Eliot, Social History and Literary Representation* (Minneapolis: University of Minnesota Press, 1987), 16 (also quoted in Ruth, *Novel Professions*, 47), 74–75.
33 Michael J. Sandel, *Liberalism and the Limits of Justice* (Cambridge and New York: Cambridge University Press, 1998), 74.
34 Margaret Holmgren, "Justifying desert claims: Desert and opportunity," *The Journal of Value Inquiry* 20, no. 4 (1986): 268).
35 Rawls, *Theory of Justice*, 274; my emphasis.
36 Rawls, *Theory of Justice*, 275–76.
37 For a critical reading of Marlow's words, see Michael John DiSanto, *Under Conrad's Eyes: The Novel as Criticism* (Montreal and Kingston: McGill-Queen's University Press, 2009), 56.
38 Sandel, *Liberalism*, 74–75.
39 Sandel, *Liberalism*, 75.

Chapter 8

MAGIC, MODERNITY, AND WOMEN AT WORK

Caroline Webb

The period immediately following the First World War has traditionally been identified as a high point in the literature of modernism. What has been much less recognized is that in England it also marked a significant period of growth in literary fantasy.¹ Some authors, such as E. R. Eddison, Lord Dunsany, and Hope Mirrlees, wrote works readily recognized as fantasy, in that they are full secondary-world fantasies.² However, a number of other writers, such as David Lindsay, David Garnett, Stella Benson, and Ronald Fraser, produced what Farah Mendlesohn has termed "intrusion fantasies," in which extraordinary events impinge on the ordinary world, or "liminal fantasies," in which at least some characters in that world accept the fantasy events as natural.³ In various ways, these authors' fantasy works are modernist in method and concern. Like more famous modernist fictions, they address issues arising in the post-war re-evaluation of social structures, relations, and purpose, focusing in particular on the individual consciousness. They examine the changes to daily life, both social and physical, produced by the impact of the Great War and developments in technology. In this essay, I explore how two of these writers, Stella Benson and Ronald Fraser, portray and perceive women at work in their respective post-war fantasies *Living Alone* (1919) and *Flower Phantoms* (1926). These two novels both focus on women in work situations during or immediately following the war, and explicitly or implicitly interrogate either the nature of that work itself (*Living Alone*) or the nature of women and their roles in post-war English society (*Flower Phantoms*). In so doing, both writers also offer an account of the function of art in human life.

Prior to the war, the roles of women in England had been much disputed. The jobs available to working-class women were limited and menial, while women of the higher classes were only gradually gaining economic power and the freedom to engage in certain kinds of work, including journalism and secretarial activities. The dominant expectation was still that women whose families could support them would perform only unpaid domestic labor in the family home.⁴ During the war, however, many such women became involved in war work, like Benson, along with their working-class sisters. The exigencies of the war, during which England's male population was drastically reduced, drew women of all classes into a range of activities from which it was subsequently difficult to exclude them. Nevertheless, the nature and place of women remained a thorny issue.

Living Alone and *Flower Phantoms* are in many ways highly dissimilar, but both engage with the rapidly changing attitudes to working women in the post-war period. Benson's novel is full of incident. *Living Alone* deploys techniques we have since come to identify with magic realism, introducing into wartime London a witch who battles her German counterpart on a broomstick, and the dead mixing with the living in a church during an air raid. The narrative style is light and witty, offering ironic comments on social institutions and practices of the late 1910s, and highlighting the unsatisfactory nature of work—whether as traditionally gendered or as available to women through the conditions of the war—to women seeking emotional or intellectual fulfillment. *Flower Phantoms*, on the other hand, is a deeply serious and slow-moving novella that describes its protagonist's experiences poetically and uses fantasy as a narrative device to represent the intensity of her interior life. The surrounding characters—her family and fiancé—anxiously observe her detachment from emotional engagement in, and preparation for, marriage, which they see as her major social duty. Both novels involve forms of magic, in Benson's case explicitly so, but their treatment is different. Benson identifies magic, in effect, as that which escapes the customary: across the novel magic operates as art, transforming the everyday and allowing even the most apparently conventional of characters to access experiences and emotions they usually suppress. Fraser is more mystical, portraying his protagonist as engaging in dialog with sentient flowers—an experience she then herself transforms into artistic representation. What both novelists have in common is that they offer astute though diverging evaluations of contemporary work in England and the place of women—especially women of the middle classes, Virginia Woolf's "daughters of educated men"[5]—in work.

Stella Benson, born in 1892, joined the women's suffrage movement prior to the Great War. During the war, she assisted the war effort as a gardener, and also performed charity work in London's Charity Organisation Society, assisting poor women in the East End. The society was a conservative one, engaged in philanthropy for the deserving poor; her biographer Joy Grant notes that Benson was reprimanded for "dispensing what was disapprovingly termed 'promiscuous charity.'"[6] Its activities were typical of the kind of volunteer work that had been considered suitable for a woman of the upper and middle classes in Victorian times; the move of such women to land work, meanwhile, had been encouraged during the Great War, as there was a shortage of male agricultural workers.[7] Both of Benson's wartime activities make their way into her third novel, *Living Alone*, published in 1919. *Living Alone* opens, in fact, with a charitable committee meeting. The committee comprises six women, at least two of whom are (like Benson herself) from the upper classes, but, notably, is chaired by the only man, who is Mayor and a grocer, and to whom even the more aristocratic women somewhat reluctantly defer. Benson quickly sketches the work that had become one of the more acceptable activities for middle- and upper-class women from the late nineteenth century, and finds it wanting. She depicts the committee members as fixated on class position and formulaic responses, while the at-first-unnamed Sarah Brown, one of the novel's central characters, is seen doodling with boredom. Benson's narratorial comment inversely deploys the diction of turn-of-the-century warnings against vice: "Gay heedless young people set their unwary feet between the flowery borders of [the Charitable path], the thin air of resigned thanks breathed by the deserving poor mounts to their heads like wine; committees lie in wait for them on every side ... they run rejoicing to their doom."[8] To the narrator, whose views seem to align with Benson's, committee work itself is soul-destroying.

This mocking deprecation is supported by the action of the first chapter, in which the meeting is interrupted by the dramatic incursion of a young woman, a Stranger, who disrupts the committee's expectations completely. Although she admits to stealing a bun, calling down a reprimand for not working to earn her food, she declares that she had had a hundred pounds earlier that day; when rebuked for "squander[ing] all that money" instead of investing it in England's War Loan, she declares that she has indeed "squandered" it by spending it in just that way, indicating that she operates with a quite different set of values from those of the committee.[9] Thereafter, Benson's Stranger consistently undermines the committee's values, and, implicitly, the very nature of its work. The committee automatically require her name and address; the Stranger undercuts this classification of human beings through labels, especially labels implying a socio-geographic location, by offering several alternatives, none of which she identifies with. To her the formal name-and-address is a game of pleasant sounds, where to the committee it is a way of categorizing, and indeed mastering, the objects of its assistance. Similarly, the Stranger extols the pleasure of giving a gift that exceeds expectations—quite the opposite of the committee's practice, which clearly focuses on providing a carefully measured assistance to appropriately qualified recipients. In so doing, she supports the rejection of committee work more self-consciously voiced by the narrator.

No one quite knows how to deal either with the Stranger or with the magical experience she provides before departing; the narrator insists that committee experience has disabled the members' capacity to respond to and understand the extraordinary. As she explains, "The more committees you belong to, the less of ordinary life you can understand. When your daily life becomes nothing more than a daily round of committees you might as well be dead."[10] Benson's portrayal of charitable committees lacks the animus Dickens directs against his Mrs. Jellyby and Mrs. Pardiggle, who respectively neglect and constrain their children in order to carry out unwanted charitable projects.[11] Instead, Benson represents her committee members as fundamentally decent and well-meaning human beings who have become separated from what is best in their own lives and selves by the mechanical round of their social labors—a standard trope of modernist fiction. The intrusion of the Stranger, soon self-identified as a witch, begins a strange series of events that gradually transforms the lives of several members of the committee, not least the protagonist, Sarah Brown. It becomes clear that Benson's view of modernity is of a more disconnected world than Wordsworth's or even Dickens': interactions are random, and not just Sarah but most of the characters seem condemned, knowingly or not, to live alone, occasionally making gestures that signal the possibility of a warmer response to life. The social expectations of the worlds they inhabit, including their shared practice of committee work, have functioned to deaden and deny such responses.

Benson's condemnation of the effects of modern work is not confined to the conventional social and urban activities of this rather Victorian committee, but extends to forms of labor traditionally associated with other classes, which were also becoming a potential activity of the middle-class woman during the war. Later in the novel, Sarah Brown travels to the Parish of Faery to assist in war work there. Ill and tired, she loses pleasure in hoeing beans—especially when she accidentally digs up a fairy nest—and slows down: "'I can't hoe any more,' she said. 'There are twenty-five more beans, but I can't hoe them.' 'Why should you?' asked the nearest fairy indifferently. 'The foreman never notices if we shirk. We always do.'"[12] And indeed the dragon overseer approves Sarah's neat hoeing at the end of the day without noticing that she has failed to finish her task. Agricultural labor was for centuries essential to English prosperity and even survival, and the middle-class women who engaged in it in the war were encouraged to be proud of freeing up men to fight by "doing their bit."[13] In *Living Alone*, however, Benson critiques the actual practice of modern land work. The task is not glorified but remains an increasingly painful duty. There is no suggestion that the hoeing of beans is a productive activity that will assist in feeding people; the local "fairy" women are easily distracted, while Sarah herself and the dragon overseer seem more interested in, respectively, numbers and neatness than healthy beans.

Meanwhile, class division is still in operation. Although Sarah has journeyed hopefully to the Parish of Faery and her fellow workers—from their description clearly farm women—are labeled fairies, implying a potentially positive magical capacity, Sarah's hopes of connection and magical satisfaction are unfulfilled. She feels herself detached from the other workers; as the narrator wryly comments, she is "conscious of that touch of scorn always felt by the One towards the Herd,"[14] suggesting an isolation such as that sardonically glorified in Joyce's *A Portrait of the Artist as a Young Man* but in this case without any clear intellectual or aesthetic reward.[15] Instead the focus is on the painful labor itself as a solitary experience for the suffering Sarah. Despite the absence of mechanical aids to farming, Sarah's approach to it bears the earmarks of early factory work. Agricultural labor is seen here as arbitrary, productive of destruction (the fairy nest) and exhaustion, without any obvious fulfillment. Although Sarah's particular sufferings are personal, her fellow laborers' and the overseer's indifference to any actual outcome from their activities locates these as pointless, rather than productive.

Benson's critique of work in wartime England further extends beyond the jobs available to middle-class women to the work Sarah's land duties enabled: military action. For this Benson moves away from light parody of her own real-world activities to a fantastic depiction of aerial combat. In chapter 6, the witch engages in an air battle over London against a German witch—a dog-fight on broomsticks. The dog-fight itself is amusingly described, as Benson adds charming touches such as the German witch's use of a cloak as a parachute. But the replacement of airplanes with broomsticks has a more serious purpose: it allows Benson to depict a face-to-face encounter, including substantial dialog, between enemy fighters that would not have been possible in most of the combat situations produced in the new, technologically sophisticated fighting of the Great War. The German witch makes a clichéd speech about the vile practices of the enemy English, to which the English witch responds with a correction: "'This is really rather funny,' [the English witch] said. '... You've been reading the *Daily Mail* and misunderstanding it. The whole of that quotation applied to Germany, not England. It's Germany that's being naughty. You made a mistake, but never mind, I won't repeat it.'"[16] Benson points to the hollowness of standard war propaganda through the perceptions of the English witch, whose approach to all social matters is fresh and naïve. The witch notices absurdities. She is, nevertheless, engaged in a dog-fight—significantly, an activity from which English women were then and for long after debarred. Parodying male military adventure, Benson represents the encounter as one between clear perception and mechanical pomposity, rather than more conventionally as between good and evil. The witches' apparently inadvertent disclosure of the identical principles fighters of both sides have been called to defend suggests that the fight itself, with its slapstick action, is both mistaken and risible. Although the German witch does not appear to listen to the English one, the broomstick battle enables a recognition of mirrored misconceptions not available to actual fighters. Propaganda, Benson suggests, is the same on both sides, and has impelled men of both countries into activity that is in itself merely destructive—not instructive, as the German witch argues—while forcing women to replace them in the land work that is depicted in the following chapter as likewise futile.

Benson extends her implicit critique of this particular war to critique of the values involved in war itself, as the German witch insists on the need to "exterminate vermin in their lair" and attack the English home, while the English witch defends the home as a source of individual value: "It is at home that people are kindly ... Nobody is taught anything stupid or international at home. You can bring death to a home, but never a righteous scourge. Nobody feels scourged or instructed by a bomb in their parlour, they just feel dead, and dead without a reason."[17] By placing the fresh-visioned woman at the heart of the dog-fight, in place of the trained fighting man, Benson challenges the purpose of fighting itself. In Benson's vision, women undertaking the traditional female work of the committee are deadened by it; women taking on the socially sanctioned replacement of men as agricultural workers are exhausted and unproductive; and women imagined as replacing male fighters expose the activity of fighting as ultimately meaningless.

In *Living Alone*, the counterforces to the deadening nature of work in a fractured and besieged community are love, which Sarah glimpses fleetingly, and magic—the fantasy version of art itself. Before she leaves the committee room, the Stranger casts a spell from a bag labeled "magic" that makes the beauties of an English country April appear before the committee and evokes some quite surprising responses. Through the witch's magical revelation of April, the members of the committee are provoked to a range of emotions, as becomes gradually evident across the novel. Sarah Brown herself is moved to a diatribe against her own charitable work: "All habits, all habits ... Does Love make her voice heard through a committee, does Love employ an almoner to convey her message to her neighbour?"[18] Meanwhile the witch's own art is represented not as work but as a lack of encumbrance: intriguingly, Benson proposes that "witches and wizards ... are people who are born for the first time,"[19] refuting the idea of the artist as aged magus or old soul. It is the witch's direct and unfettered vision that enables her to assist others to see, and her own actions appear spontaneous rather than confined by habit, convention, or rule. But by depicting art as magic and its practitioner as spontaneous and whimsical, Benson removes art from the realm of modern work, which therefore remains unredeemed.

Benson's sketches of women at work fill out her portrayal of modernity as a space of disconnection containing random encounters and generally abortive activities. Sarah's attempts to form connections fail; the house of *Living Alone* is a house in which the inhabitants pursue their own activities outside the limits imposed by others' expectations, but also with little close engagement. Even Sarah's final charitable act, to take the witch to America to escape the Law, turns out to be a futile one: the witch immediately decides that America is antithetical to magic, and flies back to England, assuring Sarah that magic thrives on martyrdom and the wrath of the law. Magic, the force that drew the members of the committee to feel that their private feelings had been understood and responded to—in other words, art itself—cannot serve institutions, but must resist them. The witch's own brief engagement with war work—the dog-fight over London—has shown precisely her distance, and Benson's, from the values that have structured English work during the war. Charitable committee work, the traditional approved site of the conservative middle-class woman, is deadening; agricultural work, the new work of the land girls to which such women were being given access during the war, is exhausting and ultimately futile. Even fighting, still a male-only province, is seen as absurd. Magic, that mysterious activity practiced by the witch, sits outside of organized work altogether; its main function in the novel is to teach its recipients, especially Sarah Brown, just how alone they really are. In this it seems representative of modernist art itself, including Benson's own novel. The fantastic method of *Living Alone* can be seen as a representation of the witch's magical vision—a vision that sees directly into the absurdity and aimlessness even of apparently well-regulated modern work.

Both work and art are very differently portrayed in *Flower Phantoms*, third novel of the author Ronald Fraser. *Flower Phantoms*, first published in 1926, has been described by Brian Stableford in *The Encyclopedia of Fantasy* (1997) as a "magnificently bizarre botanical fantasia."[20] It focuses on a young woman called Judy, whose profession is never named. The introduction to the recent Valancourt edition calls her a "professional gardener," as she works in the various gardens and plant houses at Kew Gardens,[21] but it seems clear that she is rather a botanist, as the narrator notes that her brother Hubert controls the family income "apart from what she earned by scientific journalism."[22] Judy is evidently the daughter of an educated man; her father has left a house near Kew Gardens, a very prosperous neighborhood, and "a moderate annuity," and her Uncle Henry is "in charge of Kew Gardens."[23] As such, she represents that class of women who were just emerging from the domestic expectations of the previous century; it is significant that, though at work in Kew Gardens every day, she is apparently not paid to work there. For Fraser, unlike for Benson, it is women and the work they can do, not work itself, that requires interrogation. *Flower Phantoms* appears at first to present Judy as a test case: an attractive and well-brought-up young woman of good family engaging in a pursuit that combines intellectual with menial activity.

Much of the novel focuses on an apparent tension between Judy's work and her potential for marriage; significantly, almost all the action occurs either in the family home or in Kew Gardens, which is represented not as a public space but as a site for individual scholarly study. Where Benson's Sarah is only tangentially connected to the social world and engages with increasing dissatisfaction in the work available to her, Judy is firmly located within the class and gender expectations of her family even as she absorbs herself in her chosen field, and it is the extent to which she can fulfill their expectations while remaining thus absorbed that is in question. Pursued by a young scholar of literature, she quickly becomes engaged to him. Their relationship, however, consists of her responding uncertainly but often skeptically to his adoration. Strikingly anticipating Woolf's *Orlando* by two years, Fraser's Roland praises his epicene beloved in chains of extravagant metaphor:

> "You look like some golden boy," he said. "Your hair . . . is cut in such a way that it seems to be a cap of gold, or helmet of saffron fire. . . . [The] eyes stare out under the shining hat like those of a cynical page in some wintry and Russian court."[24]

Judy at first finds it interesting to be described, but when she dislikes Roland's images she directly critiques them and responds with a derogatory image of her own. Judy's responses not only astonish her lover's soul, but annoy him.[25] This is a woman speaking back, where Orlando's sixteenth-century Sasha will fail to speak back in words and respond only indirectly to her adorer's very similar images.[26] Where Benson's witch simply bypassed the committee's conventional understanding of the behavior and dialog to be expected in its offices, highlighting its limits through her uncaring and even unwitting transgression of them, Fraser's Judy exercises her critical intelligence to speak metaphors, not just to hear them, and this is initially destructive of her relationship with Roland. Although we are told that she desires to feel desire, her mind distracts her, and apparently repels her lover. As predicted by many Victorian and early twentieth-century anti-feminists, exercising her intelligence appears to unfit Judy for heterosexual marriage.[27]

As the novel progresses, however, Judy finds her passions aroused by other elements in her life. It turns out that her relationship with the plants she studies is not after all a wholly professional or intellectual one; she begins to sense presences within the plant houses. This fantasy element in the novel, the flower phantoms themselves, is strongly implied to be Judy's own fantasy. She is clearly aware, for instance, that "for [Roland] there was no voice in the silence; there were no eyes among the plants,"[28] and that recognition quenches any hope that he might share her state of mind; later, she realizes "that she herself had created [the] curious experience" of conversation with a cactus.[29] Increasingly, however, the narrative endorses her experience of conversations with the flowers, removing such framing moments and presenting the experience as real. Fraser adopts the modernist focus on the individual consciousness to represent Judy's interior life, like Woolf with Septimus Warren Smith in *Mrs. Dalloway* two years before.[30] The reader is thus drawn into a world that depends on the senses with which women had been for so long associated; yet rationality is still part of the experience, as it is in the dialog imagined by Joyce's Stephen Dedalus in the "Proteus" episode of *Ulysses*.[31] Judy's conversations with plants are philosophical as well as sensual; she is chilled by the philosophy of the Water Lily, and respectful of that of the Sacred Fig. As her passion increases she comes increasingly to dream of and seek out the exotic Orchid, who is figured as a seductive Eastern prince. Yet her scientific attitude is still at work here, and she shocks herself by her sudden thought "Oh, how wonderful it would be to dissect an orchid! To cut one's lover open and slit him up, and separate him part from part . . . ! How would a flower like to dissect a woman?"[32] Science and sexuality seem entwined in this woman, and each seems to destabilize the other. Similarly, Judy's move from the apparently scientific image of dissecting a plant (or plant/lover) to speculation about how a flower might feel if given the corresponding opportunity is narratively disturbing in its startling invitation to an empathic shift.

When Judy touches the real orchid, her experience is highly erotic: "Gently she touched the flower with her fingers and ventured a little pinch, and threads of flame ran through her nerves from his body of white fire."[33] The description evokes post-Freudian associations of genitals with flowers: the passage, and indeed much of Judy's experience, could be read as a thinly veiled metaphor for the discovery of the delights of masturbation. This was, after all, also a time when sexuality, especially female sexuality, was being explored and examined more overtly than before the war. Judy's scientific work seems here to be represented as sublimation of, or perverted expression of, her sexual nature as a woman. Yet even when she escapes from her home in the night to go to the plant houses—subsequently earning her conventional family's suspicion that she is meeting some unsuitable lover—she does not choose visionary union with the phantom orchid as fulfillment. The seeming story of oddly sublimated sexual desire again takes a twist: Judy requires her plant lover to take her to the Buddha, and when before him wishes that she may "be a flower for a little while, so that I might know them, as surely you know them."[34] Fraser then provides an extensive vision of plant life—sensory, illuminated by light. The representation of botany as a professional, scholarly activity has vanished under the pressure of Judy's sexualized but still spiritual yearnings. Her work is here transformed into an intense identification with the imagined life of the flowers.

The last section of the novel appears to underline the conflicts between sensuality and intellect, work and domesticity, that Judy's passion for her flowers has demonstrated. Her lover, her brother, and especially her mother, are variously dismayed and appalled at her behavior in escaping to the Gardens at night. Judy nevertheless affirms that she will marry Roland; the story appears to be heading for a resolution that will locate her plant passion as an adolescent experience to be matured from, preparing her for an ordinary heterosexual marriage. Again, however, Fraser surprises his readers. Left alone to digest her experiences, Judy becomes an artist: "She had no need of the Gardens, she perceived, for she herself, a flower, was the creator of flowers. They claimed life of her mind."[35] She paints and draws, "watching the curious and individual ways of her genius ... in a rage to finish, intolerant of impediments, fierce for her children."[36] This is a vision of art as work that encompasses mind and body, Judy's intellectual study of plants and her physical and emotional passion for them, and figures that as the traditionally maternal labor of the artistic creator.

Fraser concludes the passage with the statement that "Her body died. She floated like a nebula high among stars, and had ineffable pleasures."[37] But Judy's body has not in fact died; rather, it has been translated into the life of her mind, and both survive the intensity of her visionary experience.[38] When she emerges from her absorption in her artwork, Judy discovers that the financially shrewd and ruthlessly pragmatic Hubert, whose commercial values she has despised, has been expecting all along that her peculiar behavior would end by producing something financially valuable. Judy's art is not denied but affirmed, as Hubert identifies her as a client and negotiates for a commission to promote her artwork. Her role as a contributor to the commercial world, as opposed to the domestic, is after all endorsed.

"You don't mind my being a little mad, now?" she inquired.
"Nothing is mad that results in financial advantage."
"But what do you say, now, about my being economically independent?"
"You're not economically independent. You're dependent on me."
"I really feel," she admitted, "that part of my success will be due to you."[39]

The revelation that Hubert has suspected her artistic abilities and connived to give her freedom is both belated and somewhat implausible. Hubert's main gift to Judy, prior to his offer to market her art, has in fact been the sort of benign neglect common at the period to many fathers, brothers, and husbands who took their women's happiness for granted. Fraser's apparent endorsement of Hubert as the superior male who can perceive his sister's true desires and capacities while she herself struggles with them coheres with his often-idealizing depiction of women as intuitive beings rather than, or at least more importantly than, intellectual equals to men.[40]

Nevertheless, Fraser affirms that Judy's mind and passions have joined to produce art; although she determines to marry Roland, she does so now in the knowledge that he recognizes and salutes her abilities: "You are a poet and artist. Reality, call it what you like, looks out of these flowers."[41] Their relationship is no longer that of Astrophil and Stella, poetically eloquent adorer and object of adoration; Roland, whose literary phrases have so failed to move Judy, acknowledges that his study of literature "has at any rate given [him] understanding"[42] of what she has achieved, thus freeing her to acknowledge both love and physical desire for him. In a reversal of traditional accounts of the male artist genius supported by his adoring wife, Fraser represents Judy as the creator, Hubert and Roland respectively as enabler and admirer.

Fraser's novel thus tests and challenges post-war debates about the nature of women and their relationship to work. Judy's extraordinary merging of intellectual and physical passions in her botanical study turns out not to disable her capacity for heterosexual marriage. Instead she achieves a new status as artist, even genius, whose scholarly attention to her objects of study enables the expression of talents that complement and are supported by those of her hard-headed brother. Such a complementarity was advocated by 1920s theorists of sex-difference such as Arabella Kenealy, and it is noteworthy that Fraser does not conclude with a portrait of Judy as scientist. However, his final depiction of Roland as supporting and admiring her artwork, rather than the converse, suggests a belief in women's capacities that goes beyond most such writing. *Flower Phantoms* enchants by its vision of a transformed eroticism, as well as of the sensorially informed spirituality that is a persistent theme in Fraser's writing, but it also offers a serious statement about the capacities of women to work and to create art at a time when these capacities remained subject to debate and doubt.[43]

Both Fraser and Benson depict women's work during and in the aftermath of the First World War as a troubled space. For Benson, the work available to middle-class women, whether the traditionally sanctioned work of a charitable committee or the newly permissible activity of agricultural work, is ultimately soul-destroying and unfulfilling, while imagined female engagement in the traditionally masculine task of fighting merely reveals the absurdity of such conflict. Benson depicts the experience of contemporary modernity as one of social disconnection, and her characters' experiences of work emphasize the futility of their labors. Fraser's focus on Judy's consciousness, by contrast, depicts Judy's scholarly work both as absorbing in itself and as preparing her for an artistic role—thus, incidentally, fusing science and art, often thought to be irreconcilable. His portrait of the artist emphasizes not only female interiority but also female passion, and effectively demonstrates how exercise of intelligence by a woman can have positive results for society as well as for her domestic relationships. While Benson represents work as disabling or even irrelevant to women, Fraser depicts Judy's botanical studies as intrinsically connected to her fulfillment as a woman, an artist, and a human being.

It is significant that in both novels fantasy becomes the agent for revelation: Judy's visions prepare for her artistic creation, while the witch's magic liberates those caught in the deadening routine of charitable work and enables a fresh and critical perspective on human relationships within the modern world. These novels, like much of the fantasy writing of the period, attracted attention in their day but have been comparatively little studied. Yet both *Living Alone* and *Flower Phantoms* demonstrate the capacity of fantasy to illuminate experiences and concerns in the real world. The imagined incursion into a wartime committee room of a witch unconstrained by the expectations of the time allows Benson to reflect ironically on the destructive nature of those conventions and the hollowness of modern labor, especially for women. Fraser's portrayal of Judy as engaged in a series of sexual and spiritual encounters with flowers similarly undercuts modern expectations of the well-brought-up young woman, and extends debates about the nature of women and their relationship to work. Both novelists disrupt conventional understandings not only of female roles but of narrative—Benson through her sketches of a fantasy London overlaid with magical encounters, Fraser through his vivid representation of Judy's intensely imagined experiences as reality. In so doing they register English society during and after the war as the site of a re-evaluation of both work itself, and women's relationship to it, in which only art retains transformative power.

Notes

1 Brian Attebery has demonstrated the use of mythic method in the period by fantasy writers, not just recognized modernist authors, in *Stories about Stories: Fantasy and the Remaking of Myth* (Oxford: Oxford University Press, 2014).
2 See E. R. Eddison, *The Worm Ouroboros* (1922; New York: Ballantine Books, 1967); Lord Dunsany, *The King of Elfland's Daughter* (1924; New York: Ballantine Books, 1969); Hope Mirrlees, *Lud-in-the-Mist* (1926; London: Ballantine Books, 1972).

3 See Farah Mendlesohn, *Rhetorics of Fantasy* (Middletown, CT: Wesleyan, 2008); David Lindsay, *The Haunted Woman* (1922; N.p.: Positronic Publishing, 2013); David Garnett, *Lady into Fox*, in *Lady into Fox and A Man in the Zoo* (1922; London: Hogarth Press, 1985), 1–91.
4 Gender roles had become more distinct in the nineteenth century, with increasing emphasis on the role of woman as nurturer. "The home became the middle-class man's retreat from the world of business and competition, and the wife who presided over this retreat was not to be sullied by paid work herself. Domestic work was also unsuitable." Gail Braybon, *Women Workers in the First World War* (1981; New York: Taylor & Francis, 2012), 18.
5 Virginia Woolf, *Three Guineas*, in *A Room of One's Own and Three Guineas* (1938; Oxford: Oxford World's Classics, 1992), 155.
6 Joy Grant, *Stella Benson: A Biography* (London: Macmillan, 1987), 62.
7 In 1915 the Permanent Secretary of the British Board of Agriculture wrote to the County War Agricultural Committees recommending the recruitment of women for agricultural work, and in 1917 a Women's Land Army, with its own uniform, was established. See Bonnie White, *The Women's Land Army in First World War Britain* (London: Palgrave, 2014).
8 Stella Benson, *Living Alone* (1919; Sioux Falls, SD: NuVision Publications, 2008), 9.
9 Benson, *Living Alone*, 10.
10 Benson, *Living Alone*, 10.
11 See Charles Dickens, *Bleak House* (1851; London: Bradbury and Evans, 1853), especially 25–32 and 71–5.
12 Benson, *Living Alone*, 77.
13 White, *Women's Land Army*, 56. White further notes that "The press presented [Land Girls who died in the course of their duties] as brave and enduring ... Their work contributed to Britain's war effort and in the end would be justified by Britain's victory," *Women's Land Army*, 74.
14 Benson, *Living Alone*, 75.
15 James Joyce, *A Portrait of the Artist as a Young Man* (1914; London: Penguin Books, 1992).
16 Benson, *Living Alone*, 62–3.
17 Benson, *Living Alone*, 64.
18 Benson, *Living Alone*, 44.
19 Benson, *Living Alone*, 19.
20 Brian Stableford, "Fraser, [Sir] Ronald," *The Encyclopedia of Fantasy*, ed. John Clute and John Grant (1997), at *The Encyclopedia of Science Fiction*, http://sf-encyclopedia.uk/fe.php?nm=fraser_ronald
21 Mark Valentine, Introduction to *Flower Phantoms*, by Ronald Fraser (Kansas City, MO: Valancourt Books, 2013), v.
22 Ronald Fraser, *Flower Phantoms* (1926; Kansas City, MO: Valancourt Books, 2013), 3.
23 Fraser, *Flower Phantoms*, 3.
24 Fraser, *Flower Phantoms*, 5.
25 Fraser, *Flower Phantoms*, 5.
26 Virginia Woolf, *Orlando: A Biography* (1928; Oxford: Oxford World's Classics, 1992).
27 See for example Arabella Kenealy, "The woman of average brain ... attains the intellectual standards of a man of average brain only at the cost of her health, of her

emotions, or of her morale." Arabella Kenealy, *Feminism and Sex-Extinction* (London: T. Fisher Unwin, 1920; Project Gutenberg, http://www.gutenberg.org/files/37964/37964-h/37964-h.htm), 155.
28 Fraser, *Flower Phantoms*, 18.
29 Fraser, *Flower Phantoms*, 26.
30 Virginia Woolf, *Mrs Dalloway* (1925; New York and London: Harcourt Brace Jovanovich, 1953).
31 James Joyce, *Ulysses* (1922; New York: Vintage, 1961).
32 Fraser, *Flower Phantoms*, 50.
33 Fraser, *Flower Phantoms*, 51.
34 Fraser, *Flower Phantoms*, 66.
35 Fraser, *Flower Phantoms*, 74.
36 Fraser, *Flower Phantoms*, 75.
37 Fraser, *Flower Phantoms*, 74.
38 Judy's experience of "floating like a nebula" recalls Kenealy's account of how the Woman-brain can oscillate between the extremes of hysteria and catalepsy "in which she exists detached from earth and its material needs and consciousness ... withdrawn into the Inner, and potential, zones of Life and Mind," Kenealy, *Feminism and Sex-Extinction,* 157.
39 Fraser, *Flower Phantoms*, 77.
40 See for example Fraser's portrait of Lychnis in *Landscape with Figures* (London: T. Fisher Unwin, 1925).
41 Fraser, *Flower Phantoms*, 78.
42 Fraser, *Flower Phantoms*, 78.
43 See Woolf's depiction of Lily Briscoe, assailed pre-war by Charles Tansley's dismissive "Women can't paint, women can't write," in *To the Lighthouse* (1927; New York: Harcourt Brace Jovanovich, 1981), 48, published a year after *Flower Phantoms*, and the narrator's concern with similar dismissals in contemporary newspapers in *A Room of One's Own* (in *A Room of One's Own and Three Guineas* [1929; Oxford: Oxford World's Classics, 1992], 1–149).

Chapter 9

THE DISCLOSURE OF WORK IN THE POETRY OF RON SILLIMAN

Christopher Oakey

The Language poet Ron Silliman begins his autobiographical poem "Albany" (1980) with a fragment that reads "If the function of writing is to 'express the world.'"[1] The possibility that the "function of writing" lies somehow in "express[ing] the world" leads Silliman to his childhood in the San Francisco Bay Area, and to related glimpses into his adult life:

> My father withheld child support, forcing my mother to live with her parents, my brother and I to be raised together in a small room. Grandfather called them niggers. I can't afford an automobile. Far across the calm bay stood a complex of long yellow buildings, a prison.[2]

"If the function of writing is to 'express the world,'" it is a very personal sort of "world" that initially emerges. The cruelty of Silliman's father, and the effects this had on Silliman and his brother, are followed by an image of the preceding generation and the racist terms wielded by his grandfather. Silliman tries to resist the forms of cruelty modeled by his father and grandfather by attending to them poetically and thus rendering them manageable as objects of self-understanding. If reference makes the past an object for critique, however, the effects do not vanish. His mother's poverty persists in his present inability to "afford an automobile," which is symbolically reflected through the darkened glass of the prison that lies "across the calm bay."[3] The prison is a metonym for the forms of racial tension and poverty that Silliman's grandfather also embodies. It also symbolizes the family unit, closed off, confining, but inseparable from its historical and geographic identity.

Behind each of these elements lies a culture of poverty and violence bound to particular forms of work. Though this is less apparent at the start of "Albany," when Silliman returns to his poem decades later in his prose autobiography, *Under Albany*, the importance of work to its meanings and its form is stark.[4] Factory culture in particular, he reveals, had a profound impact on his family and his life growing up. "I do not recall," Silliman writes, "a time in which I was not the absolutely poorest kid in my class."[5] He remembers again his grandfather, who was

> first-line management all the years I was growing up, a foreman in the newspaper pulping operation.... Although we drove right past the plant every time we took 80 through Emeryville ... he never took either my brother or I to the job.[6]

Silliman's grandfather was the breadwinner of the family in which Silliman and his brother, Cliff, were raised.[7] In all of his years of working at the newspaper pulping plant, Silliman writes, "I never once heard him speak of his work with satisfaction or pleasure."[8] "Albany" begins, therefore, by turning not only towards Silliman's childhood in the town of Albany, but even more specifically to a symbolically prison-like relationship with a guardian who was himself bound to a culture of factory work and working poverty.

It is in light of this that we can say that Silliman's postmodern poetry continues, extends, and alters the modernist concern with industrial modernity in light of a postmodern reconfiguration of work and its presentation in poetry. In "Albany," Silliman's concern is explicitly a factory culture, and one shaped by the forms of work that were central to modernity and which were troubled by modernist literature. In other places, however, the modernist relation of the individual to cultures of work boils over into a postmodern interrogation of the culture of work, disconnected from the sorts of modernist narratives of the individual that would give it even the dark glamour of individualized alienation. Both in the autobiographical "Albany" and elsewhere, moreover, the connection between work, cruelty or violence, and forms of entrapment runs throughout Silliman's oeuvre in ways that bring the personal experience of *a* world, such as that which launches the autobiographical "Albany," into contact with *the* world as experienced by and as the culture at large.

This essay offers a new approach to Silliman's work in light of these concerns. I argue that the forms of work that Silliman addresses in his poetry are of just this type: limiting and marginalizing frames that either directly or indirectly install the conditions of physical or psychological violence around individuals. As part of this, I argue that work has a special place in Silliman's poetry because it joins two of his key thematic concerns. These are a concern with the social system currently in place—including the way of life that emerges for individuals out of its social conditions—and the particular, autobiographical life experienced by an individual within that culture. These forms of life are approached, by Silliman himself, through the term "Actual life."

Autobiography and portraiture

In the group autobiography, *The Grand Piano*, Silliman writes that:

> Actual life—or maybe as my old comrades in the anti-Stalinist left would have put it, "actually existing life"—is, after all, what it's all about. The mind/body problem doesn't exist without breath, without dance, sex, digestion, anxiety, colonoscopies, smelling flowers, blinking, drinking OJ straight from the container, scrunching your nose, stumbling over small objects, you name it. My interest in what others call Language poetry has always been because of the access this writing gives me, as poet & reader, to all the world that is the case. That is my focus of attention.[9]

Actual life, as Silliman uses the term here, reaches both towards the personal and towards the social. The examples he uses are distinctly bodily, sustaining bodily life and expressing its drives. At the same time, these drives towards sustenance, sex, fun, etc., tie the individual into social relationships in which things like sex and drinking OJ are conceptually and economically embedded.

The list that Silliman builds in his description of "actual life" also models the challenge of his "new sentence" parataxis.[10] Which is to say that the fact that we can understand his list of bodily actions as "actual" relies on our being able to decode the contexts in which they are meaningful. Christopher Nealon notes this when he writes that the Language poets' forms reflect a larger response to capital.[11] He writes that when Silliman "describes [Jack] Spicer admiringly as 'flooding the text with a surfeit of incommensurable meanings'" he is offering a phrase that "is particularly illuminating as a self-description of Language writing practice, not least the working of the 'new sentence.'"[12] Such a flood, Nealon argues, offered Silliman "a formal means" by which to "meet the encroachments of mass culture and its attendant forms of political control."[13] If one can comfortably inhabit the troubling juxtapositions of violence, domesticity and geography at work in the beginning sentences of "Albany," for instance, it must mean that one is already too literate in those forms of violent relation and in the linguistic milieu in which the violence also exists and is reproduced.

In her reading of "Albany," Marjorie Perloff argues that if Silliman's characteristic new-sentence parataxis resists attempts to project a coherent lyric subject at the center of the poem, there is nonetheless something authorial and autobiographical at work.[14] Perloff emphasizes the term "autobiography" in order to reclaim a notion of representation as a frame for understanding Silliman's poetry. To this end she quotes Silliman himself from their private correspondence:

> In a letter to me (10 January 1998), Silliman comments, "... The whole premise of <u>Albany</u> (or at least a premise) was to focus on things that were both personal and political, so when Gale called it seemed like the right place to begin. *That poem always has been my autobiography, so to speak*"[.][15]

Autobiography is a provocative term to bring into contact with a poetry as ideologically opposed to representation as Silliman's. The sentences in "Albany" clearly do refer to and, to some extent, represent aspects of Silliman's childhood in Albany, California. At the same time, however, the later addition of Silliman's prose autobiography, *Under* Albany, reveals a significant difference in what is accomplished in the prose and poetic autobiographies. The sentences in the poetic autobiography do not run together or accumulate into a narrative account of Silliman's childhood, nor into a unified scenic representation of the conditions of Silliman's upbringing. It is only in the later prose autobiography, also, that his grandfather is represented within hypotactic prose structures and thus accrues something that we might call "character."

For Perloff, "Albany" is autobiographical to the extent that it presents a language tied to both a geographical area and to Silliman's history within it. Bob Perelman, however, describes the effect of Silliman's writing differently, as a kind of mass portraiture (as opposed to Perloff's argument regarding self-portraiture) where individuals and things are referenced, but where none is singled out for "novelistic" forms of attention.[16] It represents collective existence by means of a cumulative succession of glances. This assessment both loosens the grip of the personal over the poem and allows Silliman a greater degree of artistic control. Where, for Perloff, Silliman's world is "the world as I found it," for Perelman it is also especially the world as Silliman chooses to arrange and present it.[17] In fact, these positions are relatively close to each other. Sitting as they do at the intersection of the private and the public, Silliman's poems look both inward to the personal and outward to the socio-cultural, often within the same (new-)sentences. Rather than use hypotactic structures of representation, the poem "Albany" radiates outwards from the autobiographical impulse, presenting a formal disclosure of the moment in which Silliman's childhood took place, bound both to private autobiographical experience (a life) and shared cultural forms (a way of life). In looking back to Silliman's childhood, "Albany" therefore turns a postmodern form of poetic attention upon the social forms and social consequences of modern work.

In order to further interrogate this process, I take guidance from the philosophy of Martin Heidegger. In Heidegger's essay, "What are Poets For?," the realities of economic and cultural modernity are provocatively tied to a "danger" located in the essence of technology and technological production— what Heidegger calls the "Americanism" of the modern age. Heidegger's concept offers a way of interpreting the forms of work presented in Silliman's poetry. In what follows, I look briefly at what it means to perform a Heideggerian reading of Silliman's poetry. I then examine how Silliman's poetry uses new-sentence parataxis to disclose the forms of violence, anonymity, and de-personalization at work in work in the Enframed culture his poetry addresses, before returning to "Albany." As we will see, the poem's autobiographical perspective leads to a disclosure of the intimate connection between violence and dailiness in the culture of the town.

The Heideggerian project

In essays from the 1960s and 1970s, the Language poets argued for breaking away from the historical progression of capitalism by articulating an end-point to its self-propelling and consciousness-forming logic. In "Disappearance of the Word, Appearance of the World," Silliman writes that the process through which words "*become* commodities" leads to language being taken as a conduit to reality, wherein its material features are erased in favor of representative, referential realism.[18] Language is simultaneously effaced and fetishized. After this, "Freed from recognition of the signifier and buffered against any response from an increasingly passive consumer," Silliman writes, "the supermarket novelist's language has become fully subservient to a process that would lie outside of syntax: plot."[19] This argument takes fictional realism as not just a literary genre but an ideology of language—one, moreover, that creates "[a] world whose inevitability invites acquiescence; capitalism passes on its preferred reality through language itself to individual speakers."[20] For Silliman, this means that realist or even representational writing (prose mimesis and poetic self-expression) is both an outcome and reinforcement of the broader cultural conditions and relations for which contemporary American capitalist culture might be criticized. Therefore, a self-conscious poetics—what Silliman refers to as a "gestural" poetics—might for him free language use from capitalism's control over the means of representation.[21]

Steve McCaffery has used Language writing's connection between poetic and economic form to argue for a connection between Language poetry and "the Heideggerian project."[22] Language poetry aims to disentangle language, by means of immanent critique, from the control it wields over one's relation to the world. This marks Language poetry out as a continuation of one of Heidegger's key aims: to free thinking from the relation to being dictated by a language gone "out of tune."[23] Implicit in this understanding is therefore the argument that the postmodern characteristics of Language poetry represent a continuation of preoccupations of European and Anglo-American modernism. Postmodernism, in its configuration as Language writing, erupts into the scene of modernist alienation by self-consciously reconfiguring the relation between the individual and the social being of the sign.

Although I draw this parallel between Heidegger's philosophy and the strategies of Language poetry, it is important to recognize that the affinity this implies is a complicated one—and not only because of their respective political leanings. The energies of Language poetry's grammatical, syntactical, and formal interventions aim at a destabilizing critique of the ideology embodied within, produced by, and producing the means of production: capitalism. For Heidegger, the effect is almost entirely opposite. Poetry for Heidegger aims at re-grounding human being within being as a whole. The poetry Heidegger turns to is typically lyric, and is turned to for its insights into being more than for acts of formal destabilization. This is in addition to the fact that, in his essays on the work of art, Heidegger ties poetry's re-grounding of language to ideas of nation redolent of his Nazism.[24] In short, where Heidegger's notion of the poem recalls the founding of political states, the Language poetry notion enacts post-structuralist critiques of the ideologies and economic relations upon which states are built, and these poets and their works are clearly suspicious of the sorts of linguistic and political unity that Heidegger desired.

If Language poetry continues "the Heideggerian project," therefore, it is not at the level of poetry's political outcomes or a return to the values indicated in Heidegger's diagnosis of the modern. Any continuation must, rather, rest on two points of contact between the thinking and work of the Language poets, particularly Silliman's, and Heidegger's philosophy. First is that both diagnose modernity with a similar set of problems located especially strongly in the domain of work, even if their approaches and solutions are radically different. Second, for both, poetic creation is capable of breaking the human relation to the world away from the inherited forms of production, encounter, and re-production that underlie modernity and, for Silliman, even the literary critiques of his modernist predecessors.

Heidegger, Enframing, and the work of art

In the essay "What Are Poets For?," Heidegger writes that the ground [*Grund*] of our human being is absent; it fails to appear for us, such that we stand over an abyss [*Abgrund*], disconnected from the sorts of relational belonging that characterize authentic being.[25] When Heidegger turns to Rilke's poetry for what it says of this destitution, he finds that it has its essence within the modern relationship to production, producibility, and measure. This is a destitution in man's relationship to the world and to the beings that compose it. This connection between ontological destitution and modes of production is made even more explicitly in *The Question Concerning Technology*. There, the crisis of humanity's experience of the world is part of a larger process Heidegger calls "Enframing" [*Gestell*]—a relation to being that frames everything off and predetermines meanings prior to any encounter between a person and any particular thing.[26] The essence of technology, he argues, lies in the production of a calculated, and calculable, uniformity of being, in which all beings are made part of a "standing reserve" [*Bystand*] in relation to processes of production.[27] It converts beings, including human being, and even "[t]he earth and its atmosphere" into "raw material . . . for self-assertive production" and makes this the sole register of their worldly legibility.[28] What Heidegger finds troubling thus moves toward the long history of critiques of capitalism. Indeed, like Marx, Heidegger finds work to be an issue not in itself, but in its historical configuration within modernity. Technologized production in particular forces one's being to take on technology's rhythms, rather than allowing the worker to dwell within his or her own.[29]

In this context, art takes on a special function. Heidegger argues that the artwork is the founding of the truth of being.[30] The poem founds truth by setting into itself the dynamic motions of world and earth. One of Heidegger's most famous examples is the ancient temple at Paestum. He writes that

> It is the temple-work that first fits together and at the same time gathers around itself the unity of those paths and relations in which birth and death, disaster and blessing, victory and disgrace, endurance and decline acquire the shape of destiny for human being. The all-governing expanse of this open relational context is the world of this historical people.[31]

The work gathers a unity that is "the world." This "world" is the historical and shared ontological unity of a people—their affects, aims, desires, decisions, etc.—historically borne along in the open of the *logos* (that people's linguistic milieu). At the same time, Heidegger writes, in an artwork the "earth" of which it is composed does not "disappear," as it does in other configurations of earth and world, but rather "come[s] forth for the first time ... into the Open of the work's world."[32]

The "truth" of poetry's disclosure of the world is thus formal for Heidegger as much as it is thematic; it is borne into presence through the formal means by which it brings the world into meaningful and legible presence. This is what we might call the "work" of the work of art: the appearing of world within the materiality of the artwork. In a destitute era, however, the work of the work of art takes on a new urgency, in which some must make this destitution present in the experience of the word, to make the danger at the heart of modernity available for thinking. Art is able to do this because, for Heidegger, it is neither mimetic in nature nor entirely divorced from the world. Rather, it discloses both the world *in which* it is created and the material *of which* it is created. In disclosing, it lies prior to mimesis, not re-presenting but primordially presenting earth and world, meaning and materiality, for encounter within our world.

Continuity and discontinuity

Heidegger's notions of Enframing and the work of the poem in relation to it together help us to consider how Silliman's poems approach ideas of work. In his essay on the new sentence, Silliman writes that the type of parataxis then emergent in the poetry of the American West Coast was characterized by organization around the secondary logic of formal relation rather than the primary, syllogistic logic of representational, hypotactic prose.[33] As Perelman makes clear, the effects of this change in the composition of sentence-to-sentence relations has subsequent effects on meaning: "New sentences imply continuity and discontinuity simultaneously," he writes, "in an effect that becomes clearer when they are read over longer stretches."[34] Some of the continuities that Perelman speaks of are formal. Others are conceptual, however, such as the strained unities of family and geography noted in "Albany." Indeed, it is helpful to look again at the poem's beginning sentences:

> If the function of writing is to "express the world." My father withheld child support, forcing my mother to live with her parents, my brother and I to be raised together in a small room. Grandfather called them niggers. I can't afford an automobile. Far across the calm bay stood a complex of long yellow buildings, a prison.[35]

The sentences articulate, in their strained relation, the strained familial relations of Silliman's childhood. This effect is itself perhaps simply a product of proximity and the social currency of words and roles like "father," "mother," and "Grandfather." Geography works similarly. Not only are prison and home thematically and ironically juxtaposed, but the simultaneous continuity and discontinuity of their sentence-to-sentence relation emphasizes a comparable form of geographic relation. The prison is intimately inside the everyday experience of the area: a kind of circle marking out a special and separate district. It is similar also to the home: open to the world and, at the same time, oppressively closed off.

Even in this brief excerpt from the opening of "Albany" it is clear that paratactic discontinuity is key to Silliman's disclosures because it allows for a non-scenic mode of relational co-ordination. Perelman suggests a similar role for parataxis in his reading of the poem "Ketjak":

> In the following juxtapositions—"Fountains of the financial district spout soft water in a hard wind. She was a unit in a bum space, she was a damaged child" (3)—we have switched subjects between sentences: the child and the fountains need not be imagined in a single tableau. This effect of calling forth a new context after each period goes directly against the structural impatience that creates narrative. It's as if a film were cut into separate frames. But in a larger sense, girl and fountain are in the same social space. Throughout the book, Silliman insists on such connections as the one between the girl and the wider economic realities implied by the corporate fountains. The damage that has been done to her has to be read in a larger economic context.[36]

While in "Ketjak" the autobiographical has been replaced by a broader cultural perspective, the problems of work remain prominent. The "financial district" exists as a space where the "she" whom the poem names is excluded from participating in its form of white-collar work. Perelman's reference to "frames" is significant. Parataxis produces "separate frames," but their narrative separation is unified by a larger "social frame" that renders their diegetic discontinuity legible as a form of—usually invisible but still problematic—social continuity. Parataxis, it seems, is equipped to "insist" on connections between objects within a social and economic context precisely because it is not limited by structures traditional to hypotactic realism.[37] In Perelman's example the social continuity between girl, fountains, and financial district is important precisely because it is at odds with their scenic discontinuity.

Apprehension of the socio-economic problem of the proximity of the "bum space" and "financial district" frames is dependent on the capacity of new-sentence parataxis to disclose it. This is done in deliberate opposition to the habitual invisibility of the relationship between these socio-economic entities produced by their scenic discontinuity. Moreover, the use of the sentence as a material frame works to disclose also the sort of Enframing that takes place through hypotaxis. As Silliman's argument goes, hypotaxis reifies the relations that it represents; it presupposes, as natural and inevitable, the form of relation and understanding that one can have with a particular thing. In opposition, the new sentence makes the material frame of the sentence emphatically present for attention as a meaning-making unit, and at the expense of the Enframing work conducted by hypotactic frames.

The visibility that Silliman's parataxis gives to the sentence as a unit is also key to the meanings that it gives to the forms of work the sentences reference. In the above juxtaposition of "bum space" and "financial district" in "Ketjak," work is a problem because it represents a form of economic inequality central to capitalism. The bum space exists because some people are excluded from the forms of work found in spaces like financial districts, and which bubble over, in the public sphere, both in the form of fountains and in the forms of an economically marginalized population.

In the book-length *Tjanting* (1981), however, work is an issue in a different way. It includes a degree of violence that is oddly effaced as it is disclosed; or, I should say, it is normalized in a way that again becomes uncomfortable over long stretches. Take the following excerpt:

> These hotels were built quickly after the earthquake in order to house tourists coming to the Panama Pacific Exposition, 1915, old brick, unreinforced concrete. Flat old brown cat chooses to sit atop paper bag. Mooch City. Fine blahs since pharmaceutical blah. Sitting in a hot cloud of MSG. Someone to clean up mouse noun puke, cat filth, utter verb parts. No one is watching the tortillas. Tobacco smell of his skull burned right into his shirt, hair & eyes. For a living she stands naked on a turntable carpeted lavender, while men in small latched booths deposit quarters for windows to gawk thru, to the sound of course of disco music.[38]

Though paratactic the sentences are unified by the concept of alienation and economic compulsion, for which the hotels for tourists are both symptom and symbol. They are not dwellings but spaces for housing people: a resource both alienated from authentic dwelling within the city and themselves alienating. If the sentence simply recalls a fact of the city's history, it is the history of a relation predicated upon economic dwelling, transience, and being a "tourist." The earthquake named in the first sentence marks a rupture in the city's historical being. The space of tourism that enters through that rupture carries with it the mark of Enframing. If the "flat old brown cat" intrudes paratactically with something potentially more intimate, it is inhuman and itself transient. We are immediately returned to "mooch city" with its connotations of loitering and begging.

The people then mentioned are just as anonymous as tourists, even in the city they presumably live in. Who is sitting in the "hot cloud of MSG"? Does the next sentence name or seek a "someone" to help clean up as the sentence crumbles? Who is or isn't watching the tortillas? Who is the person whose "Tobacco smell of his skull burned right into his shirt, hair & eyes"? And who is the woman who "for a living ... stands naked on a turntable" so that anonymous men can watch through small windows? Not only are these individuals nameless, but they are so often within identifiable forms of work. Some are clearly "food-service" workers "watching the tortillas" or contained within a "hot cloud of MSG." One, at least, is an erotic dancer, contained within the multiple frames of the "turntable carpeted lavender," of the small "windows" and the gazes of the men who watch through them, and immersed in "disco music."[39]

There are two important points to note. First, the frames of both the food-worker and the dancer seem to trap and anonymize the individuals, but simultaneously provide the little identity that they have. This identity is simultaneously social and poetic. They are present in the poem because they inhabit these frames, and implicitly are also present in the world, capable of sustaining their lives economically, because of these same conditions. If the work is anonymizing, substituting the frame for the individual, it also sustains them and their presence within their frames. This is emphasized by the poem's refusal to grant them presence beyond or contradictory to this mode of appearing. Second, what we find underlying Silliman's attention to these figures and their work frames is a particular form of temporality. In *Under* Albany, Silliman links this to the temporality of prisons:

> The joint has a discourse and logic that took years to learn. There are a variety of ways people can avoid telling you what exactly they've done to warrant incarceration. Even harder for an outsider to fathom is the sense of time as urgency without future. The sense was not the continuous present of modernism, but rather a perpetual one in which every moment was new, in formation. This proved ultimately to be [a] more important lesson than anything I had learned in college. Twenty-one years after leaving CPHJ, it still governs the function of time in my writing.[40]

Having worked for years on projects dedicated to prisoner welfare, the politics and socio-economics of prisons is central to Silliman's poetic encounters with his era. The temporality of prisons in his experiences in the 1970s is construed as a particularly postmodern temporality, characterized by perpetual brevity in constantly urgent moments of intensity: not a sustained present but a continual failure to sustain presentness. As a result, as Jerome McGann writes, Silliman's readers "confront time, or the sequence of eventualities, in a highly pressurized state."[41] Each new sentence is intense, pressurized, and fleeting. Their flow presents a constantly urgent presentness that is most intensely experienced in the alienated and ongoing presentness of the work frames. They mark a troubling point of contact between the two halves of Silliman's thematic focus—the personal, autobiographical life, and the shared way of life.

In this context, the glimpse of the historical event of the 1915 earthquake provides a counterpoint to the ongoing presentness. It indicates a threshold to the reader, offering a historical co-ordinate for a (then) contemporary experience that is denied to the workers that follow this moment, both historically and in the poem's sequence. The effect is to make an apparent a-temporal and a-historical presentness legible as a particular stage within the historical formation and progression of consciousness. In this stage the other, as he or she is encountered through the medium of work, is reduced to his or her work frame. This was as true in "Ketjak," of the "she" in the "bum space" and the unseen workers in the financial district, as it is in *Tjanting* of the "she" who stands on the turntable. Further, though Silliman's terms are different to Heidegger's, the resonance is undeniable. In the (then) present historical moment of the poem, people begin to appear as resources for work within the domain of social, self-assertive production. In this moment, the shared way of life seems to overcome, at least in the poem, the forms of self-presence that would allow contact with an individual's autobiographical life.

"Albany," Enframing, and violence

What we have seen in *Tjanting* is that the material frame of the sentence, foregrounded by means of parataxis, allows Silliman to stage a disclosure of the material and social Enframing of individuals within certain contemporary forms of work. The Enframing is clear, in that the work-frame dominates the manner in which the poem is able to bring these individuals into poetic presence. The Enframing is also violent in the manner Heidegger's philosophy hints that it must be. The reduction of human being to a calculably present resource for production enacts an ontological violence on humanity's capacity to *be* within the world. This Enframing recalls, also, a state of affairs named in *The Grand Piano* where the time in which Language poetry emerged was found to be fragmented, ugly, and incoherent.[42] The jobs that the Language poets found available to them there were not "agreeable," because the work available to people like Perelman, Watten, and others, was the sort of liminal and precarious work suggested by *Tjanting*.

If the violence of the sort of work shown in *Tjanting* is initially ontological—or economic, in the Language poets' terms—the "autobiographical" "Albany" reveals a violence that is far more immediate and literal. Indeed, what we see in returning to "Albany" is the intimacy it is able to articulate between quotidian life and violence within Silliman's childhood community. In the middle section of "Albany" we read:

> Her husband broke both of her eardrums. I used my grant to fix my teeth. They speak Farsi at the corner store. YPSL. The national question. I look forward to old age with some excitement. 42 years of Fibreboard products. Food is a weapon. Yet the sight of people making love is deeply moving. Music is essential. The cops wear shields that serve as masks. Her lungs heavy with asbestos. . . . Those distant sirens down in the valley signal great hinges in the lives of strangers. A phone tree. The landlord's control of terror is implicit. Not just a party but a culture. Copayment. He held the Magnum with both hands and ordered me to stop. The garden is a luxury (a civilization of snail and spider). They call their clubs batons. They call their committees clubs. Her friendships with women are different. Talking so much is oppressive. Outplacement. A shadowy locked facility using drugs and doublecelling (a rest home). That was the Sunday Henry's father murdered his wife on the front porch.[43]

The landlord's control over his or her tenants demonstrates the effects of Enframing on the town's way of life, as does the fact that gardens are considered a luxury. Both sentences suggest that these spaces emerge as living-space and recreational space, framed off from each other. "Living," "recreation," and "luxury" are Enframed predispositions for how the world might be encountered. Moreover, both are implicitly distinct from work-time. If recreation and luxury are Enframed relations to the world, both are in service to the work that makes them possible and makes them meaningful as non-work frames. Even the act of framing a garden space off from the broader geography of work sustains these Enframed and Enframing relations.

These images of Enframing might seem only abstractly critical of the geographies of work and how they structure the geographies of rest and other non-work activities. However, the Enframing that Silliman shows here is interwoven with far darker and more violent images. Amongst the sorts of sentence mentioned above, other sentences act as points of crisis in Enframing's relation to the town's population and their lives within an Enframed way of life. "Not just a party but a culture," for instance, may refer to the communist or socialist parties of which Silliman was a member, which act also as worker's parties. Not just a political party, but a culture, a community, and one founded in direct opposition to the effects of Enframing on working-class lives. One sentence asserts a culture of work producing commodities—"42 years of Fibreboard products"—and another recognizes the marks of those years upon the body: "Her lungs are heavy with asbestos." If the police, given the task of sustaining the *status quo*, hide their faces and call their clubs batons, the people fashion their social organizations as clubs. The punning brings out a political and often-suppressed violence within the social ordering, making the social club a weapon of resistance against the power of the "baton."

As it goes on, the poem's oscillation between violence and the "normalcy" that accompanies it builds to a crescendo:

> Our home, we were told, had been broken, but who were these people we lived with? Clubbed in the stomach, she miscarried. There were bayonets on campus, cows in India, people shoplifting books. I just want to make it to lunch time. Uncritical of nationalist movements in the Third World. Letting the dishes sit for a week. Macho culture of convicts. With a shotgun and "in defense" the officer shot him in the face. Here, for a moment, we are joined. The want-ads lie strewn on the table.

The implicitly abnormal way of life that comes with a "broken" home is nonetheless the one that made up Silliman's childhood and which influenced his present. Silliman's question, "but who were these people we lived with?" implies that the term "broken" carries with it an ideology that takes a particular state of affairs as an aberration. The broken, however, is nonetheless the "actual." To say it is "broken" minimizes the fact that it is the home. These are the conditions of "home"; its normalcy is violent, cruel, and Enframed. Silliman's question "but who were these people we lived with?" then links the private experience of the home to the experience of a public culture. Who is the woman "clubbed in the stomach"? This is a person with whom Silliman shares or shared a way of life in Albany. The proximity between the first and second sentences in this excerpt implies that the social relationship between strangers is like the familial relation.

The earlier punning between club and baton returns here in a dark fashion only implicit in the earlier sentence. There, "They call their clubs batons." Here, a woman is seen to miscarry because she has been "clubbed." Though not stated outright, in context the term "clubbed" implies police violence, a violence that escalates a few sentences later when another officer shoots a suspect "With a shotgun and 'in defense.'" The woman and the police are shown, by Silliman's parataxis, to already be in violent antagonism to each other. In some way, their relationship is "broken," and the poem implies that the social relationship resembles a broken home. But again, the implication in this final section of Silliman's poem is that it is not helpful to pretend that these violent conditions are somehow an aberration from other essential, true, and real conditions of daily life. Rather, the eruptions of violence against the bodies of the citizens of the town of Albany are central to the culture. This centrality is shown in the turn, after the above excerpt's opening sentences, to a campus, to shops, and to convicts/prisons/police. Education, shopping/consumption, and law and order are central to the culture rather than accidental, and all incorporate forms of violence.

Indeed, in these final sentences of the poem, the violence that emerged earlier in the autobiographical domestic space (the cruelty of father and grandfather), and which moved into the shared experience of social violence ("her lungs heavy with asbestos" and police batons), boils over into a pattern of state-sponsored violence against a citizenry. Bayonets on campus, a woman clubbed in the stomach, and the police shooting the suspect in the face, "in defense," all represent the attempt of a police force to maintain the (violent) way of life. In this, "Albany" turns its violence inwards in a new way. For Silliman, this was particularly evident in the period in which the poem was written. Around this time, protests on and around the nearby Berkeley university led to multiple clashes between student protestors and police.[44] Silliman's poem thus suggests that the violence at work in Albany is at least partly at the service of the status quo, of the conditions of production that produce the sort of working poverty that Silliman's grandfather experienced, and which constitute the form of "destitution" with which Heidegger diagnosed the era.

As with "Ketjak," in "Albany" parataxis allows for connection between units that are otherwise separated by distinct semantic frames. The facts of Enframing, such as the framed-off geographies of work and leisure, are able to sit intimately alongside their often-violent consequences. Not only does this collapse geographical and temporal distance into proximities that disclose problems both social and personal, but it also resists the sense of normalcy or inevitability that might come with hypotaxis. Indeed, rather than allowing the violence experienced within a single life to take center-stage alone, Silliman's parataxis allows him to turn outwards from his childhood to the Enframing, affects, and violence at work within a shared way of life. Many of the poems' observations reflect a violence inherent in a population being taken as a standing reserve of labor by the processes of capital. Their potentialities as humans are already decided by this frame, and the forms of violence that they experience are the direct products of a life lived in these terms. Even that Sunday on which "Henry's father murdered his wife" resists the broader socio-economic frame conjured in other sentences.[45] It marks a point of radical breakdown, an extremity that draws attention to the dominant ideology even while it does not itself resist its process or effects. Enframing, we might say, becomes particularly *visible* in Albany, and in "Albany," when its totality breaks down locally in violent encroachments on people's bodies. Specific instances of destitution, as violence and poverty, trace out destitution's ontological and economic basis behind the scenes.

Notes

1   Ron Silliman, *The Alphabet* (Tuscaloosa: The University of Alabama Press, 2008), 1. "Albany" was written 1979–80, first published in *Ironwood* 20 (1982), 112–13, and first collected in Ron Silliman, *ABC* (Berkeley: Tuumba Press, 1983).

2   Silliman, *Alphabet*, 1.
3   The prison is San Quentin, which lies across the bay from Albany.
4   Silliman italicizes the word "Albany" in the title of the autobiographical text. In this essay, I have chosen to reflect this by not italicizing the word when mentioning the title of the autobiography (*Under* Albany).
5   Ron Silliman, *Under* Albany (Cambridge: Salt Publishing, 2004), 19.
6   Silliman, *Under* Albany, 44.
7   "Albany" is also dedicated to Cliff Silliman: *Alphabet*, 1.
8   Silliman, *Under* Albany, 44.
9   Rae Armantrout et al., *The Grand Piano: An Experiment in Collective Autobiography, San Francisco, 1975–1980* (Detroit: Mode A/This Press, 2006–10), v.6, 20.
10 In Silliman's "new sentences," the accumulation of sentences into paragraphs is rejected in favor of sentence-level formal procession. The overt aim is to keep attention focused on language at the level of opaque, gestural form. See the title essay in Ron Silliman, *The New Sentence* (New York: Roof Books, 1989). It is partly this stated aim, however, that drew criticism into underappreciating Silliman's interest in "actual life."
11 Christopher Nealon, *The Matter of Capital: Poetry and Crisis in the American Century* (Cambridge, Massachusetts and London, England: Harvard University Press, 2011).
12 Nealon, *Matter of Capital*, 126.
13 Nealon, *Matter of Capital*, 128.
14 Marjorie Perloff, "The Portrait of the Language Poet as Autobiographer: The Case of Ron Silliman," *Quarry West* 34 (1998).
15 Perloff, "Portrait of the Language Poet," 175. Perloff's italics.
16 Bob Perelman, *The Marginalization of Poetry: Language Writing and Literary History* (Princeton: Princeton University Press, 1996), 67.
17 Perloff, "Portrait of the Language Poet," 175. Perelman, *Marginalization of Poetry*.
18 Silliman, *New Sentence*, 8. Emphasis original.
19 Silliman, *New Sentence*, 14.
20 Silliman, *New Sentence*, 8.
21 Silliman, *New Sentence*, 12.
22 Steve McCaffery, "Autonomy to Indeterminacy," *Twentieth-Century Literature* 53, no. 2 (2007), 215–16.
23 Heidegger, *Elucidations of Hölderlin's Poetry* (Amherst, New York: Humanity Books, 2000), 22.
24 See, for instance, Martin Heidegger, *Poetry, Language, Thought* (New York: Harper Collins, 2001), 60. There Heidegger likens the founding of being that goes on in poetry to the founding of political states.
25 Heidegger, *Poetry, Language, Thought*, 90.
26 Martin Heidegger, *Basic Writings*, ed. David Krell (London and Henley: Routledge & Kegan Paul, 1978), 309.
27 Heidegger, *Basic Writings*, 332.
28 Heidegger, *Poetry, Language, Thought*, 136.
29 See also Paul Gibbs, *Heidegger's Contribution to the Understanding of Work-Based Studies* (Dordrecht, Heidelberg, London, New York: Springer, 2011).
30 Which he also calls *aletheia* [truth]. Heidegger, *Poetry, Language, Thought*, 74–5.
31 Heidegger, *Poetry, Language, Thought*, 41.

32 Heidegger, *Poetry, Language, Thought*, 45.
33 Silliman, *New Sentence*, 91.
34 Perelman, *Marginalization of Poetry*, 67.
35 Silliman, *Alphabet*.
36 Perelman, *Marginalization of Poetry*, 67.
37 Perelman, *Marginalization of Poetry*, 66.
38 Ron Silliman, *Tjanting* (Cambridge: Salt Publishing, 2002), 95.
39 Silliman, *Tjanting*, 95.
40 Silliman, *Under* Albany, 33.
41 J. J. McGann, "Contemporary Poetry, Alternate Routes," *Critical Inquiry* 13, no. 3 (1987), 640.
42 Armantrout et al., *Grand Piano*, 2:21–2.
43 Silliman, *Alphabet*, 1–2.
44 These clashes are documented by multiple newspaper articles from this decade, including Special to *The New York Times*, "Copter Breaks up Berkeley Crowd: Stinging Powder, Dropped from Air, Ends 'Funeral' for a Gunshot Victim Copter Breaks up a 'Funeral' Protest at Berkeley," *New York Times (1923-Current file)* May 21, 1969.
45 Silliman, *Alphabet*, 2.

Part IV

CLASS IDENTITY AND CLASS CONFLICT

Chapter 10

SWEDISH SOCIAL MODERNISM: THE INWARD AND OUTWARD TURN IN EYVIND JOHNSON'S *STAD I LJUS*

Niklas Salmose

Introduction

When Swedish working-class literature[1] established itself in the transition between the 1920s and 1930s, how did it fit into the emerging, admittedly late, modernist Swedish context called aesthetic modernism? Many of the working-class writers' books discussed the dichotomy between urban and rural landscapes as well as modern communicative techniques. Thus, it was not only aesthetic modernism that was interested in describing, criticizing, and embracing the changed society within modernity. Nonetheless, working-class literature was accused of being radical in its content, but not in its form, and critical consensus is that aesthetic modernism and working-class literature are two very separate, and incompatible, phenomena. A more nuanced and developed attempt to understand working-class literature in a modernist way is to be found in Michael Denning's polemical attitude towards the separation between aesthetic modernism and Cultural Front literature during the Depression. He names the latter *social modernism*, as a literary tradition that demonstrates both continuity and rupture with modernism, a third modernist wave.[2] The concept of social modernism, according to Denning, is a way of crediting working-class literature with a radical rather than a reactionary literary style, combining the symbolic power of modernism with the revolutionary politics of social realism.[3]

As a result of the delay of high modernism in Sweden, modernism coincided to a greater degree than in other countries with social working-class literature. Consequently, Swedish working-class literature is *more* accentuated by modernist features than its international contemporaries, and the great divide between the two traditions in Swedish literary history is unfortunate and partly incorrect. In an effort to correct this perception, this chapter will study how a prominent working-class writer, Eyvind Johnson, had already commenced a fruitful collaboration between modernist techniques and social concerns in the

1920s, and can thus be seen as an early representative of social modernism. This case is particularly compelling since analyses of working-class literature from a social modernist perspective have been limited to literature in the 1930s and later. My sample for analysis here is Johnson's third novel, *Stad i ljus* [*City in Light*], written in Paris in 1926. Johnson, who spent most of his formative years in exile in Berlin and Paris, encountered the 1920s modernist art and literary movements in continental Europe, and was heavily influenced by Proust, Gide, and Joyce. "Their influence on him," write Peter Graves and Phil Holmes in "Three Novelists of the 1930s: Vilhelm Moberg, Ivar Lo-Johansson and Eyvind Johnson," "was profound and lasting; he was to become a pioneer of Modernism as far as the Swedish novel is concerned."[4] His, from a Swedish standpoint, rather early interventions with modernist aesthetics in combination with his working-class commitment, make him the most interesting Swedish author to investigate in terms of the relationship between international high modernism and a national working-class literature. The most ambitious modernist analysis of the work is that performed by Bjarne Thorup Thomsen in his recent and illuminating article, "Marginal and Metropolis Modernist Modes in Eyvind Johnson's Early Urban Narratives,"[5] and by Sylvain Briens in "Le discours de Paris comme écriture moderniste? Les regards du flâneur dans *Stad i ljus* d'Eyvind Johnson et *Alberte og friheten* de Cora Sandel."[6] Thomsen's interpretation forms a basis for a more detailed stylistic analysis of *Stad i ljus*. Examining *Stad i ljus* from a social modernist perspective reveals how the social pathos of working-class literature (and work) intersects with modernist aesthetics in a novel. Before I inspect *Stad i ljus*, however, it is appropriate to contextualize the novel in the particular flux of Swedish modernism and working-class literature.

Working-class literature and modernism in Sweden

In regard to literary Sweden, the so-called working-class authors, active primarily in the 1930s—a group whose most prominent representatives include Ivar Lo-Johansson, Harry Martinson, Moa Martinson, Vilhelm Moberg, and Eyvind Johnson—are usually considered as representatives of a thoroughly national style of writing. Although different in literary style and content, they have much in common in terms of background. To a large degree, they had an agricultural heritage rather than coming from the industrial working class; they all worked in manual occupations for years; they were at times unemployed; and, most importantly, they lacked formal education beyond the compulsory elementary school. In Sweden, these authors are usually referred to as autodidacts, since they were all more or less self-educated, benefiting from widespread public access to libraries, political study circles, and the appearance of Folk High Schools designed for working-class people particularly from an agricultural background.

Working-class literature balances between describing the collective *and* individual experience of collective and social forces, as echoed in their genre *a priori*: the autobiography. The epithet *working-class writers* unites these authors in a shared past life experience and addresses how this actuality formed their literary content, themes, and general ambition. Since, even when they did not write autobiographies, their novels were explicitly autobiographical, their literary worlds manifested their own personal life journeys. Their agricultural backgrounds accentuated the tension between town and country to an even larger extent than what was common in the era of modernization. Their rural reminiscences, which had a bitter flavor for them, made them favor, at least initially, urbanity as a place of opportunity and freedom compared to the narrow-minded countryside.[7] However, we can observe a certain primitivism at the same time, a romanticization of the soil, fertility, and peasantry from their past. The importance of their own experiences of childhood and youth also forces them, initially, to look back a couple of decades instead of writing contemporary fiction. As the political turmoil thickened in the 1930s, "they—along with many other literary figures in Sweden—reacted to the increasingly dark international scene of totalitarianism of the Right and of the Left by coming to the defense of democracy."[8] Finally, their literary material usually dealt with social outcasts sympathetically, and depicted protagonists that also were self-educated and from a working-class or proletarian background. In a political sense, the working-class writers represent a gradual change in Sweden towards an equal welfare society as well, as instigating this very change.

How does the growth of a politically conscious working-class literature interact with the rise of high modernism in Sweden? Andreas Huyssen associates modernism with the advent of a self-conscious conflict or "great divide" between "high art and mass culture."[9] Such a divide suggests an antagonism between a genre traditionally associated with realistic aesthetics and modernism. Moreover, these issues echo in one of the more important early modernist magazines in Sweden in the 1920s, *Ultra*. Mats Jansson writes in "Crossing Borders: Modernism in Sweden and the Swedish-speaking Part of Finland" that "*Ultra* intended to become a battleground between the old and new" where the post-First World War witnessed a period of great tension which needed a fundamentally new art and aesthetics to describe it.[10] Hence, Sweden conforms to an international perspective where realist traditional aesthetics marked something of the past and were frowned upon by the new generation artists.

Modernist aesthetics, however, were never in fashion in Swedish criticism, as Peter Luthersson so convincingly argues in *Svensk litterär modernism: En stridsstudie*. The first serious attempt to introduce continental modernist ideas to Sweden was made by Pär Lagerkvist, through his programmatic *Ordkonst och bildkonst* [*Literary Art and Pictorial Art*] (1913).[11] Lagerkvist was highly influenced by modernist art, especially cubism, during his stay in Paris in the spring of 1913. He tried to manifest his new design in his collection of poetry,

Ångest [*Anguish*] (1916), by using free verse, complex metaphors, alliteration, personification, anaphora, and an expressionist articulation of universal rather than individual feelings. Fredrik Böök, professor in Literature in Lund and the diligent, leading literary critic in one of Sweden's most important daily newspapers, *Svenska dagbladet*, considered Lagerkvist no more than a formalist without any content.[12] Continental modernism in the 1910s never really became a factor in Swedish intellectual and artistic life. As Luthersson has shown, the great expressionist director Max Rheinhardt was surprised by the lukewarm reception when he visited Stockholm in 1911,[13] and the critic August Brunius' review of Picasso during the 1912 Spring Exhibition in Cologne demonstrates the general antagonism against the modern: "The Spaniard Picasso appears to be a shady character. He is almost the only one in the group who is untalented, or weakly talented, in terms of color treatment. He can draw, and his cubistic fantasies are a master drawer's nightmares from overexertion and poor digestion."[14] Furthermore, Lagerkvist's modernist dramas in the 1920s received mostly negative press: "Modernity, fine! But modernism, No, it should stay in Berlin."[15] Stockholm was a provincial place compared to Berlin or Paris. Greta Knutson-Tzara reported this particular provincialism and naïvety. In an interview in a Swedish newspaper in 1934, she responded that "[i]t is not strange that people forget about art in times like these. Everything is politics. You never know what will happen next. It is only here in Scandinavia one does not feel the volcano growl under one's feet!"[16]

The ideas of continental high modernism seemed to hit Sweden just as it started to fade in the rest of the world. The most important advocate for high modernism was undeniably Arthur Lundkvist, whose first collection of poetry, *Glöd* [*Glowing Embers*] (1928), roared louder than most of his generation for change and a literary revolution. However, as Anders Österling wrote in his review: "These ... roars have their culmination behind them and are not very coveted; we need to find something new."[17] This explains the consensus among Swedish modernist critics that modernism came late to Sweden and did not establish itself until the 1930s and 1940s.

This new Swedish modernism, as represented by the poetry of the Young Five[18] group of poets—Erik Asklund, Josef Kjellgren, Artur Lundkvist, Harry Martinsson, and Gustav Sandgren—has, somewhat unfortunately, been named *aesthetic modernism* by Magnus Nilsson in order to emphasize its formal qualities as well as distinguishing it from the more proletarian and realistic literature that occurred simultaneously.[19] The major genre was poetry. Although stylistically different, however, Swedish early modernism and working-class literature were equally engaged in describing, criticizing, and embracing the changed society within modernity. Many of the working-class books, as mentioned before, discussed the dichotomy between urban and rural landscapes as well as modern communication such as telephone, radio, railways, and cars. These overlapping similarities are also evident in the influential modernist 1930s magazine *Spektrum*, where much attention was devoted to social politics.[20]

Another affinity, as Rochelle Wright argues, is that the two literary currents were both strongly anti-bourgeois (as well as critical to the literary institutions in Sweden in the preceding decades) although in different ways.[21] As Raymond Williams reminds us, critique against the bourgeois can come from both an aristocratic, elitist perspective (as in the case of many British modernists) *and* working-class hatred (as in Brecht or D. H. Lawrence).[22] The working-class authors endorsed the title autodidacts since it established a clear rupture from former literary tradition in choices of literary setting and topics and the aesthetic modernist poets revolted against the provincial, critical attitude towards experimental modernism in the 1910s and 1920s.[23] Even though both were clearly against the bourgeois, the modernists were not as explicit in their critique as the working-class authors were. The aesthetic modernism of the 1930s was accused of being not only formal but also unworldly, not reacting to the growling political volcano in continental Europe. In its aestheticism, it also never included the radicalism and ideological characteristics of high modernism in Europe and Finland in the 1910s and 1920s. Thus, the working-class authors did not enter into controversy with the modernists' aesthetic, formalistic program, but rather with their unworldliness and elitist escapism, which contrasted with many European high modernists' engagement with social and political dimensions, albeit through subjectivism, such as in Woolf, Döblin, Joyce, and Kafka. Still, since many of the authors in the Young Five also had working-class backgrounds, one can notice, at least on a programmatic level, a strong awareness also of the social aspects of modernism. Lundkvist wrote in 1929: "The poetry of the modern times is not to be found in old, whistling mansion avenues, in sloping, moth-eaten fences, in the red cabins situated in birch hillsides. The poet of today shall discover beauty, poetry and unsung songs in the buzz of road junctions and the roar of traffic, in the machines of the shop floors, in the seething industrial work's symphony, in the ordinary, daily human life."[24] Hence, Lundkvist embraces the typical modernist fascination with the modern world *and* the life of the ordinary, working-class man.

As mentioned above, Denning's critique of the separation between aesthetic modernism and Cultural Front literature during the Depression in the United States seems also to apply to documents like Lundkvist's 1929 program. Denning names Cultural Front literature *social modernism* in order to demonstrate its combined continuity and rupture with modernism. Denning's social modernism is an updated version of Kenneth Burke's 1935 address to the American Writers' Congress, "Revolutionary Symbolism in America." "The title," writes Denning,

> carries two meanings: it is both a discussion of the role of symbols in revolutionary politics *and* a juxtaposition of "symbolism"—the word that had become the shorthand for the arts of the modern—with "revolution," thus figuring a "revolutionary modernism."[25]

To me, Denning's social modernism is informed more by a sense of a modernist continuity than a fissure. Referring to the socially engaging literature of the 1930s in the United States as radical (as most critics do), as "one of the few important avant-gardes,"[26] and as a third-wave modernism,[27] in the spirit of Fredric Jameson's concept of *late modernism*, Denning stresses how modernism develops into a more socially conscious aesthetic art form in the Depression and its aftermath. This is in line with Benjamin Balthaser, who acknowledges that "Denning's formulation not only recovers the aesthetic value of Popular Front literature, but, as importantly, it recovers the revolutionary potential of the modernist project."[28] Laura Browder adds to this when she recognizes the need to "rethink modernist fictional techniques in the light of their contemporary political experience."[29] Like Denning, Browder wants to eliminate the dominant belief that working-class literature is a prolongation of realist aesthetics.

In essence, social modernism combines social pathos with a radical and experimental aesthetic form, which sets it apart from a diversity of social realisms. Denning also identifies how modernist strategies permeate the social consciousness in his analysis of John Dos Passos's *U.S.A.* trilogy (1930–6), where he addresses cubist and cinematic influences on Dos Passos's narrative style, but the discussion of particular modernist stylistics in social modernism is by no means the dominant aspect of his analysis. Neither Barbara Foley in *Radical Representations: Politics and Form in U.S. Proletarian Fiction, 1929–1941*,[30] nor Browder, provides any close readings that display how exactly modernist aesthetic techniques are used in correlation with social ambition. Similarly, Nick Hubble in *The Proletarian Answer to the Modernist Question* is less interested in style in proletarian fiction than the cultural oscillation between individuality and collectivity. Although occasionally referring to Virginia Woolf, interior consciousness, and cinematic montage techniques, his monograph, in his own words, "is neither a book about modernism *and* proletarian literature nor a comprehensive survey of books written by proletarians *containing* modernist features; but the complex cultural mapping of a relationship explored by the detailed analysis of a small selection of texts."[31] In respect to these rich volumes' discourse on the social and the modern, this article aims to investigate how high modernist style is combined with a social pathos. The choice of Johnson's novel *Stad i ljus* for analysis, additionally, pulls the discourse of social modernism back to a temporal context which recent work on proletarian literature has not yet explored. Johnson himself acknowledged in "Ett decennium utan slut" ["A Decade Without an End"], part of a subsequent compilation of personal memories and reflections, *Personligt Politiskt Estetiskt* [*Personal Political Aesthetic*] compiled by Lindberger, that in combination with the international influences of modernism, Swedish 1930s fiction also contained the regional component of a historical openness to social issues.[32] Let us explore these diverse influences in his own work in more detail.

The inward and outward turn in Stad i Ljus

Johnson's third novel, *Stad i ljus*, was written during his stay in Paris in 1926. The novel's initial reception in Sweden was almost non-existent. Johnson, and his colleague and friend Rudolf Värnlund, were particularly unfortunate in the reception of their early work. Aspiring to retell their own working-class experiences in a modern form, they were practically opposed on all fronts.³³ Johnson's debut, *De fyra främlingarna*, a collection of short stories about workers and famine, was literarily torn to pieces by critic Erik Hedén.³⁴ The title of Hedén's review was "Ett kräks själsliv" ["The Spiritual Life of a Swine"]: "The only reflex such a book can provoke is this: That they even manage! That they can stand it, book after book, year after year, portraying the same, eternally passively lost swine!"³⁵

Recently *Stad i ljus* has attracted some academic attention; the most impressive analysis has been performed by Thomsen, who argues that Johnson's early work, in its "stylised and systematic mode of representation ... contributes to moving Johnson's writing increasingly away from a more conventional realist voice."³⁶ These stylized devices are, according to Thomsen, extensive use of hyperboles, surreal metaphors, leitmotifs, and personification.³⁷ One example of the latter is the use of street lamps in a short story preceding *Stad i ljus* echoing the street lamps in T. S. Eliot's "Rhapsody on a Windy Night."³⁸ In addition to these modernist stylistic features, Thomsen emphasizes Johnson's treatment of subject matters closely related to his working-class background, such as the collective forces of society, social welfare, and autodidact protagonists.³⁹

The first striking thing to note about *Stad i ljus* is that it is a one-day novel, capturing Bastille Day in Paris sometime in the 1920s. This typical high modernist genre gives both the novel intensity and is in its concentration on impressions and interior consciousness a radical step *away* from traditional realism. It follows a young aspiring Swedish author, Torsten, and his adventures in Paris during this extraordinary, yet ordinary, day. It is thus also a metafiction on writing and authorship, as well as semi-autobiographical: one café is called "The Grey Adventure," the title of Johnson's first attempt to write a novel.⁴⁰ As a story of youth, it is also a generational novel; Torsten tries in his literary ambitions to capture the modern spirit of rupture and is simultaneously a representative of the young generation.⁴¹ Torsten writes that between "our generation dated 1900 ... and the previous generation is a large black line drawn, its width four years long," alluding to the rupture of the First World War.⁴² This theme of generational spleen is also apparent in passages like the following: "Our generation does not possess a sea, which is not damned, not a flowering field, which cannot be drowned in poisonous gas. Our generation has inherited the dance hall, the cocaine, the pederasty, and the glossolalia. It is therefore wiser than all other generations, wiser than Aristotle, and is the only one which has the ability to vomit when it sees its own reflection in the mirror" (36). Torsten, thus, is a good advocate for the lost generation.

Much like Berlin in *Berlin, Alexanderplatz,* Dublin in *Ulysses,* and London in *Mrs. Dalloway,* Paris is a protagonist of its own and becomes a leitmotif in giving the narrative structure and rhythm. The narrative tracks Torsten's wanderings in the city with great precision, always giving the names of boulevards, districts, and locations. Every chapter, more or less, opens with a detailed description of the setting in order to call attention to the relationship between space and consciousness. There is also a meta-aspect to the rendering of the city. "And this is the song about the grand boulevards, stretching, developing and changing names and possessing their own fates" (119). In a café, Torsten ponders the importance of writing about one thing at a time, meticulously, in order to explore and relish the inner, artistic exploration of the city, to "make long parentheses like Marcel Proust" (68). The city is not just personified, but personified through interior monologues: "In this hour my nerves tremble of iron and steel and copper, and they sing; and their song is a song where each fully loaded tram is a tone,—and have you heard omnibuses bellow like draft oxen or elephants, bellow like heavy hungry wanderers over prehistoric plains, where the sun burns the wild grass. The happiness of the automobiles is mine,—a happiness of the air at lunch hour" (50). The city is thus granted its own, independent, narrative voice ("The song of the city"), in two short chapters (6 and 16) that function like the intertitles of a highly subjective narration (110).

Johnson was reading Proust during his Paris stay,[43] and, in true Proustian manner, the narrative not only portrays interior consciousness and phenomenological experiences using sensorial aesthetics, but also pays careful attention to Bergsonian dichotomies of duration and clock time. Torsten's consciousness, long and winding inner monologues, are constantly interrupted by the temporality of the city, announced by time markers "dinner hour," "In this hour my [the city] house is singing," "Now the time was noon" (50, 50, 47). The one-day structure, the portrayal of the city as a protagonist and the treatment of time are all typical modernist features that were not recognized in an intellectually suppressed Swedish literary scene at the time of the novel's publication. But the question remains: is there anything original in his modernist style that is influenced by his working-class heritage? Are there any hints at social modernism?

The very opening of the novel is striking in its emphasis on both collective man and the distanced narrative perspective:

See here space: it is filled with sound.
See here earth: it bears fruit, it is pregnant with life—a cluster of life, crawling, swarming, holding individuals and specimen: characters, led by their fates, by their daily deeds, by their thought, and characters without fate, who only fill a gap in the crowd.
Over them light and sound, inside them happiness or emptiness. Around them the roar from everyone for everyone. It is night. (9)

Compare this to the opening of Woolf's *Mrs. Dalloway*:

> Mrs. Dalloway said she would buy the flowers herself.
> For Lucy had her work cut out for her. The doors would be taken off their hinges; Rumpelmayer's men were coming. And then, thought Clarissa Dalloway, what a morning—fresh as if issued to children on a beach.[44]

Where Woolf's free indirect discourse balances between the implied author and Clarissa's phenomenological experience of her day, Johnson focuses on a stream-of-consciousness technique emanating from a non-subject, a force, a religion, the universe—an external perspective, an overview, a bird's-eye view of humanity. The difference between external subjectivism and internal subjectivism is also shown in Johnson's use of collective possessive and third-person plural pronouns, compared to Woolf's third-person singular. It might be a subtle difference; both authors introduce their one-day novel with a generic modernist technique of representing some kind of consciousness, but Johnson introduces the inhabitants of his Paris dated July 14 as a collective, whereas Woolf immediately alerts us that the single day in June 1923 is entirely focalized from one individual's perspective at a time. In *Stad i ljus*, the city becomes a true player, capable of reflecting and commenting on the Parisians; in *Mrs. Dalloway*, the city is equally visible, but through the sensorial experience of the Londoners (such as the repeated chimes of Big Ben). Johnson sees the world as both external and internal; true, much of the story is rendered through Torsten's imagination, but there is also a prevalent social attitude, an analytical objectivism seeing individuals as part of collectives. It is as though the modernist inward turn, as represented by Woolf, has stopped with one leg in individual consciousness and the other in social consciousness, the *outward turn*.

Another subtle difference between Woolf's and Johnson's early writings is how they treat sensorial experience and emotions. In Woolf's free indirect style, the world is sensed through the subject's consciousness, but linguistically "perfected" by the narrator. Still, the overwhelming emotional perspective is always subjective. Thomsen argues that Johnson's treatment of emotions displays "a shift from a notion of emotions as primarily subjective, as 'feeling', towards a new idea of shared affectivity."[45] This transition is displayed already in the opening, but also throughout *Stad i ljus* in the use of third-person-plural narration:

> Now the carousel is only happiness, and everyone clinging to it, following on its journey, exclaims: I am happy, we are happy.—One is happy because the air is saturated with happiness and each and every one laughs because others are laughing; and each shout, each raptured whisper, each smile is born out of this: WE.
> WE are a huge happiness, born by a thousand small laughters. (13)

This very passage illustrates this transition from individual to shared affection in its own move from the first-person pronoun to the third-person-plural pronoun: "I am happy, we are happy." The opening chapter depicts the world as a miniature, a micro cosmos, through the thematic use of the fair as setting. The use of the metaphor of fair, carousels, amusement parks, Ferris wheels, to symbolize the world is not unique. The originality lies in how Johnson both looks at this world as a miniature *and* focalizes the opening chapter from the viewpoint of the fair, thus managing, with a modernist voice, to methodologically apply a social attitude to his narrative.

Being a generational novel, *Stad i ljus* is densely populated, not by striving artists alone, but by all walks of life. The lower classes are emphasized through the prostitutes, homeless, beggars, tinsmiths, and stonemasons who crowd Johnson's Paris. This accentuation is carried further through recurrent references to aspects of life that are linked to these classes, such as "dirt, vermin," or through similes like music being as contagious as "cholera" (33, 22). But Torsten is also brooding on the lives of the lower- and working-class people he meets, often in a way that stresses class differences and the social and existential situation of these classes, as well as pointing a finger at those in power. "Our generation," Torsten agonizedly exclaims, "grew up in the shadow of the war swindlers, the bankruptees, embezzlers and the swindled" (36). Later on he juxtaposes the lives of the privileged with the daily, monotonous routines of the workers:

> Humans pause, move on, pause and move again. That's their lives. They work, rest, work. Sleep enters as a friend in the evening, the weariness waits at their beds as an enemy when it is morning. Morning is wait and work the afternoon is peace and work, and then arrives the night, then comes old age crawling against them, and one cannot tell if it comes as a friend or a foe. Life ends, Earth takes her stuff, but the stones remain on the streets awaiting new feet. (55)

This claustrophobic and hopeless situation is not unlike the famous scene with the struggling dog tied under the horse-drawn carriage in Luis Buñuel's film *Viridiana* (1961), which is freed by Viridiana's cousin at just the same moment as another carriage with a dog passes by.[46] In a similar deterministic fashion, the beggars in *Stad i ljus* consume meals "without dreams, just like their lives: they chew," and prostitutes live their lives "in this simple bodily feast without being a feast themselves except for others" and "[die] without lamenting death" (73, 112). In a significant interior monologue, Johnson compares our most basic needs with ordinary, social discourse:

> One day a man says to another:
>
> – It is a hundred and fifty years ago.
> – Really.
> – It is an important day, says the first, it is very warm.

- I am hungry, says the other.
- Oh really. It is dreadful hot. The tenant's association has a meeting next week, a forest party with Japanese lanterns. What do you think about the harvest this year? About the war debts? About woman's situation in society? It is dreadful hot today. What is your occupation?
- I am hungry.
- What is your opinion on the ministry?
- I want food.
- Do you belong to any religion?
- Food. (56)

This general sense of social tragedy permeates the narrative, but one remarkable fact about the focalization of events in Torsten's *flânerie* through Paris is that it is influenced to a high degree by his growing hunger, so much that one might actually refer to *Stad i ljus* as a starvation or hunger narrative. It is not only that Torsten constantly reminds us about his own starvation, such as in his dialog with the stray dog—"Now we seek starvation death together. Are you hungry?"—but starvation is granted a wider social and global, even human, dimension: "Starvation was a Being who entered into people's homes and made them skinny and hollow-eyed" (26, 29). And later on: "As I said before, these were the times when Starvation still existed on Earth. It even existed in Stockholm. It existed in the autumn, the good season when we harvest" (41).

The notion of starvation is quite unlike the exaggeration of gustatory aesthetics to be found in many modernist texts, either in a sensorial hyperbolic way, as in Joyce, or as a nostalgic memory in Proust. Michel Delville writes in his insightful gastroaesthetic analysis of modernist and avant-garde literature and performance that "the Modernists considered eating habits as a reflection of sociological, aesthetic, and psychosexual issues," situating food and the senses affiliated with it within modernist modes.[47] Conversely, Michel Delville and Andrew Norris explore the opposite of food narratives in *The Politics and Aesthetics of Hunger and Disgust: Perspectives on the Dark Grotesque* (2017), investigating the consequences of starvation and embodiment from social and political perspectives.[48] They write that "[s]tudying the aesthetics of hunger amounts to addressing hunger not only as a sensation but also as the object of philosophical and political reflections and speculations about self-definition and social identity."[49] This is particularly true of starving artists' narratives, such as *Stad i ljus*. Delville and Norris explore how starvation or fasting alludes to the political and social contexts of starvation artist narratives. "Another dominant preoccupation of hunger fiction," they write, "is to explore the physiological and material condition of the failed, starving artist," as well as analyzing "hunger both as a symptom and the cause of diverse forms of alienation and resistance to social assimilation."[50]

Delville and Norris's analysis of Knut Hamsun's *Sult* [Hunger] (1890) is relevant here both because *Stad i ljus* is reminiscent of the earlier narrative and because we know that *Sult* influenced Johnson.[51] Delville and Norris call into question Robert

Bly's influential interpretation of *Sult*: "Robert Bly has ventured that Hamsun's protagonist unconsciously chooses to suffer the pangs of hunger in order to attain a higher level of artistry and awareness ... Bly's neo-surrealist interpretation of Hamsun's novel ... clearly underestimates the novel's naturalistic outlook and obliterates the deep sense of social and cultural fatalism that pervades the story."[52] This is much like Torsten's vagabondish starvation in *Stad i ljus*: there is never a sense that his starvation is self-imposed in any way, not even subconsciously. In fact, the ingenious narrative within the narrative about the registered letter Torsten is waiting for, containing money, informs us not only of Torsten's temporary fate, but also how these letters include "the bread of tomorrow" for many world citizens (27–9). The addressed "You" that opens this digression on the importance of a registered letter establishes its universal character (27). Johnson also turns the material story of the registered letter containing money for starving people into an allegory of hope. These letters are "Hope, blind fate, the spark" in a world in turmoil (29). Torsten clearly acknowledges that hunger is not a romantic state of mind where an artist can transcend the materialistic world: "You do not think about literature, about art, about the roaring sea or playing children in a beautiful park, you just think about food" (82). Therefore, the starving stroller in *Stad i ljus* comes to represent, in a rather unusual modernist way, a blatant social critique of class difference and capitalism. Johnson's use of the trope of hunger thus corresponds with Maud Ellmann's analysis of artist starvation narratives by Yeats and Kafka: "The image of the starving artist in their work seems to stand for the crisis of high art in bourgeois culture; that is, for the exclusion of artists from the life of commerce and their proud refusal to be 'fed' by capital."[53] Delville and Norris's identification of alienation in *Sult*—"the starving vagabond suffocates in an overpopulated, indifferent space of urban conformity and ruthlessness"[54]—is equally true for Torsten in *Stad i ljus*.

The most original aspect of *Stad i ljus*, though, is how starvation informs the novel's style. *Hunger*, for example, is still a product of 1890s naturalism, whereas *Stad i ljus* utilizes the social component of work, class, and starvation to create an associative stream of consciousness that is clearly affected by, and an embodiment of, starvation. The hungrier Torsten becomes the more fragmented become his sensorial and cognitive impressions:

> He watched the dog which kept close to him.
>   ... that brute. I wonder where it comes from? If it only was cooler. If one would have been in the countryside after all. One should have had a car. (53)

These associations and fragmentations are regularly explained as being part of his starved imagination. Örjan Lindberger writes that the state of hunger affects Torsten's impressions, which alternate "between fatigue and exultation, hypersensibility, susceptibility to moods"[55] and thus employ a typical modernist feature, stream of consciousness, to communicate the sensation and inner reality of poverty and fatigue. This to me seems to be a very conscious use of a high modernist device in the service of the social concerns of a working-class writer. Hunger becomes subjective and yet a political phenomenon.

In this analysis, I have offered a reading that is situated between high modernist aesthetic strategies and social concerns normally attributed to working-class literature. In its consistent use of first-person interior consciousness, *Stad i Ljus* is very far away from social realism; yet, there is a compelling oscillation between a universal, extreme omniscient perspective and individual experience. Through the internalization of hunger, fatigue, class, and poverty, the emotional layer of capitalism and social politics becomes featured in a different way than in traditional working-class literature. The one-day narrative is traditionally associated with the modernist inner turn, in contrast to the epic quality of working-class novels. Instead of illuminating the temporal development of characters within a particular setting, so common in naturalist fiction, *Stad i ljus* crystallizes in detail the angst of non-privileged humans in a hostile world, without polemically counterpointing poor against rich. The novel successfully employs what I would like to call both an inward and an outward turn.

Johnson's own working-class background and social pathos sets him apart from most literary modernist authors, although he was formed within a stylistic tradition learned from the European high modernists he admired, such as Joyce and Pound. Denning's term *social modernism* has hitherto been reserved for working-class literature from the 1930s and onwards. As mentioned above, Denning favors the idea that social modernism is a continuation of high modernism, situating the radical, young deconstructionist voices of the high modernist generation within a stronger socio-political awareness. His, and other critics', analyses of the modernist influence on working-class literature tend to see social realism as infused by aspects of high modernism, rather than the other way around. Denning's own application of the concept of social modernism to American folk front narratives in the 1930s still emphasizes content over modernist style. Thus, there is an inconsistency between Denning's definition and the way it is applied. By contrast, *Stad i ljus*, written during the heyday of international high modernism, foreshadows the social concerns of the working-class literature of the 1930s *within* the discourse of a high modernist style. This sets it apart from Denning's use of social modernism as an analytical tool. *Stad i ljus* is a convincing example of a novel that fully shares both the formal concerns of high modernism and the social concerns of later working-class literature. It represents an original attempt to infuse social and political ambition with modernist techniques, combining both an inner and an outer turn, embracing the collective through the individual, and vice versa.

Notes

1   The term *working-class literature* is often used synonymously with *proletarian literature*. Nick Hubble offers a brief survey of the historical definition of

proletarian literature in *The Proletarian Answer to the Modernist Question* (2–6), where his main definition is a literature about workers but not necessarily written by workers (2). Thus, he takes a more thematic stand than the ordinary political definition offered by Marxist critics. Nick Hubble, *The Proletarian Answer to the Modernist Question* (Edinburgh: Edinburgh University Press, 2017). I use the term working-class literature for three reasons: One, I want to avoid the Marxist politicized understanding of the proletariat as not a classification of a social group of people but rather a political category. Two, in a Swedish context, the term *arbetarklasslitteratur* (literally, working-class literature) is more dominant than *proletärlitteratur* (proletarian literature). Three, the use of the word *working* connotes the social, physical, material aspect of labor. For the purpose of this essay, I define working-class literature to mean literature by working-class authors, which reflects the definition most commonly used in the Swedish context.

2 Michael Denning, *The Cultural Front: The Laboring of American Culture in the Twentieth Century* (London, New York: Verso, 1998), 122.
3 Denning, *Cultural Front*, 122.
4 Peter Graves and Phil Holmes, "Three Novelists of the 1930s: Vilhelm Moberg, Ivar Lo-Johansson and Eyvind Johnson," in *Aspects of Modern Swedish Literature*, ed. Irene Scobbie (Norwich: Norvik Press, 1999), 277–8.
5 Bjarne Thorup Thomsen, "Marginal and Metropolitan Modernist Modes in Eyvind Johnson's Early Narratives," *Scandinavica* 54, no. 2 (2015), 61–90.
6 Sylvain Briens, "Le Discours de Paris comme Écriture Moderniste? Les Regards du Flâneur dans *Stad I Ljus* d'Eyvind Johnson et *Alberte Og Friheten* de Cora Sandel," *Nordlit*, no. 21 (2007), 71–89.
7 Graves and Holmes, "Three Novelists," 265.
8 Graves and Holmes, "Three Novelists," 265.
9 Andreas Huyssen, *After the Great Divide: Modernism, Mass Culture, Postmodernism* (1986; Basingstoke: Macmillan, 1988), viii.
10 Mats Jansson, "Crossing Borders: Modernism in Sweden and the Swedish-speaking Part of Finland," in *The Oxford Critical and Cultural History of Modernist Magazines: Volume 3, Europe 1880–1940 Part 1*, ed. Peter Brooker, et al. (Oxford: Oxford University Press, 2013), 675.
11 Pär Lagerkvist, *Ordkonst Och Bildkonst: Om Modärn Skönlitteraturs Dekadens. Om Den Modärna Konstens Vitalitet* (Stockholm: Lagerströms, 1913).
12 Peter Luthersson, *Svensk Litterär Modernism: En Stridsstudie* (Stockholm: Atlantis, 2001), 64.
13 Luthersson, *Svensk Litterär Modernism*, 118.
14 Luthersson, *Svensk Litterär Modernism*, 111. My translation.
15 Luthersson, *Svensk Litterär Modernism*, 129. My translation.
16 Luthersson, *Svensk Litterär Modernism*, 209. My translation.
17 Luthersson, *Svensk Litterär Modernism*, 261. My translation.
18 The phrase Young Five refers to an anthology of poetry from 1929 in which their work appeared.
19 Magnus Nilsson. *Den moderne Ivar Lo-Johansson: Modernisering, modernitet och modernism i statarromanerna* (Hedemora: Gidlunds förlag, 2003), 229–39.
20 Jansson, "Crossing Borders," 683–4.
21 Rochelle Wright, "The Martinsons and Literary History," *Scandinavian Studies* 64, no. 2 (1992), 263.

22 Raymond Williams, *The Politics of Modernism: Against the New Conformists* (London and New York: Verso, 1989), 53.
23 Martin Kylhammar, *Frejdiga Framstegsmän Och Visionära Världsmedborgare: Epokskiftet 20-Tal – 30-Tal Genom Fem Unga Och Lubbe Nordström* (Stockholm: Akademeja, 1994), 10.
24 Artur Lundkvist, "Maskinen Och Människan," (1929). My translation.
25 Denning, *Cultural Front*, 122.
26 Denning, *Cultural Front*, 121.
27 Denning, *Cultural Front*, 122.
28 Benjamin Balthaser, *Modernism: Race and Transnational Radical Culture from the Great Depression to the Cold War* (Ann Arbor: University of Michigan Press, 2016), 21.
29 Laura Browder, "Rethinking America: Modernism and the Documentary Impulse in the Works of Dos Passos, Farrell, Herbst and the Federal Theatre Project" (Dissertation, Brandeis, 1995), 2.
30 Barbara Foley, *Radical Representations: Politics and Form in U.S. Proletarian Fiction, 1929–1941* (London: Duke University Press, 1993).
31 Hubble, *Proletarian Answer*, 40–1.
32 Eyvind Johnson, "Ett decennium utan slut," in *Personligt Politiskt Estetiskt*, ed. Örjan Lindberger (Stockholm: Bonniers, 1992), 96.
33 Birgit Munkhammar, *Hemlligskrivaren: En Essä Om Eyvind Johnson* (Stockholm: Bonniers, 2000), 71.
34 Munkhammar, *Hemlligskrivaren*, 71–3.
35 Munkhammar, *Hemlligskrivaren*, 73. My translation.
36 Thomsen, "Marginal and Metropolitan," 65.
37 Thomsen, "Marginal and Metropolitan," 67.
38 Thomsen, "Marginal and Metropolitan," 67.
39 Thomsen, "Marginal and Metropolitan," 67–77.
40 Örjan Lindberger, *Norrbottningen Som Blev Europé: Eyvind Johnsons Liv Och Författarskap Till Och Med Romanen Om Olof* (Stockholm: Bonnier, 1986), 166.
41 Lindberger, *Norrbottningen Som Blev Europé*, 167.
42 Eyvind Johnson, "Stad i Ljus: En Historia Från Paris På 20-Talet," in *Stad i Ljus / Stad i Mörker* (Stockholm: Bonniers, 1950), 36. All translations from this text are mine. Subsequent citations are given parenthetically in the text.
43 See Briens, "Le Discours De Paris," 84–5.
44 Virginia Woolf, *Mrs. Dalloway* (1925; London: Vintage, 2000), 1.
45 Thomsen, "Marginal and Metropolitan," 80.
46 Luis Buñuel, "Viridiana," Films Sans Frontières, 1961.
47 Michel Delville, *Food, Poetry, and the Aesthetics of Consumption: Eating the Avant-Garde* (London: Routledge, 2008), 3.
48 Michel Delville and Andrew Norris, *The Politics and Aesthetics of Hunger and Disgust: Perspectives on the Dark Grotesque*, Routledge Interdisciplinary Perspectives on Literature (New York and London: Routledge, 2017), 3.
49 Delville and Norris, *Hunger and Disgust*, 8.
50 Delville and Norris, *Hunger and Disgust*, 40.
51 Lindberger, *Norrbottningen Som Blev Europé*, 168.
52 Delville and Norris, *Hunger and Disgust*, 41–2.

53 Maud Ellmann, *The Hunger Artists: Starving, Writing, and Imprisonment* (Cambridge, MA: Harvard University Press, 1993), 70.
54 Delville and Norris, *Hunger and Disgust*, 42.
55 Lindberger, *Norrbottningen Som Blev Europé*, 168. My translation.

Chapter 11

PERCUSSION AND REPERCUSSION: THE HAITIAN REVOLUTION AS WORKER UPRISING IN GUY ENDORE'S *BABOUK* (1934) AND C. L. R. JAMES'S *BLACK JACOBINS* (1938)

Sascha Morrell

Four years before the Afro-Trinidadian critic C. L. R. James published his celebrated study of the Haitian Revolution (1791–1804), *The Black Jacobins: Toussaint L'Ouverture and the San Domingo Revolution* (1938), the Jewish-American writer and left-wing activist Guy Endore presented a fictionalized account of the origins of the conflict in his experimental novel *Babouk* (1934). Both texts are formally innovative within their respective genres, and each imaginatively reworks the archive in ways that challenge reigning accounts of Haitian history. In particular, both emphasize the role of the laboring masses in the Haitian Revolution to connect past and present struggles, turning the Haitian conflict into a symbolic harbinger of global worker uprising which reverberates beyond racial, temporal, and geographical boundaries.

This essay will focus on how Endore and James reclaim "voodoo" from its association with racial savagery in both colonial historiography and popular representations of Haiti in the 1930s, presenting it instead as a positive medium for worker solidarity and revolutionary organization in colonial Saint Domingue, while insisting on the modernity of the Caribbean sugar plantation as a capitalist enterprise. James's emphasis on the role of *vodou* ritual in fostering slave insurrection in *The Black Jacobins* finds precedent in Endore's *Babouk*, in which the eponymous hero's revolutionary consciousness is awakened by the sound of *vodou* drums, and the rise of black workers against their white masters is presented through a stylized clash of different drumbeats. Each text presents *vodou* ritual not as a primitive hangover but as a distinctly modern form of cultural syncretism which arose to facilitate bonding among workers from different African backgrounds brought together in the production of commodities for the world market—even as it continues to serve as a marker of a specific racial and colonial experience.[1] For although each text encourages proletarian identification with the Saint Domingue slaves regardless of race, each also suggests that the division of labor along racial lines in the colonial context made it inevitable that the slaves themselves would racialize their grievances. They convey what contemporary scholars of the "Black Atlantic" increasingly recognize: that among the most enduring products of slave labor in the Americas was racial tension, and even, to some extent, the very concept of racial "blackness."[2]

The resonances between *Babouk* and *The Black Jacobins* are hardly surprising: for one thing, Endore and James were working from common sources and within a broad Marxist framework; moreover, both were writing against the background of the United States' military occupation of Haiti (1915–34), during which *vodou* was suppressed as a potential locus of resistance.[3] It is even possible Endore's novel was known to James prior to writing *The Black Jacobins*, for *Babouk* received its most favorable review in the Trotskyist *New International* (which James not only read but would contribute to from 1939).[4] But either way, the case would be less one of direct influence than imaginative affinity, for James himself had already made innovative use of ritual drumming to "modernize" the Haitian Revolution in his play *Toussaint L'Ouverture: The Story of the Only Successful Slave Revolt in History*, which was written over 1932–4 although not performed until 1936, and which anticipates some of the tensions and motifs of the 1938 study.

Sounding Black Jacobinism

Act 1 of James's play *Toussaint L'Ouverture* presents a kind of fictionalized "primal scene" of the Haitian Revolution in which its most celebrated heroes—Dutty Boukman, Toussaint L'Ouverture, Jean-Jacques Dessalines, and others—are present at a mass slave gathering in the woods around Le Cap which supposedly preceded the outbreak of insurrection in 1791. The beating of drums offstage accompanies a *vodou* ceremony officiated by Boukman, who urges his fellow workers to emulate "the white slaves in France" who have "made everybody free" and "divided the property," thus encouraging labor solidarity across racial lines.[5] Next, the untutored Dessalines stresses the imbrication of race and labor struggle in the colonial context when he leaps forth from the crowd to proclaim, "No more work ... If white man want bread let white man work ... I, Dessalines, will work no more. Liberty!" Stage directions explain that meanwhile "the drums are beating faster, as if quickened by Dessalines' speech" as "with deep passion the crowd takes up the word: Liberty! Liberty!" (55), and "[t]he drums beat louder as the crowd goes off, and then begin to grow fainter" while "Liberty or death! is the password with which they [the slaves] bid each other farewell" (56).

James thus creates a complex soundscape in which the watchwords of Enlightenment philosophy become inseparable from black percussion, and the rhetoric of individual speakers is diffused into a chorus of slave voices which is amplified by the drums and flows beyond the edges of the stage at the scene's closing. This is consistent with James's assertion in stage directions that "they, the negro slaves, are the most important characters in the play" and that "Toussaint did not make the revolt. It was the revolt that made Toussaint" (54).[6] James's expressionist use of offstage percussion likely drew inspiration from that in Eugene O'Neill's *The Emperor Jones* (1920), but whereas the thump of a "tom-tom" from the wings in O'Neill's play exemplifies the use of Africanist figures in modernist primitivism to symbolize the possibility of civilized man's reversion to a savage condition, James's drums sound the entry of a black workforce into revolutionary modernity.[7]

The rhythms of revolution continue to resonate across space and time in James's celebrated historical study *The Black Jacobins* (1938). In Chapter IV ("The San Domingo Masses Begin"), James describes how slaves traveled from miles around Le Cap Français "to sing and dance and practise the [*vodou*] rites and … make their plans."[8] Even as James asserts that "Voodoo was the medium of the conspiracy" in 1791, he is comparing the restive workers to a "modern proletariat" and asserting that their uprising "was, therefore, a thoroughly prepared and organised mass movement" (86). *Vodou*, on this view, should neither be condemned as a remnant of premodern "savagery" nor celebrated as the expression of some atavistic pan-African identity, but must be understood as the cultural work of a modern proletariat "organising for revolution" (86).

Seamus O'Malley has argued recently that "modernism … interrogated historical narrative and its formal assumptions,"[9] and in these terms, *The Black Jacobins* can be read as a work of *modernist* historiography, for—even as it seeks to provide an alternative, revisionist narrative of the Haitian Revolution—the text incorporates fictional strategies and displays its own limitations (and unresolved contradictions) in ways that promote dissatisfaction with the pretense of coherence and impartial authority in the work of "professional white-washers" (14). In *The Black Jacobins*, James gives a version of the mass *vodou* service of 1791 which—while not so bold a reimagining as his stage version—makes no small use of creative license. Dramatic scene-setting and striking imagery ("the sucking of the blood of a stuck pig") precede a speech from Boukman invoking "the voice of liberty" alongside "[t]he god who created the sun" (87), which appears in direct quotes as if word-for-word, but citing no sources. James has found novel means of "making history new": rather than questioning the demonizing speculations of early white commentators, who had sought to associate the slave uprisings with heathen barbarity through lurid visions of animal sacrifice and blood ritual, James unapologetically adopts such details as facts and even puts them on display—in the service of a very different narrative.[10] Rather than serving as an index of savagery, the *vodou* ceremony now becomes central to a story of worker uprising unparalleled in its "scope and organisation," with the slaves conceiving plans on a "massive scale" with a "Papaloi or High Priest" as chief organizer (86).

James's desire to emphasize collective ritual as a medium for resistance is apparent from the opening chapter, where he contrasts the slaves' outward submission and their "secret pride and feeling of superiority to their masters," and relays what he describes as their "favourite song":

Eh! Eh! Bomba! Heu! Heu!
Canga, bafio té!
Canga, do ki la!
Canga, li! (18)

James asserts without authority that "for over two hundred years the slaves sang it at their meetings," and even purports to provide a translation: "We swear to destroy the whites and all that they possess; let us die rather than fail to keep this vow" (18). None of James's sources provide authority for the translation, and recent research has shown it to be an invention, loosely based on the translation of a different chant ("Aya Bombé") first recorded by Drouin de Bercy in 1814.[11] This should not be considered careless scholarship, however. Rather, as with his recreation of Boukman's prayer, James's creative manipulation of his sources can be read as an act of generic sabotage, exposing flaws in dominant modes of writing source-based history. It is an attempt, however impossible or imperfect, to counteract the limits of the archive when it comes to giving voice to unlettered slaves (and a broader reminder that the role of different groups and cultural practices in shaping history may not be in proportion to the traces they leave in print).[12]

It will be noted that James's rendering of the "Bomba" lyric emphasizes race ("We swear to kill the whites"), but when the chant reappears (now without its "translation") as the epigraph to Chapter IV, it serves to introduce the comparison of the slaves to "a modern proletariat," and the accent has shifted from race and colonialism to labor struggle more generally (86–7). Over the course of *The Black Jacobins*, James variously compares the rebel slaves of Saint Domingue to "the peasants in the Jacquerie or the Luddite wreckers" (88) to modern factory workers and miners—even as he continues to foreground the role of *vodou* in their revolutionary organization. As in his earlier play, *vodou* drums beat in time with French Revolutionary slogans: at a meeting led by Toussaint in Port-de-Paix in 1796, for instance, dances accompany the cry of "Long live liberty, long live equality!" (152–3), and the black masses honor Toussaint's Constitution of 1801 with their songs and dances (253). James also foregrounds the role of *vodou* in military preparations, describing how "the women and children sang and danced in a frenzy" while "their priests (the black ones) chanted the wanga [*ouanga*]" to rally the fighters (117). Again, following Toussaint's arrest in 1802, James reports that "the drums were beating and calling the people to revolt" (334).

Crucially, James's conception of "Black Jacobinism" does not imply the unilateral influence of the French on the Haitian Revolution. In *The Black*

Jacobins, Edward Said suggests, "events in France and in Haiti criss-cross and answer each other like voices in a fugue."[13] A more fitting comparison might be the "polyrhythm" characteristic of Afro-Caribbean percussive traditions, as James presents a complex system of repercussive interaction between events on both sides of the Atlantic. As Claudius Fergus notes, James has his black Jacobins singing their vengeful "Bomba" chant "long before La Marseillaise," thus giving primacy to the slaves' own culture and spontaneous organization over the influence of French Revolutionary slogans or Enlightenment philosophy.[14] Yet James gives the opposite impression when he describes the Saint Domingue slaves as "hospitable to the boldest conclusions of revolutionary thought," contending that they "had heard of the [French] Revolution and had construed it in their own image":

> The white slaves in France had risen, and killed their masters, and were now enjoying the fruits of the earth. It was gravely inaccurate in fact, but they had caught the spirit of the thing. Liberty, Equality, Fraternity. (81)

We might think of this in terms of syncopation, with events in France taking the on-beat, and Haiti the off-beat for a time. But the accent continues to shift and, in one striking passage, James proclaims the simultaneity of these movements and makes them part of an unfinished history of class struggle:

> [a]t the same time as the French, the half-savage slaves of San Domingo were showing themselves subject to *the same historical laws* as the advanced workers of revolutionary Paris; and *over a century later* the Russian masses were to prove once more that this innate power *will display* itself in all populations when deeply stirred.... (243, emphases added)

That James should emphasize rather than downplay the role of *vodou* in this context is crucial: as in his play *Toussaint L'Ouverture*, James invites readers to hear the beating of *vodou* drums as the expression of this "innate power," reverberating across space and time.

Structurally, *The Black Jacobins* can itself be considered a polyrhythmic text, wherein criss-crossing narratives—of race and class struggle, of ideal principle and spontaneous resistance, of individual and collective agency—mingle their distinct but interlocking rhythms. There is tension in the study's very title, where the colon pits the plural ("The Black *Jacobins*") against the singular ("*Toussaint L'Ouverture* and the San Domingo Revolution"). James evidently wants to emphasize the role of the working masses, and his admonition in the preface that "Toussaint did not make the revolution. It was revolution that made Toussaint" (x) recalls the near-identical statement in his earlier play *Toussaint L'Ouverture*, cited above. But in the theater, James could utilize non-verbal sound (including percussion) and the physical presence of bodies onstage to foreground the agency of the working masses despite a lack of primary sources.

Such strategies were not available in writing *The Black Jacobins*, and notwithstanding James's readiness to creatively manipulate evidence, Toussaint tends to steal the limelight as an exemplar of principled leadership and individual "genius" (127, 133, 256, 272).[15]

In order to claim both Toussaint and *vodou* for an inspirational narrative of successful proletarian uprising, James must downplay divisions that arose between the working masses and the revolutionary leadership precisely over questions of forced labor and *vodou* practice. Numerous scholars have pointed to the irony that Toussaint fought against slavery but "reintroduced compulsory labor rules" in an effort to preserve the system of large-scale plantations as the basis of national prosperity.[16] Meanwhile, he and subsequent Haitian leaders recognized *vodou* as a potential breeding ground for resistance and sought to suppress it accordingly.[17] But James effects strategic elisions and juxtapositions to convey an impression of greater continuity between *vodou* folk practices and Toussaint's politics as part of a larger black Jacobinism. For instance, the *vodou* ceremony at which Boukman bids his fellow slaves to "[t]hrow away the symbol of the god of the whites" (i.e., the Catholic cross) in order to dedicate themselves to "liberty" (87) sets the scene for Toussaint's "entrance into history" (90), and only much later will James admit in passing that Toussaint "encouraged the practice of the Catholic religion" (246).

More broadly, James contradicts himself regarding Toussaint's relations with the ex-slaves following their ostensible emancipation. For instance, he acknowledges that Toussaint's laws "insisted on ... the necessity for work," but maintains that they did not involve "one class oppressing another" and were "rooted in the preservation of the interests of the labouring poor" (247), only to admit within a page, "No doubt the poor sweated ... so that the new ruling class might thrive" (248). As well as stressing Toussaint's affinity with radical Enlightenment philosophy, James claims him as a precursor for later Marxist thought. Tracing a line from Toussaint reading his Abbé Raynal to black workers reading Lenin in the twentieth century, James compares Toussaint's letter to the French Directory of November 1797 (proclaiming the ex-slaves' readiness to sacrifice their lives for liberty) to both "Paine on the Rights of Man" and "the Communist Manifesto" (197), only to admit that Toussaint ruthlessly suppressed labor uprisings under his own administration, and thereafter "confined the workers to their plantations more strictly than ever" (279).[18]

The sleight of hand evident in James's championing of Toussaint as working-class hero reminds us that *The Black Jacobins* is a genre-bending text written in pursuit of multiple, sometimes incompatible aims. If it is primarily a rigorous and pioneering source-based history, it is also committed to the project of bolstering the inspirational narrative of the Haitian Revolution as an instance of successful slave revolt, and an image of Haiti as a successful black republic. What James does differently from many previous writers who had pursued that project is to emphasize the role of African-derived cultural practices in facilitating that success, recognizing *vodou* as the medium of a modern labor movement that would "shift the economic current of three continents" (25). In this, and in his creative exposition of the limits of the archive, James can be recognized as an early exemplar of what Samantha Pinto calls "a Caribbean modernism... which developed narrative strategies and counter-discourses... distinct from white European and American modernists' appropriation-invention of 'African' primitivisms."[19]

"No romance this": Guy Endore's Babouk

Whereas James's *The Black Jacobins* exposes the limitations of historical discourse from within, Endore's *Babouk* launches its assault on official history through the ostensibly escapist medium of historical adventure romance. Juan Suárez and others have sought to demonstrate "the embeddedness of modernism in popular culture," foregrounding the "selective appropriation of popular expressive forms" within "modernist aesthetics."[20] In *Babouk* we see the opposite, as Endore turns genre fiction to political ends through the strategic appropriation of elements of modernist aesthetics.

Endore had begun to experiment along these lines in *The Werewolf of Paris* (1933), in which the suppression of the Paris commune of 1871 provides a story of real-life capitalist "werewolfism" which threatens to overtake the supernatural horror story.[21] Notwithstanding its departures from commercial formulas, *Werewolf* became a *New York Times* best-seller, and Endore was commissioned by Century publishers to write another historical romance, this time with a Caribbean setting and an exotic "voodoo" flavor. What Endore instead produced, following an inspiring visit to Haiti and a year's research into Haitian history and culture, was a genre-bending novel about the economic roots and enduring political significance of the Haitian Revolution. Century rejected *Babouk* as too incendiary, and no publisher would touch it except the left-wing Vanguard press.[22] In *The New International*, reviewer Florence Becker recognized *Babouk* as "a new sort of novel" suited to "readers who may have to run—or fight—at any moment," but the book failed to replicate *Werewolf*'s popular success, and certainly spurred no mass political action.[23] Yet in its hybrid, fragmentary form, Endore's experiment in "pulp modernism" lays bare connections James would examine in greater depth in *The Black Jacobins*, not least through its "modernizing" treatment of *vodou*.

Babouk's eponymous hero is an ingenious storyteller whose creative powers are diminished after he endures the middle passage and years of slave labor in Saint Domingue, but then are revived and turned to revolutionary ends through the collective culture of *vodou*. The prose is characterized by abrupt tonal and perspectival shifts, and narrative progression is continually disrupted by the interventionist narrator's excursus on political and economic questions, historiographical critique, and the inclusion of fragments from other texts, including colonial travelogues and legislation.[24] Like *The Black Jacobins*, *Babouk* layers multiple historical frames of reference through bold trans-temporal comparisons and proleptic projections, such as the self-reflexive moment when Endore's narrator sardonically begs the reader's pardon for comparing the execution of the slave rebel Mackandal to contemporary lynchings in United States, admitting dryly, "That was an anachronistic slip. This is a novel about an eighteenth century Negro."[25] At another such moment, the narrator pulls back in the midst of a polemic on how historians privilege the wealthy, this time making his apology directly to the hero: "but Babouk, we have gone beyond your century" (96). Such disclaimers are thoroughly disingenuous for, structurally, the novel insists that readers relate Babouk's struggle to other locations and time periods, including their own.

In *The Black Jacobins*, James maintains that Africans transported to the West Indies "entered directly into ... a modern system" of vast plantations, with "gangs of hundreds" working in "huge sugar-factories" (86). Endore conveys the same point through scenic and sensory description when the slave-ship carrying Babouk first nears the coast of Saint Domingue, and the captives in her hold begin to scent "a sharp, disturbing odor," identified by the narrator as "the odor of industry" (45). This emanates from the "vast industry" of sugar refineries, distilleries, and brickyards—from which the smog creates a "red glow" on the horizon, reminiscent of the "dark satanic mills" of mechanized mass production (all the more appropriately since, as Endore points out, the Industrial Revolution in Europe was fed by raw materials produced on slave plantations) (15). Far from offering the escapist exoticism of jungle island adventure, Endore renders the setting of Babouk's enslavement all too recognizable for American readers in industrialized urban settings (45).

On Babouk's first arrival, the seasoned slaves look to him like "zombies," and readers witness the process of Babouk's own "zombification" through years of mindless toil, which is described in terms consistent with twentieth-century critiques of deadening factory labor.[26] Babouk's body is transformed, becoming "heavy, chunky with muscles that had learned to function fourteen or more hours a day," until finally "his muscles began to act of themselves and even sixteen hours of uninterrupted hard labor could not tire him" (81–5). Imprisoned within this automaton-like flesh-machine, Babouk's consciousness becomes inaccessible both to himself and the narrator:

> What was Babouk thinking of?
> Nothing.
> Perhaps he had forgotten why he was working so fast, so hard. (81)

There is, admittedly, some irony in this emphasis when *Babouk* is considered in its immediate historical context at the height of the Depression, when the greatest threat facing working-class Americans was not long hours but unemployment and underemployment. Moreover, this disproportionately affected African Americans, who were typically "the last hired and the first fired", as W. E. B. Du Bois emphasized in his speech resigning from the NAACP in the year of *Babouk*'s publication.[27] But as will be seen, *Babouk*'s protest against the "unmapped" global division of exploiters and exploited (179) operates over a much longer time-span.

Babouk's creative powers revive when he is "struck full in the chest" by a "simple but subtle drum beat" from a nocturnal dance gathering (86). The bodily impact of this rhythm elicits a startling "surcharge" of sound from Babouk, putting an end to "the silence of years." This begins as a rush of wordless "noise" but soon becomes a "cataract of words and sentences" in multiple languages and "unknown tongues," expressing "all that his soul had ever wanted to say," and including the following chant:

Eh! Eh!
Bomba!
Heu! Heu!
Canga bafio té! (86)

This is the same chant James would include in *The Black Jacobins*, but the novelist takes less creative license than the historian and leaves it untranslated, thus keeping the focus on the words' rhythmic and sonorous properties as a unifying force. When the chant is repeated at a later gathering—now as "the chant of initiation"—the narrator states "[w]hat the words meant not even the singers knew clearly, but the power was there nonetheless" (154). That said, Endore's narrator does now offer some rendering gloss on what the slaves intend to express in repeating the chant:

Death to the whites!
We swear to kill all whites
Or be done to death by them! (155)

This rendering bears a striking resemblance to James's "translation" in *The Black Jacobins*, and if James was indeed familiar with Endore's novel, it may be that he followed Endore's lead in appropriating de Bercy's translation of the "Aya! Bombé" chant for the better-known "Bomba!" lyric.[28]

In any case, Endore anticipates James in associating the chant with racial resentments, while pointing to an economic basis for those resentments. To emphasize race *is* to emphasize class in a context where the division of labor coincides with the color line—hence the reference of *Babouk*'s narrator to the "hard *labor* for life to which his [Babouk's] *color* had condemned him" (95, emphases added). In response to Eugene Gordon's complaint in *The New Masses* that *Babouk* emphasized "race war" at the expense of class solidarity, Endore countered that blacks could hardly "unite and fight" with whites if there were "no whites to unite with."[29] This chimes with James's contention in *The Black Jacobins* that, whereas the workers in Paris were "passionate allies" of the rebel slaves

(120), the "small whites" in Saint Domingue could see no common cause with black workers "for whatever a man's origin ... here his white skin made him a person of quality" and "no white man did any work that he could get a Negro to do for him" (33).[30] In Endore's novel, the last-instance derivation of racial categories from productive relations is dimly theorized by Babouk himself, when he adapts the biblical story of Cain and Abel to explain how all men were black "in the beginning," until one day Cain refused to work and sought to appropriate the fruit of Abel's labor, whipping him to death and then turning pale in fear of God's vengeance (171). It is left to *Babouk*'s narrator to connect the discourse of racial difference with the quasi-racial language of class, pointing out how the ruling classes in Europe cite the "bad grammar and unwashed hands of their peasants and workers" to rationalize their exploitation just as the colonial masters insist on "those minute differences of black skin and heavy lips" in their slaves (169). Like James, who notes in *The Black Jacobins* that "the international movement was not then what it is today," Endore hopes 1930s readers will be advanced enough to identify with the Saint Domingue rebels regardless of color, even if the rebels themselves inevitably "thought in terms of colour."[31]

This is made easier by Endore's resistance to exoticizing treatments of *vodou*. When *Babouk*'s narrator describes the slaves' supernatural beliefs as "the last refuge their minds possessed," without which "they must resign themselves to being beasts of burden," Endore traces a direct line from labor exploitation to the production of folklore and *vodou* ritual (84). As Ramsey observes, Babouk is not presented as a "conduit to some primordial black spirit, but as a ... revolutionary cultural *worker*" who is "creatively preparing his listeners to throw off their oppressors."[32] Crucially, this is collaborative work: Endore's modern artist is no isolated genius but participates in a dynamic continuum of collective cultural practices comprising many voices and modes of expression—folklore, drum, dance, song, along with the daily acts of subversion and sabotage (breaking tools, malingering, and so on) through which slaves frustrate their masters. Such radical, collaborative cultural work affords some resonance with various projects associated with the Popular Front in the 1930s, such as the Workers' Dance League (later the New Dance Group), founded in 1932 to develop dance as a "weapon" in the labor movement.[33] As an index of how Endore privileges "history from below," one of *Babouk*'s most astonishing features is the complete absence of any reference to Toussaint L'Ouverture—the figure who had overwhelmingly dominated positive treatments of the Haitian Revolution hitherto.

Consistent with *Babouk*'s emphasis on the collective, the scene where the drumbeat releases Babouk's verbal "surcharge" is repeated and collectivized when the rhythms of a militant Don Pedro (*Petwo*) dance prove "contagious":

> Spectator after spectator found his throat expanding *involuntarily*; from *tense* lips *explosive* cries issued. One after the other they leapt into the midst of the dancers[.] (124, emphases added)

As an earlier chapter explained, the cult of Don Pedro aims to "fuse the numerous and conflicting tribes of slaves ... into one vast organization that all over the western world should overthrow the domination of whites" (87).[34] The dance proceeds "in deadly seriousness, in earnest sweat," but the planter is dismissive (125), and as the drumming continues for a week around Le Cap, still "the whites [are] unaware" (148). Like the doltish planter in James's play *Toussaint L'Ouverture*, who interprets the drums offstage as a sign that his slaves are "happy, dancing in the forest,"[35] the colonists in *Babouk* "conside[r] the drum only the passion for rhythm" of inferior beings with "the lowest conception of music" (148).

Babouk's name obviously recalls that of Boukman, the revolutionary figure closely associated with *vodou*, but it may also echo Babeuf, thus alluding to the French labor radical François-Noël Babeuf, often claimed as a forerunner of "the socialist tradition that would come to be closely identified with an industrial proletariat," and who is cited as a champion of the workers in James's *The Black Jacobins*.[36] Endore's wordplay in naming his hero thus fuses Afro-Caribbean associations with radical Enlightenment philosophy in a manner consistent with James's concept of "Black Jacobinism." But far more decisively than James, Endore presents the Haitian Revolution as a collective grassroots movement independent of European influence. At one point, his shape-shifting narrator turns sociologist and insists:

> [the white] discourse upon the rights of man, *that* had not caused the revolt ... These Negroes knew only the difference between a life of forced labor dictated by the lash and a life of general idleness with spells of work dictated by personal necessities, *and in that they knew all they had to know for them to rise up and slaughter their jailers*. (177, emphases added)

At bottom, *Babouk* urges, the revolution was not inspired by abstract ideals but by the lived experience of labor exploitation.[37]

In Endore as in James, "voodoo [is] the medium of the conspiracy"[38] which inaugurates the Haitian Revolution. But whereas James will stray only so far beyond the record to fill out this picture, Endore is at liberty to imagine events and interactions without record, and numerous scenes in *Babouk* depict the progress of the conspiracy from the slaves' perspective, showing the growth of revolutionary solidarity among the workers through a range of expressive practices. Perhaps the most striking is a comic sequence in which Babouk introduces the idea of flatulence as a natural "human drum" (134). At a meeting which draws slaves from multiple plantations, Babouk describes a powder used to induce flatulence at dance gatherings, thus breaking down inhibitions and providing "assistance to [the] drumming" (134). Distributed at one of the whites' social dances, Babouk claims, the powder had the same leveling effect, revealing that a white man "has a drum too, and can play on it as well as we blacks" (135). The recognition that both masters and slaves alike have bodily "drums of their own" provides reassurance that the whites are "not so much different from us" (135).

The joke then passes into a wider dialog comprising unidentified voices from the gathering, with free indirect narration representing the communal viewpoint:

> "My master would do it this way," one visitor would say, and my mistress thus.
> And then each visitor in turn had to demonstrate.
> Yes, and it was good to laugh, too, and imitate the sound that this or that person should make. (136)

Babouk's storytelling thus initiates the very "loosen[ing] up" and "abandon" of individual agency to collective play that it describes (134). Nothing could be further removed from the "nightmare bell" which regulates the "laborious days of the week" (103) than this carnivalesque living drum, as it comically reclaims the body from its reduction to a quantity of labor power. In this context, to adapt George Orwell's famous phrase, "every fart is a tiny revolution." That the fart imitations are not rendered phonetically except as a "bang!" reinforces the drum analogy, and that the farts are referred to as "drums" and "guns" interchangeably reinforces *Babouk*'s association of drums with black militancy. The joke of the human drum gathers ominous overtones when Babouk points out that if black and white fart alike, then likewise would the white masters "howl" and "bleed" if stabbed or whipped like their slaves (135).

The tension building in *Babouk*'s later chapters breaks out in a bloody insurrection which is ultimately suppressed by the colonists, resulting in Babouk's capture and execution. But the death of the novel's eponymous hero is not the end. In an extended section of formal experimentation somewhere between prose poetry and play script, Endore presents a stylized contest of different drums—a white "dum didi dumdum" and a black "tom-tom"—which foreshadows the ultimate triumph of the slaves' cause as the revolution unfolds. That cause is larger than the rebels themselves realize: the drum battle might be presented in black-and-white terms, but as the rhythms of black resistance gain ascendancy, they come to stand less for race revolt than for deracialized labor struggle against "that unmapped land, the land of property" which "covers the world" (178-9)—blowing up any remaining pretense that *Babouk* is only the story of "an eighteenth century Negro" (53).

Initially, the opposition of the "dum didi dumdum" of the white imperialists to the "tom-tom" (180-1) of black resistance might appear simplistic, even crass.[39] In particular, the "tom-tom" motif recalls the modernist primitivism of the kind seen in Vachel Linsday's notorious *Congo and Other Poems* (1914), a self-styled "Study of the Negro Race," which creates percussive effects through repetition, heavy meter, capitalization, and onomatopoeia ("boomlay boomlay BOOM") to convey what it calls "Their Basic Savagery."[40] But Endore's still cruder "tom-tom" exposes itself as an ironic *reductio ad absurdum* of primitivist stereotypes. *Babouk*'s wry narrator explicitly associates the "dreadful tomtom" with mass culture cliché:

> Who has not read a hundred stories, seen a dozen plays, of the dreadful tomtom of the savages. A thousand authors have blathered of the dreadful tomtom of the blacks, the terror of the jungle. How one's spine shivers in a cosy room to read of dark jungle sorcery, of the black man's cruel witchcraft. (181)

This is especially intriguing as a reflexive nod to the kind of escapist genre fiction Endore had been commissioned to write, and which he launches his critique from within.

Anticipating James's suggestion that "the cruelties of property and privilege are always more ferocious than the revenges of poverty and oppression" (88–9), *Babouk* suggests that the greater "terror" lies not in idle stories of island savages, but in the normalized forms of systemic violence associated with colonial domination and economic imperialism.[41] Crucially, the "tom-tom" enters the text as the white drum's "strange echo" (180), creating a sense of percussion and retributive repercussion, in which subaltern violence is justified by its dialectical relationship to the greater brutality of the oppressor. The "terrible white man's drum" is "backed by gun and cannon," and its deceptively decorous "dum didi dumdum" issues a "proclamation to the world": "Master of the world is the white man! Obey him! Sweat for him! Kneel before him!" (181). Such horrors are all too real and so widespread as to be almost mundane, a point the narrator drums home with rhythmic anaphora: "No romance this. No mystery. No magic" (181). To adapt Benjamin's famous formula, the drumbeat of civilization is the drumbeat of barbarism.

As the civilized/savage divide breaks down, so too is the black/white divide superseded. Readers' sympathies are increasingly enlisted on the black side as the white man's drum threatens to take over, with direct pleas in a hysterical first-person plural—"Help! The white man is after us!" (180)—set against the implacable imperialist rhythm:

> Dum didi dumdum! Dum didi dumdum!
> Oh God! stop the white man's drum of war!
> Dum didi dumdum! Dum didi dumdum!
> Oh God! it is coming nearer! (181)

But the black man's drum resurges, with a triumphant crescendo from "tom-tom" to "TOM-TOM," and its beat no longer calls only to "blacks" but makes a direct address to "*you* universal bootblacks," thus moving through wordplay from race to class. The drum now urges not only "you whose skins are dark" but all workers "black or yellow or red or white" to beat out "TOM-TOM!

TOM-TOM! TOM-TOM!" as a proclamation to the world in the name of equality for all (182, emphasis added). Having shown over the course of the novel how transported workers from different African backgrounds could overcome their differences through the syncretism of *vodou*, Endore now imagines this logic being extended across still greater cultural divides, with the drums uniting workers against their oppressors in various contexts worldwide—from mines to factories to fields and city streets (182).

The white man's drum which has "girdled and conquered the globe" (182) comes to stand for the global capitalist system itself, and, far from being a symbol of the exoticized other, the clichéd "voodoo tom-tom" is universalized as the rhythm of worker uprising, as relevant in the United States or Europe in the 1930s as in Saint Domingue in the 1790s. Spatio-temporal distances collapse as the black drum's message is interpreted for different contexts: "Halt! Halt, you English who murder the multitudes of your own race in mine and factory to enrich the few!"; "Halt! Halt, you Germans who poison your own superior race in chemical factories ... to stuff gold in your coffers!" (182). Like James aligning the rebellion in Saint Domingue with mass movements "over a century later,"[42] Endore's time-traveling tom-tom refers the uprisings on the plains around Le Cap to what the chapter earlier described as the "perpetual war between ... those who have not and those who have" (179).

Still, Endore remains attentive to what Du Bois called the "vertical fissure" of race as a barrier to class solidarity in the United States and elsewhere, recognizing the relative autonomy of race struggle over and above class division, and—like James—refusing to resolve one into the other.[43] This tension is evident in the competing catch-cries which head the final chapter: "*Divide and rule*, the Policy of the Imperialists," and "*Black and White, Unite and Fight*! Modern rallying cry for world social justice" (175). The formal breakdown of narrative in Endore's novel permits a sustained irresolution as to whether the effects of the first policy have made it impossible to achieve the second.

In *Black Skin, White Masks* (1952), the Martinican intellectual Frantz Fanon describes how, meeting a white man's gaze, he felt "burdened—battered down by tom-toms, cannibalism ... fetishism, racial defects."[44] But in *Babouk* and *The Black Jacobins*, Endore and James resist the primitivist associations of Afro-Caribbean drumming and religious practices, reclaiming the rhythms of *vodou* ritual as the sound of purposeful revolt, racial in its overtones but ultimately grounded in the class solidarity of plantation workers—and reverberating across space and time in the struggle of workers worldwide.

Further ironies and limitations in the uses of Haiti by these authors warrant mention, although they cannot be done justice here. In putting the Haitian Revolution to work in the service of anti-capitalist, anti-racist, and anti-imperial struggles on a global scale, Endore and James themselves might be accused of imperialist appropriation of histories and cultures not their own, and if their "corrective" identification of *vodou* with proletarian revolution challenges primitivist stereotypes, it also elides the diversity of spiritual and social functions played by drum and dance ritual both in colonial Saint Domingue and in 1930s Haiti (which Melville J. Herskovits, Zora Neale Hurston and other U.S. writers were beginning to explore in this period). That said, the enlistment of *vodou* in the cause of the international labor movement by Endore and James is compatible with the efforts of prominent Haitian authors—among them Jacques Roumain, Jacques-Stéphen Alexis, and Rene Depestre—who alike would strive to harness the energies of Haitian folk culture in the service of "proletarian solidarity across all (false) racial barriers."[45]

Endore's *Babouk* and James's *The Black Jacobins* exhibit a modernist resistance to temporal and narrative coherence which challenges dominant modes of writing history—including those narratives of Western progress which depended on the construction of other cultures as primitive, timeless or "backward." In *Babouk* as in *The Black Jacobins*, overlapping narratives of race and class struggle, individual and collective agency, abstract ideals and embodied knowledge, create a "polyrhythm" formally consistent with the complex rhythmic structures of Afro-Caribbean percussive traditions, layering multiple frames and scales of historical reference. To borrow Endore's description of the Calenda in *Babouk*, history unfolds in a "complicated rhythm of slow and rapid beats" (118) and, in *The Black Jacobins* as in *Babouk*, the Haitian Revolution has a "beat that goes on" through the history of global capitalist development and class struggle. Endore and James are putting the past to work in the present not merely to inform, but to foster proletarian identification across space and time as well as across racial lines, in order to shape the future. As C. L. R. James wrote of Trotsky's *History of the Russian Revolution*, each text commands attention not only as history or fiction but as "a summons to action" and "a roll of drums."[46]

Notes

1 The spelling *vodou* is one of several variants preferred over "voodoo" in recent scholarship.
2 On "blackness itself" as "a practice of modernity," see Samantha Pinto, "Asymmetrical possessions: Zora Neale Hurston and the gendered fictions of black modernity," in *Afromodernisms*, ed. Fionnghuala Sweeney (Edinburgh: Edinburgh University Press, 2013), 130.
3 On the confiscation of *vodou* drums by U.S. marines, see Mary A. Renda, *Taking Haiti: Military Occupation and the Culture of U. S. Imperialism, 1915–1940* (Chapel Hill, NC: University of North Carolina Press, 2001), 213.
4 Florence Becker, "An Angry Epic," *New International* 2, no.1 (January 1935), 30–1. Available online: https://www.marxists.org/history/etol/newspape/ni/vol02/no01/becker.htm (accessed April 30, 2018).
5 C. L. R. James, *Toussaint Louverture: The Story of the Only Successful Slave Revolt in History*, ed. Christian Høgsbjerg (Durham: Duke University Press, 2013), 55. Subsequent references given parenthetically in the text.

6 See Christian Høgsbjerg, "Introduction," in James, *Toussaint Louverture*, 8, 23–6, on the play's genesis and first performances starring Paul Robeson.
7 O'Neill's play, which had likewise starred Paul Robeson in stage and film versions, was itself partly inspired by Haitian history: see Renda, *Taking Haiti*, 197–205.
8 C. L. R. James, *The Black Jacobins: Toussaint L'Ouverture and the San Domingo Revolution*, rev. 2nd ed. (New York: Vintage, 1963), 86. Subsequent references given parenthetically in the text.
9 Seamus O'Malley, *Making History New: Modernism and Historical Narrative* (Oxford: Oxford University Press, 2015), 2.
10 On scholarly myths around Boukman and the *vodou* service, see David Patrick Geggus, *Haitian Revolutionary Studies* (Bloomington: Indiana University Press, 2002), 73.
11 See Alasdair Pettinger, "'Eh! Eh! Bomba, hen! Hen!': Making Sense of a Vodou Chant," in *Obeah and Other Powers: The Politics of Caribbean Religion and Healing*, ed. Maarit Forde and Diana Paton (Durham: Duke University Press, 2012), 86–7.
12 Joan Dayan makes a similar point in calling for a "*vodou* history" of the Haitian Revolution in *Haiti, History and the Gods* (Berkeley: University of California Press, 1998), 54.
13 Edward Said, *Culture and Imperialism* (New York: Knopf, 1993), 338.
14 Claudius Fergus, "'We Are Slaves and Slaves Believe in Freedom': The Problematizing of Revolutionary Emancipation in *The Black Jacobins*," in *The Black Jacobins Reader*, ed. Charles Forsdick and Christian Høgsbjerg (Durham: Duke University Press, 2017), 166.
15 Decades later, James would seek to redress this imbalance in *The Black Jacobins* (and the archive from which it derives) by returning to the theater in a 1967 play of the same title, in which *vodou* drumming expresses the resistance of the former slaves to their post-revolutionary oppression: see Rachel Douglas, "Making Drama out of the Haitian Revolution from Below," in *The Black Jacobins*, ed. Charles Forsdick and Christian Høgsbjerg (Durham: Duke University Press, 2017), 278–96.
16 Philippe Girard, *Toussaint Louverture: A Revolutionary Life* (New York: Basic Books, 2016), 175, 195.
17 See Martin Munro, *Different Drummers: Rhythm and Race in the Americas* (Berkeley: University of California Press, 2010), 48; Phillipe Girard, *Paradise Lost: Haiti's Tumultuous Journey from Pearl of the Caribbean to Third World Hotspot* (New York: Palgrave Macmillan, 2005), 28–9; Madison Smartt Bell, *Toussaint L'Ouverture: A Biography* (New York: Vintage, 2008), 194–6.
18 James could not know that Toussaint had been manumitted and was himself an employer of slave labor prior to the outbreak of revolution, of which evidence was only later uncovered: see Girard, *Toussaint L'Ouverture*, 65, 115; Bell, *Toussaint L'Ouverture*, 72–3.
19 Pinto, "Asymmetrical possessions," 130–1.
20 Juan Suárez, *Pop Modernism: Noise and the Reinvention of the Everyday* (Urbana: University of Illinois Press, 2007), 2–3.
21 See Joseph G. Ramsey, "Red Pulp: Repression and Radicalism in Mid-Twentieth Century United States 'Genre' Fiction," (PhD diss., Tufts University, 2007), 127–30.
22 Ramsey, "Red Pulp," 145; Alan M. Wald, *Writing from the Left: New Essays on Radical Culture and Politics* (London: Verso, 1994), 81, 183.
23 Becker, "An Angry Epic," 31.

24 Puzzlingly, Barbara Foley mischaracterizes *Babouk* as a "conventionally realistic work" in her pioneering study *Radical Representations: Politics and Form in U.S. Proletarian Fiction, 1929–1941* (Durham: Duke University Press, 1993), 282.
25 Guy Endore, *Babouk* (New York: Monthly Review Press, 1991), 53. Subsequent references given parenthetically in the text.
26 On the zombie's association with industrial labor in the early 1930s, see Sascha Morrell, "Zombies, Robots, Race and Modern Labour," *Affirmations: of the modern* 2, no.2 (2015), 101–34.
27 W. E. B. Du Bois, "A Negro Nation Within a Nation," June 26, 1934. Available online: http://inside.sfuhs.org/dept/history/US_History_reader/Chapter10/duboisnation.pdf (accessed April 30, 2018).
28 Pettinger's account of James's possible sources does not address *Babouk*.
29 Cited in Wald, *Writing from the Left*, 181.
30 On the need to qualify Marxist categories in the colonial context, compare Frantz Fanon, *The Wretched of the Earth*, trans. C. Farrington (New York: Grove Press, 1963), 32.
31 James, *The Black Jacobins*, 278.
32 Ramsey, "Red Pulp," 152.
33 See Ellen Graff, *Stepping Left: Dance and Politics in New York City, 1928–1942* (Durham: Duke University Press, 1997), 51–5.
34 On the cult's militancy, see Geggus, *Haitian Revolutionary Studies*, 210–11 and Gage Averill and Yuen-Ming David Yih, "Militarism in Haitian Music," in *African Diaspora: A Musical Perspective*, ed. Ingrid Monson (New York and London: Routledge, 2003), 270–1.
35 James, *The Black Jacobins*, 54.
36 Cedric J. Robinson, *Black Marxism: The Making of the Black Radical Tradition* (Chapel Hill: University of North Carolina Press, 2005), 49.
37 For a comparable suggestion that the slaves' cause was "too radical to be formulated in advance of [their] deeds," see Michel-Rolph Trouillot, "An Unthinkable History: The Haitian Revolution as a Non-Event," in *Silencing the Past: Power and the Production of History* (Boston: Beacon Press, 1995), 88–9. Other scholars urge that the workers were fighting not in the spirit of communism (as celebratory treatments have often implied) but for a system of small-scale cultivation on individual plots: see Laurent Dubois, *Avengers of the New World: The Story of the Haitian Revolution* (Cambridge, MA: Harvard University Press, 2009), 6. Endore acknowledges this here in referring to "spells of work dictated by *personal necessities*."
38 James, *The Black Jacobins*, 86.
39 The term "tom-tom" itself derives from the name of an East-Indian drum (*OED*), but was widely employed in modernist representations of African culture and identity. See, for instance, Langston Hughes, "The Negro Artist and the Racial Mountain," *Nation* 122 (1926), 692–4.
40 Vachel Lindsay, *The Congo and Other Poems* (New York: Dover, 1992), 3–6.
41 Ramsey, "Red Pulp," 182 also compares these passages.
42 James, *The Black Jacobins*, 278.
43 W. E. B. Du Bois, *Dusk of Dawn: An Essay Toward An Autobiography of A Race Concept* (Harcourt Brace & Co., 1940), 205.

44 Frantz Fanon, *Black Skin, White Masks*, trans. Charles Lam Markmann (1952; New York: Grove Press, 1967), 112.
45 Munro, *Different Drummers*, 147–8; see also Margaret Heady "*Vaudou* and the marine: Jacques-Stéphen Alexis and Zora Neale Hurston on the American occupation of Haiti," *Atlantic Studies* 13, no. 2 (2016), 282–300.
46 James, cited in Andrew Smith, *C. L. R. James and the Study of Culture* (London: Palgrave Macmillan, 2010), 148.

Chapter 12

DOMESTIC HOLOCAUST: MICHAEL HANEKE'S INTRACTABLE CLASS WAR

Paul Sheehan

"Hatred of the bourgeois," wrote Gustave Flaubert, "is the beginning of virtue."[1] He composed this "axiom" in a letter to George Sand, his fellow writer and confidant, in 1867. To show contempt for the French middle classes of the Second Empire was, in Flaubert's estimation, not just a kind of duty, it was something that could make you a better person. Disputable as this claim might be, there is no question that bourgeois-baiting served Flaubert's art—from Emma Bovary, the ungratified provincial with a craving for luxury and romance, to those two thwarted intellectuals, Bouvard and Pécuchet. More than just subject matter for his novels, it gave Flaubert an enduring critical agenda. To attack the bourgeois mindset was a necessary first step on the path to political radicalism, in the middle decades of the nineteenth century; but for Flaubert it was more a question of aesthetic radicalism, which he positioned against a view of the world that had little regard for art or its practitioners.

Almost a century after Flaubert, Richard Ellmann concluded his magisterial study of James Joyce with the following remarks:

> The surface of the life Joyce lived seemed always erratic and provisional. . . . [H]is disregard for bourgeois thrift and convention was the splendid extravagance which enabled him in literature to make an intractable wilderness into a new state.[2]

Joyce's notorious financial profligacy, which Ellmann has been documenting in some detail for the past 600 pages, is turned here into a writerly virtue—unwittingly echoing, or rather updating, Flaubert's axiom. Unlike the French writer, though, whose lifestyle was unapologetically bourgeois, Joyce practiced what he preached. On the one hand, then, Ellmann is suggesting that Joyce's mismanagement of his always-meager income had positive aesthetic outcomes. On the other, he is positing a more causal relationship: that "disregard for bourgeois . . . convention" is a necessary prelude to Joyce's—and, by extension, modernism's—disregard for literary and artistic convention.

Between Flaubert and Ellmann, the modernist anti-bourgeois myth is consolidated. The charges are, by now, all too familiar: the typical bourgeois is a consumer, not a creator, is devoid of taste and blind to beauty, passion, and adventure; most egregiously, he cares more about money than art.[3] By contrast, Joyce may have been reckless with his earnings, but his financial situation was hardly unique. Which is to say: unless you had a private or alternative income stream, to be a practicing modernist in the first half of the twentieth century was a precarious and arduous undertaking. But rather than incriminate the market, or the state, or the art institutions themselves—publishers, gallery-owners, concert promoters, and so on—it was more effective simply to blame the bourgeoisie. This took shape, though, less as blame than as a deliberate and combative agenda. Matei Calinescu suggests that modernism's founding gesture was "to disrupt and completely overthrow the whole bourgeois system of values."[4] Daniel Bell is just as unsparing; modernism, he says, can be defined as the "agency for the dissolution of the bourgeois world view."[5] Flaubert's aesthetic radicalism and Joyce's "splendid extravagance" are thus retroactively shifted from defiance to insurrection, as the modernist myth acquires the cultural weight and poise of a manifesto.

These issues find a more recent outlet in Michael Haneke, the Austrian filmmaker. Haneke is one of the few European directors to have gained not just steadfast critical support but also sizable and devoted audiences in the Anglophone world. That he has done so by following in the footsteps of the modernist auteurs of the 1960s and 1970s—indeed, by positioning himself as the "last modernist"[6]—is all the more extraordinary. Haneke's auteurist background owes a good deal to literary modernism. His principal early influence, in the 1960s, was D. H. Lawrence;[7] he has directed theatrical productions of works by Strindberg and Marguerite Duras; and he has made film adaptations of Kafka, Joseph Roth, and Ingeborg Bachmann. In addition, Haneke's technical vocabulary is continental modernist through and through: elliptical, discontinuous narration, long takes, scenographic fragmentation, and a deep and abiding commitment to documenting the material surface, the granular reality, of the world that lies before his camera. In terms of content, Haneke's films make further demands on his audience by confronting crises that are more than just social or economic—crises of communication, for example, or the conflicts that arise from crises of meaning.

Yet despite these formidable credentials, Haneke's greatest contribution to late-modernist cinema may be his unsparing, surgically precise analyses of European bourgeois identity. In attempting to diagnose what it is that has ailed Europe in the past twenty-five or thirty years, Haneke's focus is the urban middle-class professional, most often within the framework of the nuclear family. Haneke is not contemptuous of this class, as were Flaubert and his modernist inheritors, but he is just as scathing when it comes to pinpointing their failures. Accordingly, he subjects them not to ridicule but to rigorous dialectical scrutiny, exposing the contradictions, shortcomings and general untenability of the positions that they try to occupy. Bourgeois subjectivity, at least as Haneke depicts it, is not just a matter of those tried and true markers of mediocrity, insularity, complacency, and so on. It is founded on the "delusions of class and privilege" that lead to self-duplicity, and that ultimately take shape as moral blindness.[8]

In his comprehensive survey of modernist cinema, András Bálint Kovács describes the kinds of protagonists that populated such films in the 1960s and 1970s: urban middle-class intellectuals and artists, who were "concerned above all with [their] inner universe[s]."[9] The exemplar was Antonioni, whose main characters were invariably wealthy, bored, and neurotic; and it is Antonioni who has most influenced Haneke in his development of a late-modernist aesthetic (although traces of Bergman, Bresson, and Tarkovsky are also plentiful throughout the oeuvre). Antonioni staged dramas of disappearance, in which empty space was rendered ominous yet enthralling, and charged with portent. But Antonioni, like other modernist auteurs, was never really interested in the world of work, concerned instead with the dramatic tension between character and environment, and the pressures of disaffected relationships. Haneke treats his middle-class characters very differently. Their occupations largely define them, as members of (Austrian or French) metropolitan elites. More significantly, we actually see them at work, performing tasks that affirm their social identities whilst underscoring Haneke's realist aesthetic.

Industriousness has long been seen as a bourgeois value—perhaps even the cardinal value. For bourgeois self-definition is oriented around hard work and honesty, as necessary pre-conditions for material wealth and comfort. In *The Bourgeois: Between History and Literature* (2013), Franco Moretti even goes so far as to identify the creation of a culture of work as the "greatest symbolic achievement of the bourgeoisie as a class." What was once regarded as a "hard necessity or a brutal duty" came to be seen, instead, as useful, efficient and vocational; in short, as a form of "seriousness." This last epithet, says Moretti, convokes a definitive detachment from the world of labor and sets the "bourgeoisie on its way to being the ruling class."[10]

As well as work and industry, the bourgeoisie defines itself through relief from work; which is to say, through conjugal family relations which, to be properly conducted, require the safe, residential space of the home. These two milieux, "work" and "home," constitute the bases for Haneke's anti-bourgeois cinema. Although he has made one film that is recognizably "post-apocalyptic"—the haunting and bewitching *Time of the Wolf* (*Le Temps du loup*, 2003)—his real *métier* is for what could be termed the "pre-apocalyptic": expositions of certain cultural pathologies, which crystallize into tightly rendered scenarios of domestic strife, whether home- or work-based. But although his protagonists are nearly always pushed to the brink, this is rarely the overture to a spectacular and cathartic denouement. Rather, the destruction that ensues is implosive and contained, allowing the tempo of wider everyday life to continue unabated.

A victim of numbers: The Seventh Continent

This is evident enough in *The Seventh Continent* (*Der siebente Kontinent*, 1989), the first of Haneke's films to get a theatrical release. It begins as a meticulously crafted social critique, covertly exposing middle-class alienation; and it ends as a kind of modernist horror story, in which the perpetrators are also the victims. Haneke presents three days in the life of the Schober family, Georg, Anna, and their young daughter Eva, who live in the northern Austrian town of Linz. Each day is set a year apart, giving a sense of the repetitive and routinized activities that constitute their lives. At the same time, it echoes one of the most celebrated of literary modernist forms: the diurnal narrative, as perfected by Joyce, Woolf, Faulkner, and Lowry. The third day-long section, set in 1989, breaks the cycle in the most decisive way. Georg and Anna leave their jobs, settle up some of their affairs—including a visit to the bank, to withdraw their life's savings—and kill themselves and their daughter.

The first two parts of this structure effectively convey one quality in particular: typicality. Insofar as the Schobers are defined by their class, their professional lives are unexceptional. Anna works as an optician, in an eyeglass store that she runs with her brother; and Georg is an engineer, although it is not clear what the company he works for actually does. His workplace suggests heavy industry, on the outside, and depersonalized, anonymous machinery on the inside. A voiceover at the start of the film, in the guise of a letter that Anna is writing to her in-laws, informs us that Georg has been passed over for promotion. However, although this might imply a potential source of frustration and despondency for the couple, it turns out not to be the case.

Haneke has said that his script was based on a newspaper article in the German news magazine *Stern*. A suiciding bourgeois family may be unusual, even a bit lurid, but the detail that captured Haneke's attention was the prelude to the suicide. The husband paid a visit to a hardware store, and came home with an impressive array of hand tools—everything that he, and his wife, and daughter needed to destroy the contents of their home. This part of the film takes up about twenty minutes of screen time, a domestic holocaust that brings it to a suitably pre-apocalyptic close. It could be seen as a "cleansing" operation: the Schobers' desire to see that the source of their discontent—or at least some of its concrete manifestations—does not "outlive" them. One shot in particular still affronts audiences. After most of the Schobers' belongings have been smashed, ripped, torn, and pulverized, we see why that last cash withdrawal was so important. With steadfast determination, Georg flushes wad upon wad of Austrian banknotes down the toilet (giving a new, yet no less scandalous, meaning to the term "money shot"). Haneke insists that a detail such as this was beyond him, as a writer-director, and that it came from the original *Stern* article.

And so the Schobers go about destroying their property with the same determination and single-mindedness that has led them to the brink of self-annihilation. But in doing so, they cannot quite let go of their bourgeois habits.

After a few tentative swings of the sledgehammer, Georg has a realization. If we are to do this properly, he says, "we have to do it systematically." Thus, the lives that they have lived, as puppets or pawns of a cruel and unyielding social order, are terminated in a not dissimilar manner. The destruction of their property becomes, in other words, a form of work, as if they are incapable of liberating themselves from the demands of order and propriety, of *doing things in the correct manner*, thus revealing how deep their conformity runs.

Their collective suicide is hinted at from the start, albeit obliquely. The opening scene, which is set in a car wash, ends with the Schobers' sedan driving past a billboard inviting them to "Emigrate to Australia"—the seventh continent of the title, so called because the last to be "discovered." In fact, when their bank manager asks them why they are withdrawing their life's savings, Anna actually tells him that it is so they can emigrate to Australia. Why do they not consider this alternative "escape route"? It has to do with how this option is presented to them. As an advertisement on a billboard it has already been corrupted by its association with the pernicious ideology that underlies their anomie. Haneke's working title for the script was "Australien"—a reference to the impossible dream of escape that haunts the Schober family, and also a cipher for the word "alien," thus defining their relationship to the bourgeois ideology that has both shaped and denatured them.

As noted above, work is no more a cause of *direct* discontent for Georg and Anna than any other element in their lives. But work is still an issue, and we can detect in some early scenes the unmistakable aura of alienated labor. Rather than show factory workers whose labor is "invisible," because inscribed into mass-produced artifacts as surplus value, Haneke highlights those forms of labor that are visible to Georg and Anna in their everyday experiences as bourgeois subjects. The first of these scenes is a shopping spree in a supermarket, the primary consumer outlet, shot at trolley-height (gathering and grasping arms are the only "human" elements here). Wine bottles, baguettes, frozen vegetables, and cuts of meat—the supermarket has always had a close relationship with the meat industry—are piled into the trolley, which glides remorselessly along the aisles. The operations of Western industrial capitalism are equally evident in a later scene at a gas station, the petroleum industry having a well-documented strategic and symbolic importance for the capitalist economies (see, for example, Jones[11]).

The motif in both these scenes, which take place in the first twenty minutes of the film, is numbers. It is not just a matter of numerical symbols—on cash registers, on gas pumps and on receipts—but more abstractly, numbers in the form of quantities of things. There are items on sale, which have a price; and there are items on shelves, infinitely reproducible copies of a particular product. Everything in this world, it would seem, is reducible to a number, and repeatable as a quantity. (The items that Georg purchases, to destroy the contents of his home, are presented in a similar way, as commodities rather than as tools.) This is a society without distinction or difference, a society that is awash with *multiples* of everything—the hell of consumer-capitalist choice. Inside this colorless and regulated world, middle-class life is figured as a kind of prison. Within its walls, and speaking through its commodities and conventions, a stark choice is issued: conform or die. In a very real sense, then, the Schober family is a victim of numbers.

The Seventh Continent may have been Haneke's first theatrical feature, as already mentioned, but it was made after he had been writing and directing television films, mostly for West German networks, over a period of about fifteen years. As it happens, the script for *The Seventh Continent* was commissioned from Haneke by the Radio Bremen German network—which subsequently rejected it, on the grounds that it contained "too many deaths for television."[12] The Austrian Film Institute then stepped in and encouraged Haneke to make it as a theatrical feature, thus implying that the collective suicide of a nuclear family does *not* connote "too many deaths" for the cinema. In film history there are, of course, countless examples of suicidal acts—many fewer, though, where they are carried out collectively, and only a handful that are presented less as desperate and impulsive deeds than as premeditated, calculated and more or less rational acts of self-erasure. Notable examples of the latter include Louis Malle's *The Fire Within* (*Le Feu follet*, 1963), whose protagonist sees life as a series of humiliations and disappointments, and so prefers oblivion; and, several years after *The Seventh Continent*, Abbas Kiarostami's *Taste of Cherry* (1997), about a man seeking an accomplice who will bury him after he is dead, in keeping with his sense of ritual.

But perhaps the closest precedent to Haneke's film is Marco Ferreri's notorious, hard-hitting satire, *La Grande bouffe* (1973). It centers on a group of four middle-aged men, all tired of their bourgeois lifestyles, who convene for a weekend and eat themselves to death. As they expire, one by one, following an orgy of weird sex and gourmet cooking, there is as much a sense of ideological indictment as there is of overindulgence. The fetishization of food is, of course, intrinsic to the bourgeois lifestyle. Dinner parties, fine dining, and culinary tourism are vital social ceremonies, as Pierre Bourdieu notes, in which "correct eating" is an "affirmation of ethical tone and aesthetic refinement."[13] Ferreri's protagonists, by contrast, pit *quantity* against *quality*, with connoisseurship ultimately flipping over to disgust. In *The Seventh Continent*, the Schobers have a final breakfast together, the table laden with delicacies both local and exotic, thus echoing the hedonistic excesses of *La Grande bouffe*. But their alimentary extravagance is much more restrained and "systematic," and rather than being the agent of their suicide, it is just a brief lead-in to it. A means rather than an end, it is there to provide sustenance for the demolition work that lies ahead of the Schober family.

Culture masks politics: Hidden

To reiterate a point made earlier, Haneke probes the limits of bourgeois subjectivity in the context of the family. In an interview following *The Piano Teacher* (*La Pianiste*, 2001), Haneke said that his goal was to establish the family as the germinating cell for all conflicts. I always want to describe the world that I know, and for me the family is the focus of the miniature war, the first site of all warfare ... whether between parents and children or wife and husband.[14]

This model of familial strife is, however, more apparent in Haneke's French films than his earlier Austrian ones. In *The Seventh Continent*, for example, mis- or non-communication is a more plausible source for the Schobers' anomie, rather than inter-familial struggle. As to *why* this should be the case—why the social dynamic of the family can be seen, not just as a locus of conflict, but as the very paradigm for *all* forms of human antagonism—we could turn to Deleuze and Guattari, and an argument that they make in *Anti-Oedipus* (1972).

The family, they contend, operates primarily as a mechanism for repression. To become a proper subject, to be made into a useful and productive member of society, the child's desires must be repressed; and it is the role of the family, as channeled through parental command, to do this.[15] The consequences are two-fold. First, the child's repressed desires become disfigured and neurotic. Second, and more importantly, the child is rendered prone to wider forms of social repression.[16] So we could say that Haneke's remark is a further consequence of this repressive mechanism—that familial conflict arises from coercive restraint, and that one of its end-points is what I am calling "pre-apocalyptic" violence and destruction.

Family relations and residential space come under threat in *Hidden* (*Caché*), the film that Haneke made in 2005. The veneer of "normalcy" is maintained more carefully here than in any other of his works (although it is, by degrees, removed); which may explain why the film has prompted more critical analysis than anything else in Haneke's œuvre. The plot turns on a series of videotapes sent to Georges Laurent, who lives with his wife and son in a chic district of Paris. He considers the tapes, which contain recordings of the Laurents' townhouse, and of Georges's childhood home, to be acts of vengeance. The avenger in question, the sender of the tapes, he believes, is Majid—a French Algerian who lived with Georges when he was a young boy, and who was on the verge of being adopted by his parents. Georges, however, had other ideas. Instead of welcoming this stepbrother/interloper into his life, he convinced his parents that Majid was ill with pneumonia. So to avoid putting their other son at risk, the Laurents banished him to an orphanage, never to be seen again. Georges's lies, then, sealed Majid's fate, condemning him to a life of hardship and privation.

The videotapes (and the matter of who sent them) are, however, heuristic devices rather than mysteries to be unraveled. The questions that they raise are generally seen in terms of guilt: colonial guilt implicating the French nation, for its treacherous and underhanded persecution of Algerians; and the repressed childhood guilt, or perhaps rather shame, of Georges, which he steadfastly refuses to acknowledge. I want to suggest a third form of guilt: bourgeois guilt, the guilt of a class that outwardly embraces such things as tolerance, equity, free speech, multiculturalism, and so on, yet secretly harbors a fear of refugees, of asylum seekers, and of non-European migrants. Although I have termed this "bourgeois guilt," it is actually more nuanced than that—because, historically, the French bourgeoisie has a less than honorable record in terms of its attitude to outsiders wanting to cross its borders. Thomas Nail, for example, describes the bourgeois reception of migrants in eighteenth- and nineteenth-century France as "not positive," hence their (re)designation as "nomads," "barbarians," and "vagabonds."[17]

When it comes to Georges and Anne Laurent, their professional activities put them in a fairly exclusive social milieu: Georges is the host of a popular literary TV show, and Anne a book editor. They belong, then, to intellectual elites within the Parisian bourgeoisie, connected intimately to the creative arts. Georges, for his part, is only too aware of how they are perceived. After the first videotape arrives, he initially blames it on the company that his teenage son keeps, dismissing it as "some idiot playing games on his pal's bobo parents." That term, "bobo," strikes us now as a bit archaic. Coined by a journalist in 2000 as a shorthand for "bourgeois bohemian," it indicated the arrival of a new hybrid class, one seemingly purpose-built for the era of digital capitalism. Insofar as the term is now somewhat outmoded, that is because it never really caught on in the Anglophone world. The French, however, took it up enthusiastically—so much so that the political magazine *Le Point* announced in 2008 a "Requiem for the bobo," believing that the class had outlived its usefulness, and lost whatever political influence it had. However, the bobo did not go away—neither as a term nor as a class—and a book published by a couple of French journalists in 2014, *La république bobo*, reasserts its importance in contemporary French society.

But even though the bobo is treated with indifference outside France, its socio-political agenda is only too familiar. The various names it goes by run the social gamut. At the corporate level, it is sometimes referred to as "caring capitalism," in which entrepreneurial materialism is combined with a few token counter-cultural gestures. Slavoj Žižek borrowed the term "liberal communism," to describe the practice of CEOs suddenly feeling the weight of social responsibility, and becoming philanthropists.[18] And at the individual level, it takes shape as "ethical consumerism," oriented around such brands as Fairtrade and Equal Exchange. So Georges and Anne are bobos, members of an educated elite and also possessors of cultural capital. Now, I want to suggest that the wider issue that Georges embodies is not just repressed guilt about France's violent colonial past, but another kind of subterfuge; one that brings Haneke's intellectual heritage to the fore.

Growing up in post-war Austria, Haneke was party to a nationwide cover-up, of sorts: the displacement of *politics* by *culture*. Although the term "culture industry" has been central to certain forms of critical theory, as a shorthand description for the entanglements of capitalism in the artifacts and operations of culture, the displacement just described works to mystify or befog that particular relationship. For Marx, a similar kind of mystification can be seen with the expropriation of labor value, examined in *Value, Price and Profit* (1898). He writes: "As [the worker] has sold his laboring power to the capitalist, the whole value or produce created by him belongs to the capitalist, the owner *pro tempore* of his laboring power." In "naturalizing" such an arrangement, this expropriative action can be concealed and the existing class structure maintained. For this sort of exchange "must constantly result in reproducing the working man as a working man, and the capitalist as a capitalist."[19]

In similar fashion, the Austrian covering-over of politics with culture was self-evidently a thoroughgoing success. Think of the European capital of classical music, Vienna, and what comes to mind are concert halls, museums, galleries, and coffee-houses—rather than the *Anschluss*, the annexation of Austria into Hitler's Reich, in which his troops marched into Vienna without a single shot being fired; or Austria's expropriation of Jewish property and other assets during the war years; or those outbreaks of neo-Nazi violence that take place from time to time, often in Vienna. The Austrian writer, Thomas Bernhard, who spent most of his 25-year career castigating his homeland, deplored this state of affairs. His parting shot was the play *Heldenplatz*, set in 1988, in which a character declaims that "there are more Nazis in Vienna now than in [1938]."[20] Now, although *Hidden* is set in Paris, it nonetheless evokes the troubling spirit of post-war Austria. In this poisonous context that they both share, culture does not signify refinement, or discernment, or civility; indeed, it is implied that such a way of thinking is itself a bourgeois affectation. Culture, rather, is a vocation-led distraction, a way of not having to acknowledge that the "delusions of social privilege" are founded on violence, discrimination, and forgetting. And the bobo, the French *bourgeois bohémien*, who has close ties to the culture industry, is the latest embodiment of this professionalized evasiveness.

Work, in *The Seventh Continent*, is displaced—from the workplace (where it is neither oppressive nor fulfilling) to the home, as the family sets about liberating itself from a vacuous materialism. Far from being liberated, though, they reveal themselves to be more work-focused than ever, unable to deny how indentured they are to order and to system. In *Hidden*, by contrast, it is not the material trappings of the Laurents' lives that are the problem, but the aura of "culture" that enshrouds them, providing a convenient distance from the exclusionist ideology on which their social privilege is founded. If the two situations are related, it is via the indices of class. The logical end-point of the bourgeois obsession with status, order, acquisition, and conformity is self-annihilation. The bourgeoisie is the suiciding class, unable to see beyond the dead-ends of social and cultural obeisance.

In addition, culture itself raises difficult questions about bourgeois identity. The bourgeoisie, as we saw above, has traditionally been suspicious of art, and subordinated it to commerce. As a result of this prejudice, the bobos in *Hidden* are less a hybridized social group than a conflicted one. More *bourgeois* than *bohémien*, the tension that they have inherited is transposed, rather than resolved, by projecting the more dubious values of their class onto the sphere of culture. As Georges Laurent's fears embolden him, the hidebound, illiberal side of his class background starts to emerge. It is, above all, a fear of loss—of privilege, of status, of authority and entitlement—that turns Georges into an agent of persecution, inciting Majid to commit a bloody and horrific act of self-annihilation. In committing this act, Majid makes visible the destructive consequences of Georges's fears—even, in a sense, reflecting back to the "brother" who spurned him the suicidal violence that underpins bourgeois identity.

And yet, the last words heard from Georg Schober, before he sets about destroying his home, are in a voiceover/letter to his parents. "I believe that looking at the life we have lived straight in the eye," he says, "makes any notion of the end easy to accept." In many ways, then, he is more clear-sighted than his French counterpart. For Georges Laurent, the impasse of bourgeois identity does not need to be resolved, when it can be screened out. Haneke's diagnostic insight is to show how this class, at least in its French bobo incarnation, turns the concept of work from a condition of the social contract into a technique for self-preservation and self-advancement.

Coda: The pathologies of privilege in Happy End

Work, class, and family are at the forefront of Haneke's most recent (and possibly final) film, *Happy End* (2017). As has been widely noted, the film is rife with allusions to the director's earlier works, both formally (its first scenes recall the tight, dehumanized framing of *The Seventh Continent*; the vignette-like structure echoes *Code Unknown* [*Code inconnu*, 2000]) and thematically (race relations, refugeeism, surveillance, euthanasia, and sexual perversion all feature prominently). On the subject of work, however, *Happy End* does much more than simply recuperate earlier critiques of bourgeois self-satisfaction. Yet in doing so, in moving beyond these prior reckonings, a loop of sorts is being closed. Almost thirty years after that outwardly content nuclear family, the Schobers, sought to erase both itself and the material signs of its existence, an even more privileged family exhibits a similarly implosive bent. Even if nothing in *Happy End* is as horrific or appalling as the third "act" of *The Seventh Continent*, the later film nonetheless deepens the abyss of discontent and dysfunctionality that has by now become Haneke's hallmark.

In fact, after a protracted yet beguiling prelude (filmed on a smartphone), *Happy End* begins with a stunning *coup de cinéma* (mimicking security-cam footage) to rival the destructive finale of *The Seventh Continent*—albeit condensed into a few seconds. The wall of a construction site, as deep as a cliff-face, collapses before our eyes, producing vast plumes of dust, visible panic amongst the onlookers, and one seriously injured worker. The owners of the construction company, we soon discover—and the parties legally responsible for the accident—are the Laurents. Haneke's archetypal French family has thus undergone a kind of apotheosis, and joined the corporate world. Anne (Isabelle

Huppert) controls and oversees the company, with an icy, ruthless manner indicating that she has inherited more than just the family business from her father Georges (Jean-Louis Trintignant), the retired, infirm patriarch. This could be seen as a return to a more classic Marxist version of bourgeois identity, where the owner exploits labor value in an obvious way. The bobo "mystification" that uses culture to screen out politics is therefore suspended; this new Laurent family does not even warrant the provisional sympathy that the couple at the heart of *Hidden* initially earned. At the same time, there are comedic elements here that are barely hinted at in *The Seventh Continent* and *Hidden*, and it is these elements that leaven the sometimes-appalling machinations of the Laurent corpocracy.

This comical turn is also warranted—or at least welcomed—because death stalks *Happy End* insidiously, as it does no other Haneke film, seeming to govern the drama. The worker injured by the collapsing wall sets part of the plot in motion, but his is not the first brush with mortality. In the earlier, smartphone-shot sequence, a woman is discreetly filmed performing her ablutions, each part of the routine helpfully captioned by the phone's user; we later discover that she has been poisoned, and see her expired body in a hospital bed. There are cues for this outcome in the earlier sequence, via a pointed juxtaposition: the smartphone suddenly jumps to a writhing hamster, dying from the anti-depressives fed it by a cruelly inquisitive teenager (recalling Haneke's 1992 film, *Benny's Video*). Although none of these ends is especially "happy" (or desired), there is one that promises to illustrate the film's title in a non-ironic way. The ailing Georges freely admits to having euthanized his suffering wife a few years ago (evoking Trintignant's role in Haneke's previous film, *Amour*); now he is hoping for a similar fate himself. After a few half-hearted solo attempts—crashing a car, attempting to buy a gun, and so on—end in failure, Georges persuades Eve (Fantine Harduin), his teenage grand-daughter (and, we gather, poisoner of hamsters and mothers), to assist him. Haneke's thesis that the bourgeoisie is the "suiciding class," depicted with such severity in *The Seventh Continent*, thus undergoes a makeover: shock and horror are now recast as pitch-black satire, at times bordering on farce.

The business with the injured construction worker, and the legal problems that ensue, highlight Anne Laurent's grasp of corporate hegemony; dealing with the worker becomes less a question of moral duty than an irritant to be swept away as quickly and efficiently as possible. A similarly no-nonsense assertiveness inflects her treatment of Rachid (Hassam Ghancy) and Jamila (Nabiha Akkari), the Moroccan servants who reside on the Laurent estate. (When the couple's young daughter is bitten by a watchdog Anne brushes it aside, declaring the suggested rabies shot to be unnecessary.) This side of work is hinted at in Haneke's earlier French films, but not really explored. For example, we only hear about Majid's parents, in *Hidden*, and learn nothing about them other than that they were Algerian, worked for the Laurents, and died in the Paris massacre on October 17, 1961.

Although their screen time is brief, Rachid and Jamila animate the condition of the migrant worker, caught in an impossible bind between liberal-bourgeois condescension (and off-handed negligence) and the fear and anxiety prompted by non-European refugees. The plight of the latter is conjoined with the situation of the servant couple—inadvertently or otherwise—by the impulsive and unpredictable behavior of Anne's son, Pierre (Franz Radowitz), who is committed to ever more extreme acts of humiliation and (self-)abasement. Two scenes in particular, tellingly based around bourgeois eating rituals, invite this juxtaposition. In the first, Georges's birthday party/dinner is interrupted when Pierre loudly and patronizingly extols the virtues of Jamila's cooking; in the second, the film's climactic scene, Pierre affronts his mother, in the midst of her wedding celebration lunch, by leading in a group of young, black male refugees, and announcing that they are to join the *uber*-bourgeois guests at their tables.[21] Anne Laurent, feigning hospitality, welcomes them to the celebration. For Pierre, playing the Laurents' "guilty conscience," migrant workers and asylum seekers are consonant with each other—which, in a sense, they are, given the precariousness and hostility that each group must face.

Anne's heartless business practices and Georges's death wish eventually come to seem all of a piece. The same morose mindset feeds both the quiet desperation of Anne's brother Thomas (Matthieu Kassowitz), deeply involved in extra-marital cybersex, and the boisterous (and buffoonish) dejection of Pierre. We feel, rather than see, the lives of these haut-bourgeois archetypes come apart. In one further "closing of the loop," the morbidly sociopathic Eve could be seen as an inversion of the enigmatic Eva Schober, fatally implicated in her parents' anomie. The Laurents in *Happy End* are, finally, as self-deceived as the bobos in *Hidden* and as resolute as the Schober family, focused intently on the demolition work that ultimately includes themselves. They reveal, in short, the perverse workings of the death drive at the heart of Haneke's class war, and show how it is tied in to one further Marx-related aspect.

Religion, writes Marx in 1843, "is the opium of the people"—at once a "universal source of consolation and justification," and an agency that grants "*illusory* happiness" to the masses.[22] No such spiritual or beatific panacea is proffered in *Happy End*. If there is an "opium of the bourgeoisie," insofar as "illusory happiness" is even attainable, it is a literal, pharmaceutical one: antidepressants, painkillers, soporifics, and "Lexomil" (a calmative for treating anxiety disorders) are insistent yet unremarkable elements in the Laurents' daily lives, enabling them to function efficiently. Eve reveals the end-point of this narcotic reliance late in the film, when she tries to commit suicide herself, by ingesting the pills that her (dead) mother has left behind. The ailing Georges's desire to be euthanized thus appears to be class- as well as age-driven, as if he were indulging a long-held wish for oblivion. It is a wish that has taken different forms across Haneke's oeuvre, as the trajectory of his anti-bourgeois critique reaches its terminus.

The clear-sighted Schobers recognize, and embrace, the death drive that is the mark of their class; it is only in the *doing* of the destructive work to which they are committed that their bourgeois blind-spots become apparent. The bobos in *Hidden*, by contrast, have a mystified, conflicted, and acutely deluded relationship to the malign aspects of their class background, and use their cultural capital as props or screens to maintain this deception. By the time of *Happy End*, the death drive is not just an inevitable outcome or destination, but implicit in the Laurents' very habitus. The regulated dosages that are part of their daily routines suggest that the distinctive aspect of their collective "death wish," neither implosive nor hidden, is that it has become routinized. The sheer mundanity of this baleful yet subdued disposition makes "any notion of the end" (as Georg Schober puts it) neither "happy" nor easily achieved.

Notes

1 Gustave Flaubert and George Sand, *The George Sand–Gustave Flaubert Letters*, trans. Aimee L. McKenzie (London: Duckworth & Co., 1922), 66.
2 Richard Ellmann, *James Joyce* (Oxford: Oxford University Press, 1982), 744.
3 See, for example, Raymond Williams, *The Politics of Modernism: Against the New Conformists*, ed. Tony Pinkney (London: Verso, 1989), 53–4; Peter Gay, *Modernism: The Lure of Heresy from Baudelaire to Beckett and Beyond* (New York and London: W. W. Norton & Co., 2008), 6; Cathy L. Jrade, "The Spanish-American Modernismo," in *Modernism*, ed. Astradur Eysteinsson and Vivian Liska (Amsterdam: John Betjemans, 2007), 823–4.
4 Matei Calinescu, *Five Faces of Modernity: Modernism, Avant-Garde, Decadence, Kitsch, Postmodernism* (Durham: Duke University Press, 1987), 119.
5 Daniel, Bell, *The Cultural Contradictions of Capitalism: Twentieth Anniversary Edition* (New York: BasicBooks, 2001), xxi.
6 See Roy Grundmann, "Introduction: Haneke's Anachronism," in Grundmann, ed., *A Companion to Michael Haneke* (Malden: Wiley-Blackwell, 2010), 6. Arguing for a more specific aesthetic, Oliver C. Speck suggests that Haneke's Austrian films characterize his "modernist phase." *Funny Frames: The Filmic Concepts of Michael Haneke* (New York and London: Continuum, 2010), 62.
7 This somewhat surprising revelation was made by Haneke in a 2014 interview. See Luisa Zielinski, "Michael Haneke, The Art of Screenwriting No. 5," *The Paris Review* 211 (2014), 169.
8 Zielinski, "Michael Haneke," 168.
9 András Bálint Kovács, *Screening Modernism: European Art Cinema, 1950–1980* (Chicago: University of Chicago Press, 2008), 69.
10 Franco Moretti, *The Bourgeois: Between History and Literature* (London: Verso, 2013), 43, 74.
11 Geoffrey Jones, *Multinationals and Global Capitalism: From the Nineteenth to the Twenty-first Century* (Oxford: Oxford University Press, 2005), 68–70.
12 Grundmann, "Introduction," 44 n. 12.
13 Pierre Bourdieu, *Distinction: A Social Critique of the Judgment of Taste*, trans. Richard Nice (Cambridge, MA: Harvard University Press, 1984), 196.

14 Christopher Sharrett, "The World That Is Known: An Interview with Michael Haneke," in Grundmann, ed., *Companion to Michael Haneke*, 587.
15 Gilles Deleuze and Félix Guattari, *Anti-Oedipus: Capitalism and Schizophrenia*, trans. Robert Hurley, Mark Seem, and Helen R. Lane (Minneapolis: University of Minnesota Press, 1983), 120–1,
16 Deleuze and Guattari, *Anti-Oedipus*, 361.
17 Thomas Nail, *The Figure of the Migrant* (Stanford: Stanford University Press, 2015), 162–3.
18 "Nobody has to be vile," *London Review of Books* 28, no. 7 (2006), 10.
19 Karl Marx, *Collected Works. Vol. 20, Marx and Engels: 1864–68* (London: Lawrence & Wishart, 1985), 131.
20 Thomas Bernhard, *Heldenplatz*, trans. Meredith Oakes and Andrea Tierney (London: Oberon, 2010), 55.
21 The identity of this refugee group can be guessed at by the events of 2016. In February, five months before Haneke began filming *Happy End*, half of the "Jungle" refugee camp on the outskirts of Calais was demolished, and its inhabitants forced into "reception centers" across France. Of the camp's 6,000 inhabitants, about a third were Sudanese (see Dearden); it is plausible that some of these would end up as drifters in and around Calais itself, prey to the ministrations of a resentful Pierre "cast out" of the bourgeois fold.
22 Karl Marx and Friedrich Engels, *Collected Works. Vol. 3, Marx and Engels: 1843–44* (London: Lawrence & Wishart, 1975), 175–6.

AFTERWORD: WORK, MODERNISM, AND THINKING THROUGH THE AESTHETIC

Morag Shiach

Modernist writers and artists were, as this volume has demonstrated, much exercised both by the specific character of the art work and by the kinds of labor required to create aesthetically significant works of art at the beginning of the twentieth century. T. S. Eliot wrote in his essay, "Tradition and the Individual Talent" (1919) that: "tradition is a matter of much wider significance. It cannot be inherited, and if you want it you must obtain it by great labour."[1] And this labor, for Eliot, included extensive reading of texts from a range of historical periods, and careful analyses of the ways in which they embodied philosophical, religious, and aesthetic ideas and modes of representation that could be made to resonate within modern poetic texts. The strenuousness of such modernist literary labor ("great labour") was typically associated, at least in the early modernist period, with intensity, with concentration of energy and of meaning, rather than with an extended scope or scale that might have been the object of literary endeavor in earlier periods. Thus, for example, Ezra Pound would write in his "Few Don'ts by an Imagist" (1913) that "It is better to present one Image in a lifetime than to produce voluminous works."[2] The proper work of the modernist poet is here represented as the creation of intense moments of insight rather than the generation of "voluminous works"—or to put it rather differently, engaging with lyric rather than epic forms of cultural representation.

Rigor, arduousness, concentration, and intensity are represented by Eliot and by Pound as the work of the modernist poet. And this kind of focus on the arduousness of literary work can also be found within the context of the modernist novel. As Andrew Kalaidjian notes in his article, "The Hardest Task: Work and the Modernist Novel" (2013):

> Lawrence writing *The Rainbow* for the seventh time, Joyce's schemas, Faulkner writing *As I Lay Dying* while working the night shift as a power plant stoker, Beckett's diminishing word count. Earning a room by one's wits, touching friends for a bit of money, whoring for the magazines, going years without writing a single page ... novelists portray their work as anything but convenient. Virginia Woolf speaks of the "horrid labour that it needs to make an orderly and expressed work of art."[3]

The intensity of literary labor (Lawrence's seven drafts of *The Rainbow*) sits alongside the economic precarity of such literary work ("touching friends for a bit of money") to produce a relation to work that is "anything but convenient" or to echo Woolf's comment, "horrid." The apparent compulsion for writers to produce and refine modernist literary works has to be understood both within and to some extent against the evidence for the economic precarity of such work, in order to grasp the dynamic that consistently produces such an "inconvenient" relation both to literary work and to literary works.

One modernist literary text that stages a particularly powerful investigation of such an "inconvenient" relation to work, while also exploring the economic dependencies associated with modern labor, is Franz Kafka's 1915 novella, *Metamorphosis*. This short fictional text has long been understood as a key modernist work of art, but it is also, I would suggest, a key modernist engagement with the experience of work. It is a literary invocation of alienation from and through labor, as well as of the coercive and precarious economic relations that underpinned work in the early years of the twentieth century.

Metamorphosis begins with the radical transformation of Gregor Samsa from "a travelling salesman" into a kind of "monstrous vermin."[4] Samsa's surreal metamorphosis into a creature with a "tough armoured back ... sectioned off by little crescent-shaped ridges" (75), is set in the opening page of the novella right next to his experience of work as a traveling salesman. In the pages that follow Gregor's experiences of work feature at least as prominently as the sensation of his utterly transformed physical body:

> "Oh, my Lord!" he thought. "If only I didn't have to follow such an exhausting profession! On the road, day in, day out. The work is so much more strenuous than it would be in head office, and then there's the additional ordeal of travelling, worries about train connections, the irregular, bad meals, new people all the time, no continuity, no affection." (76)

Gregor's relations to his work are marked by fear and vulnerability. His parents owe money to the director of the company for whom Gregor works: "once I've got the money together to pay back what my parents owe him ... Then we'll have the parting of the ways," he fantasizes (76). Getting money together proves unachievable, however, as his altered bodily state makes going to work impossible. The chief clerk from his workplace arrives at Gregor's family home to demand he comes to work immediately, warning him that "your position is hardly the most secure ... your performances of late have been extremely unsatisfactory" (83). The precariousness of Gregor's employment dominates the narrative. He cannot survive once he is no longer able to go to work, and becomes increasingly isolated, rejected, and alienated. Gregor's physical condition rapidly declines. His sister is forced to undertake exhausting office work to compensate for the loss to the family of his income, and thus "no longer had it in her to care for Gregor as she had done earlier" (113). By the end of the novella, Gregor's "conviction that he needed to disappear was, if anything, still firmer than his sister's ... his head involuntarily dropped, and his final breath passed feebly from his nostrils" (122).

Metamorphosis is a text that is fascinated by the banal, as well as driven by a fantasy of revolutionary transformation; it stages the work of literature as inhering in its capacity to generate an alternative imaginative space for the reader, beyond the naturalistic representation of the everyday. Gregor is at one level an almost excessively average twentieth-century, white-collar worker. He is dominated by the requirements of his work while being unfulfilled by them, locked into relations of economic and familial dependency, and constantly struggling against the damning judgment that his "performances of late have been extremely unsatisfactory." But the work of the novella, as an aesthetic text, is to create a very different imaginative possibility, however absurd and impossible, through which Gregor can transcend these constraints and experience himself as having a degree of autonomy and agency. As a literary "monstrous vermin" he can and does inhabit a totally different social and affective space, and can imagine, even if only fleetingly and imperfectly, other worlds. That is the work that Kafka undertakes in writing *Metamorphosis*.

Such Modernist explorations of how the representation of work can both animate and circumscribe aesthetic practices as well as informing understandings of the nature of the work of art itself, are, however, subject to various forms of critique in later years of the twentieth century. Thus, for example, Hannah Arendt was to argue in *The Human Condition* (1958)[5] for the importance of distinguishing between "labor" as an unceasing requirement to reproduce the conditions necessary to sustain human life and "work," which for her had a defined temporality and generated artifacts that could have continuing material existence in the world. Both, she argued, needed to be understood also as distinct from the category of "action," which allows for the articulation of selfhood:

> It is in the nature of the human condition that contemplation depends upon all sorts of other activities—it depends upon labor to produce whatever is necessary to keep the human organism alive, it depends upon work to create whatever is needed to house the human body, and it needs action in order to organize the living together of many human beings in such a way that peace, the condition for the quiet of contemplation is assured.[6]

Arendt's move in articulating these three distinct elements of an active human life, and also her privileging of "action" over both work and labor because of its capacity "to organize the living together of many human beings," is part of a broader challenge to the modernist idea of "work" as key to the effective, and indeed affective, connection of subjectivity and the social that emerges so strongly across the essays in this volume.

This challenge to the power and to the radical potential of "work" can be found across a range of philosophical, political, and cultural texts, from those that seek to theorize the increasing prevalence and importance of "immaterial" forms of labor within neoliberal economies and societies, to those that promote a utopian vision of human potentialities "post-work."[7] Antonio Negri and Michael Hardt's detailed account of the particular characteristics of immaterial labor in their 2000 volume *Empire*, for example, makes the case that immaterial forms of labor, which can best be understood as work that produces entities that are intangible, abstract, or ephemeral, are becoming an increasingly prominent part of the global economy. Such immaterial forms of labor also, they suggest, rely disproportionately on elements of "affective labor," a kind of working on and with feelings whose "products are intangible, a feeling of ease, well-being, satisfaction, excitement or passion," and this in turn has consequences for the subjective meanings and experience of "work."[8] Maurizio Lazzarato highlighted the same understanding in his 1996 essay, "Immaterial Labor," but stressed also the importance of "the labour that produces the informational and cultural content of the commodity" in capturing the characteristics of immaterial labor.[9] The global digital economy, for Lazzarato, shapes the character and the experience of immaterial labor in significant, and often damaging, ways. So, for these social theorists at least, work appeared to be changing in important ways in the late twentieth century. For Hardt and Negri, as well as for Lazzarato, this has consequences for the extent to which work can continue to provide the conditions for any collective political project of liberation—a project that was, for the modernists discussed in this volume, at least imaginatively possible.

In Lazzarato's more recent work, he explores the radical potential both of (particular forms of) aesthetic practice and of the deliberate "refusal of work."[10] Marcel Duchamp's "ready-mades" are for Lazzarato prime examples of an artistic practice of idleness, or as he also considers them, art objects without an artist. For Lazzarato, Duchamp's modernist aesthetic practice in the early years of the twentieth century can be read as an increasingly radical series of interventions that have the effect of refusing and critiquing the very concept of artistic "work." Such radical critique of the nature and role of work can now be found across many disciplines, articulated from a range of theoretical perspectives. One could, for example, look at the range of contributions to the conference on "Antiwork, Postwork, No Work" organized by the Centre on Modern Culture, Materialism and Aesthetics and the Department of English of the University of California at Santa Barbara in 2012. The conference argued that engagement with "work," and also with the concepts of "postwork" and "antiwork," "brings together questions of survival, social justice, new forms of subjectivity and of resistance, but also of escape toward the new and the possible."[11] Kathi Weeks's 2011 study, *The Problem with Work: Feminism, Marxism, Antiwork Politics, and Postwork Imaginaries* (one chapter of which first appeared in 2005 in a volume of essays addressing the philosophical work of Antonio Negri[12]), approaches the question of work from the disciplinary space of political theory. In her introduction, "The Problem with Work," she asks why there has not been more active resistance to the conditions of labor in the contemporary world, and makes the case that, "as a fully political rather than a simply economic phenomenon, work would ... seem to be an especially rich object of inquiry."[13]

Weeks's volume is a provocation to encourage greater political and philosophical engagement with "work," as well as to recognize the potential of a politics that does not put work at the center of theories of the social, and it also puts the case that waged labor should not be seen unproblematically as an inherent good. Similarly, Nick Srnicek has recently explored the potential advantages of a world without work, with all citizens supported through a universal basic income, while David Frayne has explored the theory and the practice of resistance to work in the early twenty-first century and James A. Chamberlain has argued that forms of social organization that rely on wage labor can be understood as detrimental to both freedom and social justice.[14]

The negative social and individual impacts of a moment when the division of labor generates and exacerbates social inequalities; when developed as well as developing economies are unable to hold out the possibility for fulfilling and secure employments to their citizens; and where the relation to sustainable employment is reimagined as an individual responsibility rather than a collectively achieved aim, are real and pressing contemporary issues, that the volumes cited above address with energy and imagination. But not all social theorists, legal philosophers, or cultural historians and critics are ready to give up on the central importance of work to the constitutions of collective and individual identities. The Jean Monnet Project, "I Work Therefore I am (European)" argued in 2017 that:

> In contemporary Europe, labor occupies a central position in human existence: since the industrial revolution it is the principal criterion of reciprocal recognition and of universal mobilization. In a multi-level governance system like the EU, through their profession people feel recognized by the others: they are. Indeed, labour is more than a mere economic relationship, it rather pertains to an identitarian process and it is an anthropological phenomenon radically influencing human existence.[15]

At a conference on "The Metamorphosis of Labour," held in Brussels in 2017, scholars, policymakers, artists, and activists from a range of national and institutional backgrounds considered the extent to which recent economic and political developments undermined both the socially and the individually constitutive power of work, but also addressed the political and policy interventions that might restore the productive connections between work and forms of social identity, and thus enable work to continue to function as "the principal criterion of reciprocal recognition and of universal mobilization." As the essays in this volume have shown, there is much to work for in retaining both the practical and the utopian power of the idea of "work."

Notes

1. T. S. Eliot, "Tradition and the Individual Talent," in *The Sacred Wood* (London: Faber and Faber, 1997), 40.
2. Ezra Pound, "A Retrospect," in *Literary Essays of Ezra Pound* (New York: Directions Publishing Company, 1968), 4.
3. Andrew Kalaidjian, "The Hardest Task: Work and the Modernist Novel," *Modern Horizons: Modernity, Ideology, and the Novel* (June 2013), www.modernhorizons journal.ca/june2013issue/
4. Franz Kafka, "Metamorphosis," in *Metamorphosis and Other Stories*, trans. Michael Hofmann (Harmondsworth: Penguin Books, 2007), 75–126.
5. See also John Attridge's brief discussion of Arendt in the Introduction to this volume.
6. Hannah Arendt, "Labor, Work, Action," in *The Portable Hannah Arendt*, ed. Peter Baehr (New York: Penguin, 2000), 167.
7. I have discussed the importance of theoretical accounts of "immaterial labor" to the understanding of the work of the modernist artist in more detail in "Labour Material and Immaterial: A Modernist Perspective," in *The Labour of Literature in Britain and France, 1830–1930: Authorial Work Ethics*, ed. Marcus Waithe and Claire White (Palgrave Macmillan, 2018), 292–309.
8. Michael Hardt and Antonio Negri, *Empire* (Cambridge, MA: Harvard University Press, 2000), 292–3.
9. Maurizio Lazzarato, "Immaterial Labour," in *Radical Thought in Italy: A Potential Politics*, ed. P. Virno and M. Hardt (Minneapolis: University of Minnesota Press, 1996), 133.
10. Maurizio Lazzarato, *Marcel Duchamp et le refus du travail* (Paris: Les Prairies Ordinaires, 2014).
11. For further details of this 2012 conference see, https://lists.lsit.ucsb.edu/archives/ihcevents/2012-May/000616.html
12. Weeks notes that an earlier version of the second chapter of *The Problem with Work* appeared as "The Refusal of Work as Demand and Perspective," in *The Philosophy of Antonio Negri. Volume One: Resistance in Practice*, ed. Timothy S. Murphy and Abdul-Karim Mustapha (London: Pluto Press, 2005), 109–35.
13. Kathi Weeks, *The Problem with Work: Feminism, Marxism, Antiwork Politics, and Postwork Imaginaries* (Durham, NC: Duke University Press, 2011), 5.
14. Nick Srnicek, *Inventing the Future: Postcapitalism and a World Without Work* (London: Verso, 2015); David Frayne, *The Refusal of Work: The Theory and Practice of Resistance to Work* (London: Zed Books, 2015); and James A. Chamberlain, *Undoing Work, Rethinking Community: A Critique of the Social Functions of Work* (Ithaca, NY: Cornell University press, 2018).
15. See http://www.iworkthereforeiam.eu

INDEX

absolute work 12, 22–4, 32
Adorno, Theodor 3–7, 10–11, 66–7
Alborough, Alan 2, 13, 96, 108
   Beautiful Objects: Asterisk, Ellipses, Hyphen 98–101
antiwork 14, 214
Aragon, Louis 3, 7
Arendt, Hannah 14, 213
Aristotle 5, 38, 169
artisan 1, 5–6, 11, 67, 77, 84, 87
autobiography 67–9, 71, 77, 83, 87, 145–8, 155–6, 158, 165, 169
autonomy 1, 4, 12–14, 21, 30, 32, 36–8, 42–6, 192, 213
avant-garde 3–4, 7–8, 11–13, 21–2, 44–5, 95–8, 108, 168, 173

Benjamin, Walter 4, 96–8, 103, 191
Benson, Stella 13, 131–2, 140–1
   Living Alone 132–7, 141
blackness 180–1, 193
bourgeoisie 3, 13–14, 21, 42, 67, 73–4, 84, 167, 174, 197–209; *see also* middle class
Bürger, Peter 3, 4, 21

capitalism 2, 67, 91, 115–16, 124, 179, 204–5
   and art 67, 84, 147, 174
   critique of 14, 117, 120, 127, 149–50, 153, 158, 174–5, 185, 192–3, 201
class 1, 54, 58–9, 83, 91, 103, 125, 133–4, 137, 174
   conflict/struggle 8, 183, 193
   consciousness/identity 1, 7, 8
   middle class 2, 10, 58, 134–6, 141, 142 n.4, 198–200, 202; *see also* bourgeoisie
   and race 187–8, 191–3
   upper class 133

working class 7, 9, 13–14, 131–2, 156, 163–72, 175, 176 n.1, 184, 186
collaboration 49, 54, 56, 58–9, 163, 188
colonialism 102, 179–80, 182, 185, 188, 191, 193, 203–4
Conrad, Joseph
   Heart of Darkness 115
   Nostromo 13, 113–27
craft 5–7, 13, 15 n.21, 21, 29, 70, 73, 77, 84, 87, 90–2, 97

Dada 1, 3, 12; *see also* Duchamp, Marcel
death drive 208–9; *see also* Freud, Sigmund
difficulty 35–6, 38–46, 52, 90, 120
disclosure 13–14, 148, 151–3, 155, 158
Duchamp, Marcel 87, 92–3, 95–8, 101, 105, 109 n.5, 214; *see also* Dada

Eliot, T. S. 39, 169, 211
Endore, Guy 14, 179–80
   Babouk 179–80, 185–93
   The Werewolf of Paris 185
Enframing 14, 148, 150–1, 153–8

failure 22, 24–5, 28, 32, 55, 97, 115, 117, 120, 126, 136, 173, 198, 207
fantasy 12, 13, 30, 32, 66, 131–2, 136–8, 141, 213
First World War 8, 67, 88, 93 n.26, 131, 140, 165
Flaubert, Gustave 23–5, 43–4, 197–8
Fordism 8, 87–8
Foucault, Michel 69
found objects 13, 57, 95–6, 98, 101, 108
Fraser, Ronald 13, 131–2, 140–1
   Flower Phantoms 137–40
Freud, Sigmund 91–2, 139; *see also* death drive

Gesamtkunstwerk; see absolute work
Gide, André 12, 38, 164
   The Counterfeiters 12–13, 37, 40, 42–6

Haiti 179–80, 183–5, 192–3, 194 n.7
Haitian Revolution 14, 179–82, 184–5, 188–9, 192–3
Hamsun, Knut 173–4
Haneke, Michael 2, 14, 198–204, 206–9
   Happy End 206–9
   Hidden 202–9
   The Piano Teacher 202
   The Seventh Continent 200–3, 205, 206–7
   Time of the Wolf 199
Hardt, Michael 88, 214
Heidegger, Martin 7, 14, 149–51, 155, 158
   "The Origin of the Work of Art" 5–6
   "The Question Concerning Technology" 6, 10, 150
   "What are Poets For?" 148, 150
high modernism 163–7, 175

identity 10, 102, 113–17, 120–7, 145, 154, 181, 198, 205–7, 215
inheritance 13, 113–27
intimacy 89–91, 156
irony 27, 42, 72, 77, 119, 184, 186

James, C. L. R. 14, 179–89, 191–3, 194 n.15 and n.18
   The Black Jacobins 14, 179–88, 192–3
   Toussaint L'Ouverture (play) 180–3, 189
Jameson, Fredric 35, 43, 128 n.12, 168
Johnson, Eyvind 163
   De fyra främlingarna 169
   Stad i ljus (*City in Light*) 14, 164, 168–75
Joyce, James 4, 134, 138, 164, 167, 173, 175, 197–8, 200, 211

Kafka, Franz 24–8
   "Before the Law" 31
   "The Burrow" ("Der Bau") 12, 28–32, 34 n.18
   A Country Doctor 25

   "A Dream" ("Ein Traum") 30
   In the Penal Colony 27, 31
   "The Judgement" 25–6, 31–2
   The Man Who Disappeared (formerly *Amerika*) 26
   Metamorphosis 14, 31, 212–13
Kittler, Friedrich 9

labor
   affective 41–2, 84, 88, 90, 214
   agricultural 132, 134, 136, 141, 142 n.7
   artistic 1, 4–5, 7, 13, 21, 60, 84, 86–7, 91, 96–7, 101, 105
   domestic 8, 10, 13–14, 59, 89, 131, 139, 142 n.4
   factory 134, 145–6, 182, 186, 192, 201
   immaterial 13, 14, 84, 88, 90–1, 214, 216
   intellectual 1, 41, 54–5, 84, 86–7, 90, 105, 137
   manual/physical 1, 7–9, 11, 52, 54, 101, 164
   movement 1, 193
   reproductive 88, 93 n.25, 213
   women's 8, 10, 13, 58–9, 88, 90–1, 131–2, 134–7, 140–1
Language poetry 2, 145, 147, 149–50, 155–6
late modernism 2, 168
Lawrence, D. H. 13, 49–55, 60, 167, 198
   "The Man Who Loved Islands" 50, 53–5, 58
   The Rainbow 211–12
   "The Reality of Peace" 51, 53
   "Study of Thomas Hardy" 50, 53
   "Why the Novel Matters" 52
Lazzarato, Maurizio 88, 214
Lewis, Wyndham 4, 44, 87–8
   Tarr 12, 37–8, 40–2, 45
love 26, 65, 73, 88–92, 136, 140, 156

magic 13, 108, 132–4, 136–7, 141, 191
Marx, Karl 36, 117, 127 n.10, 150, 204, 208
Marxism 176 n.1, 180, 184, 207
meritocracy 13, 113–15, 117–18, 120–2, 124–7
mimesis 13, 49–50, 59–60, 149, 151
moral desert 122–5; see also meritocracy

Nietzsche, Friedrich 70–2, 74, 80 n.37

office work 1–2, 9–10, 14, 24, 26–8, 32, 212; *see also* white-collar work

percussion 14, 180–1, 183, 190–1, 193
perfection 22–4, 26, 28, 29, 32
Picabia, Francis 3, 7, 12
Picasso, Pablo 87, 95–6, 166
postwork 14, 214
Pound, Ezra 13, 84, 91, 175, 211
professionalism 9–10, 66, 205
Program music 71
Proust, Marcel 23, 164, 170, 173

Rancière, Jacques 11–12
Rawls, John 123, 125–6
ready-made 1, 4, 13, 87, 96–7, 101, 109 n.5
rhythm 13, 49–52, 54–6, 58–61, 74, 150, 181, 183, 187–93

Schopenhauer, Arthur 70–1
Seejarim, Usha 2, 13, 96, 108
 50 Stories 105–8
self-quotation 77
self-representation 67–8, 73
Silliman, Ron 2, 13–14
 "Disappearance of the Word, Appearance of the World" 149
 "Albany" 145–8, 152, 154–8
 The Grand Piano (with Rae Armantrout et al.) 147, 155
 "Ketjak" 152–3, 155, 158
 Tjanting 153, 155–6
 Under Albany 145–6, 148, 154
Siopis, Penny 2, 13, 96, 104–5, 108
 Patience on a Monument: a History Painting 101–3
 Reconnaissance 1900–1997 103–4

slavery 102, 119–20, 179–90
social modernism 14, 163–4, 167–8, 170, 175
starvation 119, 173–4
Stein, Gertrude 4, 13, 83–4, 97–8
 Autobiography of Alice B. Toklas 83, 87
 "Lifting Belly" 84, 88–90
 Tender Buttons 84–7, 89–90
Steiner, George 38–9, 41; *see also* difficulty
Strauss, Richard 65–7
 Alpensinfonie 70, 80 n.30
 Don Quixote 72, 77, 81 n.46
 Ein Heldenleben (*A Hero's Life*) 13, 67–9, 71–3
 Symphonia Domestica 13, 67–9, 73–7
Swedish modernism 164, 166

tone poem 70, 72–3, 77, 78 n.8

voodoo/vodou 14, 179–85, 188–9, 192, 193 n.1

white-collar work 9, 152, 213; *see also* office work
Williams, Raymond 5, 167, 209 n.3
women's sexuality 138–9
Woolf, Virginia 9–10, 13, 49–50, 60, 132, 137, 167–8, 200, 211–12
 "Kew Gardens" 50, 57–60
 Mrs. Dalloway 138, 170–1
 "A Sketch of the Past" 56–7
 "Solid Objects" 57
 "Street Music" 55–6, 57
 To the Lighthouse 57, 143 n.43
work of art 1–5, 11–13, 21, 30, 35–6, 38, 40–4, 49–60, 150–1, 211–13
working-class literature 163–6, 168, 175, 176 n.1

www.ingramcontent.com/pod-product-compliance
Lightning Source LLC
Chambersburg PA
CBHW052038300426
44117CB00012B/1879